THE
GHADAR
MOVEMENT

ADVANCE PRAISE FOR THE BOOK

'With uncommon commitment and passion, Rana Preet Gill documents the Ghadar Movement, a heroically courageous but almost forgotten chapter in India's multi-hued struggle for freedom. This book is a scholarly salute to the sacrifices of the Ghadarites and a commendable effort in keeping their memory alive for future generations'—**Navtej Sarna, author of *Crimson Spring***

'The spark for writing such a book came to the author during her visit to the Cellular Jail in the Andaman Islands, the ultimate torture prison for the punishment of rebels against the British Raj, where more than sixty-five patriots of the Ghadar Movement defiantly put up with beastly cruelty during 1915–20. Based largely on the study of the many published accounts of the struggle available to her, this book includes her own retelling of the self-sacrificing passion and sporadic revolutionary actions of the Ghadar patriots spread over many parts of the world'—**Harish K. Puri, author of *Ghadar Movement: Ideology, Organisation, Strategy***

'An aphorism in a Ghadar tract (1913) reads as: "This is not a piece of paper. This is the battle flag." This book by a young writer, Rana Gill, flashes up the battle for freedom that has been on since the history of all hitherto existing society began. The Ghadar Movement is a glorious chapter of the war waged by simple Punjabi farmers and workers a century ago in California against imperialism. Gill takes us back in time, resurrecting the spirit of the Ghadarites who dared to dream'—**Amarjit Chandan, Punjabi poet, writer and independent historian**

'In current Punjab, the fault line between Sikh and Marxist ideology continues to widen. *The Ghadar Movement: A Forgotten Struggle* bridges the chasm by going back more than a century to bring to us the life and vision of the Ghadarites who stitched these two ideologies to launch India's freedom movement from North America. A must-read in these torn times'— **Amandeep Sandhu, author of *Panjab: Journeys Through Fault Lines***

'Rana Preet Gill, a veterinary doctor by profession, found herself attracted towards exploring the Ghadar Movement, which was started in 1913, after visiting the Andamans' notorious Cellular Jail, now a memorial and museum. A colleague wanted her to click a picture of the statue of his grandfather, Ghadarite prisoner Ram Rakha Bali, standing in Shaheed Park outside the jail. Ram Rakha Bali was one of eight Ghadarite prisoners held there, who was martyred by observing a hunger strike against the jailer's inhuman conduct towards prisoners in the most oppressive jail of the British colonial period. As the veterinarian was posted in Hoshiarpur, and as Ram Rakha Bali also came from Hoshiarpur district, this turned the young doctor into an author.

'The Hindi Association of the Pacific Coast, founded on 21 April 1912 in Portland, California, USA, got its popular name "Ghadar Party" after it brought out its journal *Ghadar* in multiple languages. The first issue came out in Urdu on 1 November 1913 from its headquarters in the USA.

'The Ghadar Movement has a long and short story. While the attempted Ghadar Movement, in the form of a revival of the 1857 uprising against the British, failed in a short time, by end-1915, it still has a long, heroic story of the resistance continuing inside jails. The party finally got dissolved after Independence in 1947 and its headquarters in San Francisco was handed over to the newly independent Indian government. There have been many chroniclers of this great struggle, including Ghadarite heroes themselves, as well as academic scholars such as Prof. Harish Puri and Maia Ramnath. Rana Preet Gill has rewritten this story in a reader-friendly manner, spanning thirty-eight short chapters with authentic factual sources. She has also linked many interconnected cases and stories of the Hindu–German Conspiracy, the Berlin Committee, the Siam–Burma angle, the Singapore revolt and the silk letters plot, among others—all woven into one refreshing narration without using academic jargon, which makes it engaging for non-academic readers as well. I hope this story of the Ghadar Movement and its part in the Indian freedom struggle will be appreciated by readers and welcome the author to the non-historians' brand of historians!'—**Chaman Lal, retired professor, Jawaharlal Nehru University, and honorary adviser, Bhagat Singh Archives and Resource Centre, Delhi Archives, New Delhi**

THE
GHADAR
MOVEMENT

A FORGOTTEN STRUGGLE

RANA PREET GILL

PENGUIN
VIKING

An imprint of Penguin Random House

VIKING

Viking is an imprint of the Penguin Random House group of companies
whose addresses can be found at global.penguinrandomhouse.com

Published by Penguin Random House India Pvt. Ltd
4th Floor, Capital Tower 1, MG Road,
Gurugram 122 002, Haryana, India

Penguin
Random House
India

First published in Viking by Penguin Random House India 2025

ISBN 9780670099900

Typeset in Adobe Garamond Pro by MAP Systems, Bengaluru, India
Printed at Thomson Press India Ltd, New Delhi

www.penguin.co.in

MIX
Paper | Supporting
responsible forestry
FSC® C010615

Chun kar az hameh heelate dar guzasht
Halal ast burdan bi-shamsher dast

When all has been tried, yet
Justice is not in sight
It is then right to pick up the sword,
It is then right to fight.

—*Zafarnama*, Guru Gobind Singh,
translated by Navtej Sarna

For my parents,
Karamjit Singh Gill and Harjit Kaur Gill

Contents

Contents

Why I Chose to Write About Ghadar

In December 2019, I went on a vacation to the Andamans with my family. At New Delhi Airport, I updated my status on Facebook. My superior, Dr Ranjiv Bali, then sent me a text on WhatsApp asking me to take a look at the statue of his grandfather's brother, Pandit Ram Rakha Bali, installed in the park facing the Cellular Jail when I was in the Andamans.

Yes, sure, why not? I replied.

A day or two later, when we visited the Cellular Jail, I saw the statue of Pandit Ram Rakha next to Veer Savarkar's, clicked pictures with it and sent them to Dr Bali. The plaque beneath the statue read:

Pandit Ram Rakha: Son of Jawahir Ram, residence Sadar, Hoshiyarpur, Punjab. In Mandalay Conspiracy Case he was sentenced to life and transported to the Cellular Jail, Andaman. When the jail authorities interfered with his right to put on sacred thread, he protested and resorted to hunger strike. He carried on for a long three months till he breathed his last in 1919.

Pandit Ram Rakha Bali was from Hoshiarpur, where I had been resident since 2013. Busy as I was with my job as a veterinary doctor, I knew nothing about Hoshiarpur's rich past.

When I came back from my trip, I tried to find out more about the Mandalay Conspiracy case but did not find too much information. I was intrigued. What was the Mandalay Conspiracy?

I had a chat with Dr Ranjiv Bali and his cousin, Colonel Vikas Bali, in Delhi, who provided some material about Pandit Ram Rakha. But still, things did not add up. Why did Ram Rakha go to jail? What was the conspiracy?

I called up my dad, who asked me to contact the Punjabi writer, Amarjit Chandan, who gave me the numbers of Prof. Harish Puri and Sita Ram Madhopuri. Both of them briefly narrated the facts to me. Prof. Harish Puri is an authority on the Ghadar Movement and has written several books on the subject. Prof. Yubee Gill was kind enough to courier me Prof. Harish Puri's book. The day I laid my hands on the book, I was speechless. This was the beginning of my Ghadar journey.

Prof. Puri's book mentioned several other books which cited even more. I accumulated all of them. Desh Bhagat Yadgar Hall in Jalandhar, the mecca of Ghadarites, came to my rescue. I made umpteen trips to the library there. I met Chiranji Lal Kangniwal, who has also written extensively on Ghadar and sought the help of librarian Gurdeep Singh, who was always willing to get the books photocopied for me.

Once the course of Ghadar was charted in my mind, there was no stopping me. I had to refrain from writing articles and short stories for newspapers and magazines, something I did regularly, because I could not work on multiple assignments at the same time. I had to make a choice. And it was Ghadar! I deactivated my social media accounts and focused all my energies on the book. I had to put a blanket ban on myself. I would read and write nothing but Ghadar. In March 2020, the onset of COVID made life uncertain and unpredictable. I held on to Ghadar and sailed through those unprecedented times.

It was important for me to retell the story of Ghadar because I was a little ashamed that I, who was born and brought up in Punjab, knew nothing about this historic movement. I wondered why I had never read a word about it when I had spent my childhood in Nakodar, which was just half an hour from Jalandhar where Desh Bhagat Yadgar Hall is located. Why is the Ghadar Movement not taught in schools, in colleges and in universities? How could I grow up and not know anything about these men, the majority of whom belonged to Punjab, my home state, who sacrificed their lives just on a whim? Ghadar became my devotion, determination, dedication and made me more disciplined. To write this book became my personal battle that I needed to win.

I am not a historian and neither do I claim to know all about the facets of the Ghadar Movement. I have read a lot and understood it through the prism of my own sensibilities and have narrated it in my words. I hope you enjoy reading it as much as I enjoyed writing it.

Chapter 1

Bombay, Bengal and Punjab Under British Rule

The Battle of Plassey in 1757 is usually taken as the starting point for the annexation of the Indian subcontinent by the British, starting from the province of Bengal.

Until around the middle of the nineteenth century, Punjab remained outside the British ambit. Among other things, the rule of Maharaja Ranjit Singh (reigned 1801–1839) was responsible for this. Prosperity thrived under his regime, the religious communities were largely united and the strong army discouraged invaders. The British and Ranjit Singh maintained a tentative peace.

The signs of British treachery were soon evident. They had waited in the wings hoping to usurp the state after the passing of Ranjit Singh. That fateful day of 27 June 1839 when Maharaja Ranjit Singh died, despondency enveloped all.[1] It would not be long before Punjab would be ripped of its sheen and glory!

Since Ranjit Singh had seven sons, multiple claims to the throne sprang up. The Dogras and the armies of the Khalsa played power games while the British waited for their turn. They fought battles in Mudki, Ferozepur, Chillianwala and Gujarat. The East India Company took advantage of this factionalism by taking sides, plotting and planning.

1

On 25 March 1849, Dalip Singh, the youngest son of Maharaja Ranjit Singh, who had ascended the throne after multiple others had come and gone, surrendered not only the Kohinoor with the throne but Sikh pride along with it.[2] Punjab became the new conquest of the British and with this, they had conquered the subcontinent in its entirety.

The Company, when it began ruling Punjab, chose to fortify the defence of the state once again. The Khalsa army that ruled the roost during the reign of Maharaja Ranjit Singh was disbanded and a new crop of men, made servile with promises and the lure of money, were incorporated to guard the state against invaders. Ten years of anarchy and mismanagement after the death of Maharaja Ranjit Singh had finally come to an end with the beginning of a new era. The measures taken by the British provided a semblance of peace and prosperity for a while. But eventually, they started throttling the populace under the burden of raised taxes, charging of remuneration in cash, the abolition of the barter system and the rise of moneylenders eager to trade in land. The rise in land prices left the Punjabi peasant feeling both powerful and vulnerable. He had a prized commodity in his hands that would bring him prosperity if sold and gloom if the possession of it was taken from his hands.

While things in Punjab went smoothly for a while, throughout India, dissatisfaction and anger against the Company's rule was rising. Soon it reached boiling point and the bubble burst.

It was in Meerut in May 1857 where the first salvo of revolt was fired when the soldiers raised their voice against the use of greased cartridges presumed to be laced with cow and pig fat. The cartridges had to be bitten open before loading and this enraged the sensibilities of both Hindus and Muslims. From Meerut, the wave of discontentment travelled to Kanpur, Lucknow, Benares, Allahabad, Bareilly and Jhansi. The enraged fires threatened to embroil the entire country. This uprising had the support of local leaders, such as Tantia Tope, Rani Lakshmibai, Nana Saheb and Begum Hazrat Mahal, as well as that of the public but it failed to assume the role of a nationalist movement. Its impact in Punjab was further reduced with the Sikh rulers of the princely states of Punjab choosing to back the Company, foiling the possibility of any uprising in the region.

The 1857 revolt would become the precursor of the Ghadar Movement in the coming years. It brought an end to the rule of the East India Company. The British Crown took over the administration and Queen Victoria decreed that all her subjects would be treated equally, including Indians, giving false hopes to the natives.

Let us look at what happened in Bombay and Bengal, after the events of 1857. The happenings in Bombay and Bengal are closely connected to the Punjabi struggle to rid itself of British influence.

Bombay

Before the advent of the Company, it was Chhatrapati Shivaji who had emerged as a potent force in the region against Mughal rule and carved out an independent kingdom. After the failed revolt of 1857, the festival of the Hindu God Ganapati and the celebration of the lore of Shivaji became the early manifestations of opposition to tyranny. By 1893, the celebrations had started becoming grand. They were encouraging the people to come forward and be a part of a glorious history, which was theirs to celebrate. Men and boys were being given lessons on self-defence, taught the art of physical combat with sticks and encouraged to take up physical exercises. The neglected tomb of Shivaji was resuscitated once again and the ghost of the past began haunting the minds of those who were alive. It gave birth to power in a new mould, the cast of which was beginning to thicken.

The Chapekar brothers were amongst those born and brought up on the valorous tales of Shivaji. They would form the Society for Removal of Obstacles to the Hindu Religion by giving rousing slogans and hard-hitting statements to stir up not only the curiosity of their own people but of the rulers who were watching them, keeping tabs on them, the signs of worry creasing their brows.[3]

In 1897, the Bombay-Poona region was infested with the plague, killing thousands. Walter Charles Rand, the then plague commissioner, instituted a house-to-house search to ensure safety measures, which did not go down well considering the orthodox mindset of many Brahmins in Poona. If the fever against oppression was rising, this particular act of transcending boundaries raised the bar. Tempers were now blistering and would not cool down. Rand was assassinated by the Chapekar brothers on the day of Queen Victoria's Diamond Jubilee. It was a powerful message to the rulers amidst the celebrations of their crown's anniversary. The Chapekars were hanged for this offence, but the seeds of rebellion did not die down with the loss of their lives.

Bal Gangadhar Tilak was vociferous in his support for this emerging movement against British rule. His newspaper, *Kesari*, was widely read. At a time when many papers were government mouthpieces, *Kesari* had the audacity to defy the authorities by publishing views that generated an unease amongst the police and the public for the spark it was generating. In one of its articles, it said, 'Every Maratha, to whatever party he may belong, must rejoice at the Sivaji festival. We all are striving to gain our lost independence, and this terrible load is to be uplifted by all of us in combination.'[4]

Tilak emerged as an extremist leader of the Congress whose other side was represented by moderates like Gokhale. Under his influence, revolutionaries like the Savarkar brothers and Shyamaji Krishnavarma led the banner of revolt from foreign lands.

Bengal

If the sensibilities of those in the Bombay province were shaken by the strict measures enforced by the then plague commissioner, Bengal too was shaken by another decision that came out like a bolt from the blue, initiating them into the cause of freedom. Bengal was the first state to be annexed by the Company after winning the Battle of Plassey in 1757 against the Nawab of Bengal, Siraj-ud-Daulah. United Bengal comprising Bengal, Bihar and Orissa, with a population of 78 million, was getting unmanageable for the administration.[5] The signs of belligerence were beginning to show and were becoming a cause of worry for the British government. The announcement of the partition of Bengal was made in July 1905 and was carried out the following October.[6]

There was an outcry amongst the masses, leaders and revolutionaries against this move, which was eventually completed by the then Viceroy of India, Lord Curzon. The region of Bengal was finally divided on 16 October 1905 on the distinct lines of religion into two parts: one consisting of Western Bengal, Bihar and Orissa and the other of Eastern Bengal and Assam.[7] One region was clearly Muslim-dominated and the other had a Hindu majority. This was the first step to conflagrate communal passions, the divisive fumes of which would keep the flame of English rule burning for years to come, until they would depart, making this line permanent.

The revolutionary activities that were being carried out in Bengal before its partition now catapulted to a different level. Though this division did not remain for long and Bengal was eventually united after some years by Lord Hardinge, it provided the impetus for making it a worthwhile cause. It led to the evolution of an extremism that was missing in Bengal earlier, which was now followed by a string of political murders, dacoities, the creation of secret societies and a cult of revolutionaries who would be acknowledged and worshipped by people as far away as Punjab.

The division of Bengal gave way to the rise of the Swadeshi movement. 'Boycott foreign goods, use local'—this message of abstinence from foreign goods and the practice of self-reliance spread from Bengal consumed the entire nation. Tilak promulgated it in the Ganapati and Shivaji festivals in Bombay, Ajit Singh and Lala Lajpat Rai pushed it into Punjab along with their own 'Pagri Sambhal Jatta' movement. And this was preached in other parts of India as well by revolutionaries who extended full support to this call for help from Bengal. Mounds of foreign goods smouldered everywhere in India, inflaming latent passions, spreading a new wave of freedom that had been crushed in the revolt of 1857.

The division of Bengal touched an emotional chord. The day of the division was announced as a day of mourning. Bengalis fasted with no fires being lit in their kitchens. People of the divided Bengals tied *rakhis* on each other's wrists. They held prayer meetings and seminars, they berated and wept at this injustice, at this division.[8] It brought every individual from Bengal, far removed from political affiliations, into a frame of national consciousness. The people who had only been concerned about earning their daily bread were made to think about their state as a home, their country as a nation whose essence was being lost, whose stature was being demolished by a rule that was the root cause of all problems. It was deemed to be a collective loss and the movement gained a larger meaning. It soon acquired proportions where it was not about Bengali unity any more; it was now about national pride.

The anti-partition movement in Bengal gave rise to secret societies, the formation of new groups, the resurgence of old ones with a new vigour and the inculcation of young men into all kind of activities deemed seditious by the incumbent government. The Anushilan Samiti and Dacca Anushilan Samiti were the bigger groups with several smaller branches.

Punjab

The revolt of 1857 had not garnered much support from the Punjabi populace and local rulers, but it did give rise to a number of movements advocating reform. One amongst them was the Kuka movement, initiated by Balak Singh of Hazro village.[9] The followers called themselves Kukas or Namdharis and wore handspun cloth and flat turbans, often with rosary beads around their necks. The movement emphasized that its followers stay away from stealing, lying, committing adultery and abstaining from the use of tobacco, alcohol or meat of any kind. This movement was particularly progressive for it questioned the age-old, depraved customs of female infanticide, marrying girls off at a young age and the prevalent custom of giving large dowries, which was one of the factors leading to the peasantry getting into debt. The sect also stood firm against casteism and advocated the use of swadeshi and the boycott of foreign goods. The reforms this movement advocated were way ahead of its time and were later taken up by the father of the nation, Mahatma Gandhi, when he launched the non-cooperation movement. The movement lost its impact when its head, Ram Singh, was arrested and deported to Burma.

The Nirankaris, Radha Soami, Singh Sabha and Arya Samaj were other progressive movements in Punjab that had their impact on the people, making them aware and conscious about their rights.

For the British, the threat of rebellion necessitated the build-up of a large army not only to control internal dissidence but also to ward off invaders. To maintain a strong army required money, which came in the form of taxes from the Indian populace. A collective sum of 18 million pounds came from the Indian public while a contribution of 2,57,000 pounds came from the Empire's exchequer. Apart from this expenditure, which came at the cost of the Indian populace, other expenses followed, necessitated by the then Viceroy Lord Curzon's need to maintain British supremacy over the Persian Gulf and other regions in South Asia. Money was taken out of the Indian kitty to pay for several expeditions to Tibet as well as the honorarium to the Emir of Afghanistan, the sultan of Muscat and the sheikhs of the Gulf.[10]

While the money for public works was getting depleted, taxes were getting gargantuan and the man with the plough reeled under the repercussions of these measures.

The Punjab peasantry was affected by multiple factors. It was not only the shrinking lands under their control that were either being sold or mortgaged, it was the increase in population as well, which was making the situation unbearable. With more mouths to be fed, fewer resources and a landholding that was gradually slipping away from their grasp, the peasants were close to penury. Still, despite the gradually diminishing resources and lack of opportunities, many people believed in spending extravagant amounts on the pomp and show of rituals. Simplicity, though advocated by various reforms and movements, did not make much headway. The money required for such ostentatious rituals either came from the mortgaging or selling of land.

The arrival of the plague in 1898 that attacked almost all districts resulted in 29,92,166 deaths from 1898 to 1918. It wiped out entire families in Punjab and left a trail of destruction.[11] Subsequent attacks of the plague did not elicit any kind of favourable response from the government. Instead of curbing the disease, the district administrators let it spread, hoping that it would die of its own accord.[12] Medical officers were withdrawn from their duty and put on military duty during the First World War, leading to the death of more than 2 lakh people.[13]

Instead of reducing the burden on the farmer, the taxes levied remained stable and the revenue to be earned from the land kept on increasing, leading the dispossessed farmer to rely on moneylenders, who were gaining credence and acquiring importance in the sequence of events. All this was not conducive for the welfare of the farmer.

If the Punjab peasantry was in dire straits, the artisans too had a rough time under the British regime. Local handicrafts got no support from the government and had to compete with cheap imported goods from England, which were marketed with élan. The future of artistry was bleak.

To ease the density of population and ebb the growing misery, the government decided to take some measures to rectify this situation. They dug canals with the purpose of rehabilitating some of the population out of the congested areas to ease the pressure on land. The Upper Bari Doab Canal was dug in 1861 with this same motive and the region of Sandal Bar between the Chenab and Ravi rivers became home to many who were given land at minimal rates. For a while, this gave an illusion of prosperity but the greed to extract more from the impoverished peasantry again played havoc with the lives of the farmers.

To discourage the selling and mortgage of land and to protect the peasants from the moneylenders, the government brought about the Land Alienation Act in 1900.[14] The attachment of land and mortgages were forbidden and so was the sale of land from agriculturists to non-agriculturists.[15] A clear-cut division of agriculturist and non-agriculturist castes was made. The rights of the peasants were saved but the seeds of a new kind of racial separatism were sown on the basis of economic interests. The links between a Jat Sikh and a non-Jat Sikh farmer were severed, putting them in different camps.[16]

The Land Colonization Bill in 1907 further enraged the people as, in the garb of securing the land, it imposed strict conditions against its transfer. The new conditions of maintaining the land in a prim and proper state and the planting of trees added to the woes of the peasantry. The culmination of these new repressive acts led to agitation in the state of Punjab.

By the early 1900s, the repression of these laws would not only give rise to deep-rooted resentment in the populace, it led to the rise of many leaders who came to the forefront to lead with an iron will.

Ajit Singh, born on 23 February 1881, in Khatkar Kalan, Nawanshahr district of Punjab, was a prominent leader who had risen out of the Punjab peasantry and was the uncle of the great revolutionary Bhagat Singh.[17] He founded the Indian Patriots Association and a newspaper, *Peshwa*, along with Sufi Amba Prasad.[18] He would later join hands with his associates to form the Bharat Mata Society.[19]

In a gathering organized in 1907 at Lyallpur, the editor of the *Jhang Sayal* newspaper, Banke Dayal, recited his poem, 'Pagri Sambhal Jatta' (literally translated as 'Guard your turban, peasant', with the turban being a symbol of the peasant's honour, which would diminish if his land was taken away from him, as the new laws sometimes did).[20] This became the anthem of this movement, stirring the hearts of thousands of people awakening to a revolt. Agitations and demonstrations became the norm of the day and soon Ajit Singh and Lala Lajpat Rai would be arrested and exiled from their motherland.[21]

Both these leaders would be deported to Mandalay, a place in Burma, an Indian territory then, to be jailed for six months. Ajit Singh would later move to Persia where he would collaborate with Sufi Amba Prasad to lay the foundation of a revolutionary centre.[22]

The scenario in the early 1900s in Punjab was fertile and inflammable. Soon, the exodus began. Economic depredations and the lure to earn well attracted many.

They boarded ships sailing to faraway south Pacific countries such as Fiji. Later on, they would discover the excitement and freedom of Canada, a dominion of the British government and breathe free from oppression in America. There they went with hope brimming, the pride of being British subjects reflecting in their gait and love for their nation enveloped in a tiny corner of their hearts.

Chapter 2

The Exodus Abroad: Emigration
of Punjab Peasantry

The middle rung peasantry was the hardest hit with harsh tax regimes and the need for ever-increasing revenues. It became imperative for them to escape the stench of poverty, driven by the lure of earning more and supporting their families back home. The recurring plagues that wiped out generations of families created a scare and many families began sending at least one son out of the country. This was their way of ensuring that the family name survived. To raise the money required to send sons abroad, moneylenders offered money against land, which had become a prized commodity by virtue of increased land rates.

Soon, these men landed on the South Pacific coast islands, in Burma, Malaya, Singapore, China, Iran, Egypt and East Africa as watchmen and guards. They were able to earn much more than they would have earned at home. They not only sent money back home, they also sent stories of lands with opportunities to their people, luring them to these shores.

And then they heard tales of lands that were rich and posh and offered even more pay than what they were earning. They came to know about Canada, a dominion of the British Empire and the United States of America.

Canada to these expats seemed like home for they saw Canadians as British subjects and therefore considered it their right to move freely to any country under the rule of the empire that was governing their own country as well. Did not the Queen say that she would consider all subjects as her own? They believed they had the independence to choose their destination amongst the countries under British rule as dictated by the queen herself.

Agents of the Canadian Pacific Railway Company also lured Punjabi peasants to travel to the dominion of Canada to work in lumber mills or clear land in British Columbia or do farming in California.[1] Before the arrival of Punjabis, the country had witnessed an influx of Chinese and Japanese citizens. In a move to thwart the Chinese entry, a head tax of $500 was proposed, which led to a reduced number of workers from China entering the Canadian market.[2] With Japan, things were settled more amicably by agreeing on a cap on the number of workers to 400 entering every year.[3] This reduction in the number of workers was a loss for the shipping companies. To compensate for these losses, they began a drive to encourage Punjabi peasants to become labourers by advertising high wages offered in the faraway lands as a lucrative proposition.[4]

The Punjabis who moved to Canada initially settled in and around Vancouver city in the province of British Columbia. The climate suited them. It was more or less like Punjab. Warm in summers and cold in winters. This area was being cleared of jungles in the early 1900s and it required labour. Railway lines were being laid to connect the different provinces. The employment opportunities were immense and there were no restrictions on their arrival. They were being let in and this gave them confidence in their belief that they were indeed equals.

The first group arrived in March 1904—five Sikhs bearded, turbaned, wearing European-style clothing sailing on the ship, *Empress of India*. Ten more came on the *Empress of Japan* later on. In 1905, only forty-five Indians managed to reach Canada, but in the coming years, their population increased.[5] The experience of these early expats would prove crucial in directing the future course of action.

The environment in America was also conducive since it bordered Canada and promised greater freedom. The borders were unguarded and even travel to and from India did not require a passport before the beginning of the First World War in 1914. All they needed was a ticket for a ship to move from one country to another. Some therefore moved to the state of California where they started working on vast stretches of farms as unskilled labourers and fruit pickers.

Besides farms, well-built and sturdy Punjabi peasants formed an efficient workforce that was readily employed in the sawmills of the neighbouring state of Oregon, mainly in the cities of Astoria and Portland. They were quick to learn the intricacies of this trade and were very efficient in handling and sawing logs in a short time. Their efficiency rate was double that of the local worker for they often worked double shifts with minimal breaks, unaware of their right to ask for remuneration for the extra work. This penchant for work would be exploited by employers and become a cause of consternation, leading to feuds between the locals and the expats.

The Punjabi peasants working as labourers were mainly concentrated on the western coast of Canada and America around three areas:

1) Areas in and around San Francisco in California state where they worked on farms.
2) The cities of Oregon, Saint John, Portland, Seattle and Astoria near River Columbia, located between the states of Oregon and Washington. Their work was mainly in lumber mills.
3) The cities of Vancouver, Victoria and New Westminster in the state of British Columbia in Canada. Here they mainly cleared forests for newly laid railway tracks.[6]

The 'Hindus', as they were called, had proven themselves to be efficient workers and were much in demand as their credibility rose in Canada and America. They were encouraged to bring in more people of their own. By 1908, there was a considerable increase in the number of Indians living in Canada.

The majority of the influx came from the Doaba side of the Punjab. The districts of Jalandhar and Hoshiarpur, which were the most populous districts with their populace possessing comparatively smaller landholdings, were the first to leave. This immigration to foreign shores went unchecked as the British government was aware that disgruntled peasantry in the state could pose problems and so they were happy to let them go. These early settlers settled on the West Coast because less mechanized work was available and the jobs there involved more physical labour. The East Coast of the US was the hub of machinery that required technical knowledge, which these illiterate peasants lacked. The West Coast became their mecca and their earning ground.

A farmer who earned six to eight annas back home was earning $1.25 to $2 per day as a labourer and these earnings rose to $2.50 to $3 on being promoted to the higher rank of a foreman. During the season of picking and packing fruit, these wages further rose to $3 or $4, which was equal to Rs 9 or Rs 12 in Indian currency.[7] These enhanced incomes gave a boost to their economic prospects and created a win-win situation for both the Punjab peasantry and the British government. The owners who employed them were very impressed by their dedication and sometimes went to the ports and hired them right on arrival.

Among those who sought their fortunes in the US and Canada were Sohan Singh Bhakna and Pandit Kanshi Ram, who would later emerge as important figures in the Ghadar Movement. Delving into their personal histories and journeys provides some insight into the life situation of the early immigrants.

Sohan Singh Bhakna

Bhakna was born into a Jat Sikh family in 1870 in Khutra Khurd village in Amritsar.[8] His father died when he was only one year old. He learnt Gurmukhi from the village *granthi* (typically the person in charge of the gurdwara, who often doubled up as a part-time teacher) but was deprived of a proper school education. The village had no school and his stepmother, who was overprotective, did not give him permission to go to a city.

Once he was sixteen, he took charge of his landholding from his grandmother, who had been the sole person in charge after the demise of his father. Bhakna, naïve in the ways of the world, fell into bad company. His so-called friends used to gather around him and made him spend on them, often taking loans worth thousands from him. Bhakna spent ten years of his life caught up in this turmoil, unable to figure out the real purpose of his life.[9]

Awakening came when Baba Kesar Singh, a Namdhari Sikh, came to the village and exhorted people to shun the evils of society.[10]

When the family faced a financial crisis, Bhakna decided to head for foreign shores. He reached America in April 1909 and started working in a timber factory in Astoria.[11] This soft-spoken, hardy yet gentle peasant was soon acknowledged as something of a leader amongst the expats.

In a few years, the Punjabi immigrant community in Canada and America started reaching out to one another and coalesced into groups. A gurdwara was built in Vancouver, which formed a common meeting point to share their joys and grievances in a communal environment. The Khalsa Diwan Society was also formed in Vancouver to represent the rights of Punjabi expats. Similar safe harbours—gurdwaras—came into existence in California and Oregon as well. The shrine not only gave them a place to practice their religion but also the courage in numbers and a determination to protect their rights and identity.

Pandit Kanshi Ram

Kanshi Ram belonged to an agricultural family and was born in Badi Madoli village in Ludhiana district on 13 October 1883.[12] His father, Pandit Ganga Ram, was the owner of a business in the village and also undertook priestly duties. The additional income raised the prospects of the family, giving them a good life.[13]

Kanshi Ram was a keen student and was the first literate from his village, which made his achievements extra special to his father. As was the norm then, Kanshi Ram was married at the fairly young age of fourteen.

Completing his matriculation, he joined a telegraphy course and then went to Ambala to work as a clerk where he started earning Rs 30 per month.[14]

His desire to do well in life took him to foreign shores and he ended up at Portland, Oregon. Initially, he worked in a bomb-manufacturing unit but later, he went on to become a contractor in one of the lumber mills that employed Punjabi peasants. A disciple of Sufi Amba Prasad, he was a revolutionary at heart. He had a special affinity for people from his homeland and his state. This was evident from the fact that his place was open for Indians, especially Punjabis, to seek any kind of help at any time of the day. His home also became a meeting point for Punjabi labourers to discuss sundry issues bothering them. Jawala Singh Thatthiyan, another Punjabi with revolutionary ideas, had a place in Holtville that became the meeting point of the other Punjabi peasants with revolutionary ideas. Sohan Singh Bhakna, Harnam Singh Tundilat, Udham Singh Kasel and Ram Rakha were working around Portland. Whenever they got time, they used to come to Saint John and stay with Kanshi Ram. They read about the fight for freedom by other natives and nations published in journals and newspapers. This association of minds acted as a crucible, giving rise to a burning rage inside them. By the end of 1908, there were around 3500 Indians in Canada.[15]

Chapter 3

Joining the Army and the Police

Another suitable option to escape the clutches of poverty for Punjabi men was to join the British Army. The loyal role played by Punjabis, especially Sikhs, during 1857, had opened the avenues for recruitment of more people from Punjab. The province had not only remained unaffected during that time but the local armies of the various kings had sided with the English, helping to quell the few mutinous attempts that had arisen in certain pockets.

There was a certain prestige attached to the army job. The men recruited in the British police and army were held in high regard and treated with respect and awe back home. The salary of Rs 7 to Rs 9 per month, which was later increased to Rs 13, was handy to fight the poverty back home.[1] Most of those recruited in the army belonged to the central Punjab districts of Lahore, Jalandhar, Hoshiarpur and Ludhiana.

These men from Punjab were used to not only strengthen the borders of the state and country or to fight off invaders from the east but they also conquered new lands for the British. They were sent to Afghanistan, Iran, Egypt, Burma and Singapore. Life in the army promised excitement and an exposure beyond the stagnant life of home. After leaving the army, these men often longed to travel and left their homes for better pastures. The South Pacific Islands and the cities of Malaya, Hong Kong, Thailand, Sumatra,

Shanghai and Manila witnessed the influx of these ex-army men along with peasants for jobs.[2]

At the diamond jubilee celebration of Queen Victoria in 1897, England invited a delegation of Indian military men to witness this historic event in London. The men who were a part of this delegation were bedazzled by the sights and sounds of a developed nation. They further travelled to the foreign shores of Canada and America, which fuelled their desire to live in this part of the world. When they came back home, many resigned from their jobs and began their journeys abroad. With their medals tinkling on their uniforms, they considered themselves to be British subjects and expected a rousing welcome from the Dominion of Canada. They adapted to the ways of a foreign country by changing the way they dressed, conversing in a smattering of English and Punjabi, and were less conspicuous than their peasant counterparts, who chose to dress in conservative garb and were more rustic in their habits.

Pandit Ram Rakha Bali

Born in 1886 in Sasoli village, Hoshiarpur, Pandit Ram Rakha was the third son of Pandit Jawahir Ram, who had migrated from Lahore.[3] Sasoli was the ancestral village of Ram Rakha. His father used to run a shop in Lahore, but economic hardships forced him to move back to the village that was dominated by Ravidasia, Gujjars, Pandits and Muslim teachers. Baba Hakim had started a primary school on his land and Ram Rakha was an illustrious student of that school.

Sasoli was an unusual village. Originally part of the *jagir* of Todarmal, Emperor Akbar's wazir, its Hindus and Muslims managed to live together peacefully without too many issues. An old mosque in the village had, in fact, been divided between them for their places of worship.

Financial difficulties at home forced Ram Rakha to seek employment. His education strengthened his credentials and he joined the police.[4] He undertook his first assignment in Burma, then a British territory. Later on, he travelled to China, Malaya, the Philippines and Hong Kong wearing the British uniform.

After quitting service, Ram Rakha moved to Canada, where he encountered racism. He would soon become the flame lighting up thousands of hearts in a foreign land.

Harnam Singh Sahri

Harnam was born in 1884 in Kahri Sahri village in Hoshiarpur district and belonged to a rather prosperous family.[5] Due to the demands of a large landholding, he was not able to continue his studies and started supporting his father in his work. But young Harnam's mind was not on agriculture. He was in a continuous state of vexation and attempted to look beyond the ordinary. Eventually, the family's fortunes dipped and he witnessed their descent from landowners to mortgaged labourers.

The changed dynamics forced him to join the army in 1903.[6] He was sent to Burma where he made his own *jatha* (group) in the barracks of his regiment and started encouraging his colleagues to leave the service of the British police. He would often tell them, 'What is this life of ours? For a mere eleven rupees, we are selling our soul to the Englishmen! And creating slaves out of a free country. We tighten the noose around already enslaved countries, pushing them further into the swamp of slavery. How come we are so mad that we do not do anything for our nation?'[7]

When asked why he had joined the service of the British when he was so against them, he would laugh it off saying that it was his way of wanting to experience life under the British rule.

Eventually, he came back home after an eighteen-month stint. In 1904, he left for Hong Kong to join the electric tram company where he was employed for three years.[8] The success story of Canadian immigrants and the lure of higher wages drew him to Canada. He reached Victoria and came into contact with revolutionaries such as G.D. Kumar and Taraknath Das, with whom he would later found the Hindustani Association.[9]

But before that, he would travel back and forth to Seattle and gain admission in Lincoln High School to continue his education. After forming the Swadesh Sewak Home in Vancouver in 1909, Harnam and G.D. Kumar began publishing the monthly newspaper *Swadesh Sewak* in January 1910.[10] The newspaper carried articles from *Bande Mataram* and *Indian Sociologist*, newspapers printed by revolutionaries in Europe. It was similar to *Free Hindustan*, another newspaper brought out by Taraknath Das.[11]

The Swadesh Sewak Home was modelled on the London-based revolutionary Shyamaji Krishnavarma's India House.[12] It was not only a meeting point for migrant workers, it also ran a school for migrant children on its premises and arranged English classes for the immigrants.

Part Punjabi, part English, *Swadesh Sewak* caused quite a stir. Its circulation increased not only in Canada and America but also in the Sikh regiments of the British Army. It spoke to the natives in their own language, exhorting them to revolt against British rule. Its incendiary tone raised the hackles of the government, which was wary of any seditious element encroaching on its strong base, the army.

Sahri, along with Kumar, was active in building communication channels with the Indian peasants working in the lumber mills, the construction industry and railway stations. His movements came under the scanner of the British government and he was deported from Canada when he was trying to cross the border, though this would not discourage him from his revolutionary work.[13]

The Swadesh Sewak Home was closed down because it was under constant surveillance but this was just the end to a new beginning.

Harnam Singh Tundilat

Born in 1884 in Kotla Naudh Singh village in Hoshiarpur, Tundilat joined the British Army in 1902.[14] His family, struggling with financial difficulties, had no other option but to let him go. He was an artist at heart. Whenever he got the chance, he would sing with ardour, recite the Gurmukhi alphabet with panache and narrate the timeless ballads of Heer Waris Shah with eloquence.[15]

While in the army he came to know about the countries of the South Pacific coast where earnings were better. He made up his mind to leave the army and venture out. After the mandatory service of three years in the army, he decided to call it quits.

He left for America in May 1906.[16] He travelled by rail to Calcutta and later boarded a British ship to Hong Kong from where ships would be changed for further travel. In those days, there were hardly any ships that travelled directly from India to Canada and America. And for those who undertook this journey, the ticket prices were far beyond the means of a modest man. Hong Kong was the transition point from where tickets were sold, ships were changed and journeys continued.

There were fifty-two Punjabi passengers on the ship that carried Tundilat.[17] The number of immigrants to Canada and America were now climbing up steadily. He too joined the lumber mill like many others before him and was one amongst fifteen Indians living in Bridal Veil. Their lodgings were at a distance of 30 miles from the abode of Pandit Kanshi Ram. These men would meet frequently in both Bridal Veil and Portland.

The men who wore the English uniform with pride eventually realized the price it was extracting from them. Their pride was nothing but a betrayal of their motherland. And the price they ended up paying was very high. This knowledge, when it gained a foothold inside them, grew considerably, making them relinquish their pride along with their uniform. And they walked away on a solemn quest for their own independence from servility, meeting other comrades on their way and paving the way for a brotherhood. Together, they would fight the servitude of their people, putting their pride in the freedom of their nation.

Chapter 4

Revolutionaries in Exile

In the first decade of the twentieth century, the British came down heavily on those who opposed them. Whenever the government encountered opposition from Indian revolutionaries, the noose was tightened around them. They were deported or imprisoned and their activities restricted. It was difficult for high-spirited revolutionaries to serve their cause by staying in the motherland when such constraints were imposed on them. The way out was to leave the nation to formulate plans and trajectories that could be put into practice back home.

Japan was an anti-British nation that had proved its resilience in the past. America proved to be a mecca for such revolutionaries because it supported the just fight of men of any nation or creed. It was a fertile ground for liberalism, Marxism and communism. It did not impose restrictions on anti-British activities on its soil before the advent of the First World War when it became a British ally in 1917. This would wreak havoc on the activities and lives of revolutionaries working on American soil.

In Punjab, Ajit Singh and Lala Lajpat Rai became forced exiles after being jailed in Mandalay, Burma, for their sharp rhetoric against the government and its policies and for inciting people to rise up in revolt. The voice of the Kuka movement was also quelled by deporting its head, Ram Singh, to Mandalay Jail, in the 1870s.

Europe, especially England and France, became a hive of activity for the revolutionaries who felt asphyxiated by British high-handedness in India. It is a duality that while the British were high-handed with the Indian public, they let the Indian revolutionaries thrive in their own land, which allowed the passion of freedom to resurge with an exhilarated spirit. Before the idea of freedom reached the West Coast of Canada and America, it had been kept burning bright by these revolutionaries in Europe. The Ghadar Movement existed long before the *Ghadar* newspaper was born. It went by different names, but the essence was the same.

Shyamaji Krishnavarma

Born in Kathiawar, then a province in Bombay, in a family of modest means, he received the help of a generous mentor and completed his education. A meritorious student, he was affected by the incidents of that time. The Chapekar brothers were executed for the murder of Commissioner Rand and Tilak's voice was being throttled. At the young impressionable age of twenty-one, he moved from Bombay to England.

The change of place only gave him the impetus to do his heart's bidding with a renewed surge of enthusiasm. He joined the premier University of Oxford, completing his BA and MA, and he studied law as well. He made contacts and aligned with different factions who were sympathetic to the cause of Indian freedom. He made a mark when he began publishing his own paper.[1] The *Indian Sociologist* was subtitled 'an organ of freedom' and carried on its masthead two quotations by the English sociologist, Herbert Spencer, whom Krishnavarma worshipped:

> Every man is free to do that which he wills, provided he infringes not the equal freedom of any other man.

Resistance to aggression is not simply justifiable but imperative. Non-resistance hurts both altruism and egoism.[2]

The journal included a self-explanatory column, 'Ourselves', which highlighted the excesses committed by the British government on the Indian populace. It intended to let the British public know of the atrocities committed by their government on the natives enslaved by them. The journal soon gained notoriety for it was being seen as preaching sedition right from the home of the English.[3]

On 18 February 1905, Krishnavarma founded the Indian Home Rule Society.[4] The name was a misnomer for it was not Home Rule he demanded along with his followers. He did not want to reconcile with a half-hearted dominion rule. He wanted it all as he demanded complete freedom.[5]

That same year, in July 1905, he bought a mansion at 9, Queen's Wood, Highgate and named it India House.[6] It was officially opened on 10 July 1905 with a grand launch. It was to serve as a boarding house for Indian students and was also his residence. Krishnavarma had acquired quite a fortune because of his hard-working nature and austere practices. Even Gandhi was all praise for him when he said:

He lives on a land which he has purchased. Though he can afford to live in comfort, he lives in poverty. He dressed simply and lives like an ascetic. His mission is service to his country. The idea underlying his service is that there should be complete Swaraj for India and that the British should quit the country, handing over power to Indians. If they do not do so, the Indians should refuse them all help so that they become unable to carry on the administration and are forced to leave. He holds that unless this is done the people of India will never be happy. Everything else will follow Swaraj.[7]

In December 1905, Krishnavarma announced three travelling scholarships of Rs 1000 each to young Indians desirous of completing their education abroad with the spirit of nationalism burning in their heart. They were not to take up posts with the Indian government after completing their education but promote the national cause instead. Along with it, he proposed six lectureships of Rs 1000 each to enable people of merit, authors and journalists to visit abroad.[8]

His scholarship scheme attracted many meritorious scholars, among others, Vinayak Damodar Savarkar.[9] Krishnavarma's India House, which housed students irrespective of their caste, was soon dubbed the 'house of mystery' and the activities of the Indian Home Rule Society came in for censure. Krishnavarma had no option but to move out of England to the favourable environs of Paris. Savarkar, his favoured disciple, took charge of India House and the Indian Home Rule Society. Krishnavarma continued publishing the *Indian Sociologist*, initially from England and later from Paris. It was, however, banned in India from September 1907 since it was deemed to feature highly volatile content.

Vinayak Damodar Savarkar

Born in 1883 in Nasik, a Chitpavan Maharashtrian Brahmin, alumnus of Fergusson College, Poona and Bombay University, Savarkar was a trained revolutionary who had been dabbling with fire before he was recommended by Tilak to Krishnavarma as a potential candidate for his scholarship scheme.[10]

The events that happened in Bombay, especially the hanging of the Chapekar brothers, had a marked influence on a young Savarkar, who was only fourteen at that time. A disciple of Sri Agamya Guru Paramhansa and influenced by the teachings of Tilak, he had in him the flair to rouse the passions of those who had a deep devotion for him.[11]

In Bombay, he had formed an association called the Rashtriya Bhakta Samuha (society of devotees of the nation). One year later, he formed another association that was more organized than the previous one and was called Mitra Mela. From this association, he chose recruits and grouped them under the banner of Abhinav Bharat (Young India).[12] A devotee of Italian revolutionary and activist Giuseppe Mazzini, who had played a crucial role in spearheading the Italian revolutionary movement, Savarkar had his heart set on learning more about the organization of European secret societies. This could be one of the reasons for his prompt acceptance of the scholarship offered to him. On the lines of Mazzini's Young Italy, he named his association Young India. His brother Ganesh Savarkar was his close ally in all his activities.[13]

Following the partition of Bengal in 1905, the Savarkar brothers followed Tilak's footsteps, heeded the clarion call from Bengal and burnt mounds of foreign clothes. The cause of Swadeshi and Swaraj was fuelled by the energies of these young men. Before he left for England, Savarkar urged his followers, 'Organize all the people, fill their minds with one thought and with all the strength in your blood, attack the *mlecchas* (foreigners).'[14]

Savarkar arrived in England in July 1906 at the young age of twenty-two. He started residing in India House and registered for a law degree that he was never able to complete because of his revolutionary preoccupations. He had a flair for writing that got transfused with his fight for freedom. He used to edit a journal, *Vihari*, in Bombay. In England, he translated the biography of his idol Mazzini into Marathi,[15] which carried an introduction where Savarkar made comparisons between politics and religion. The book was sent to India to his brother for publication in Poona and it proved to be a smashing success. Around 1000 copies were sold every month. It was taken out in processions, as if it were a sacred religious volume.

Another book that established Savarkar's writing prowess and added to his stature was *The Indian War of Independence*. Written in Marathi, the book became the bible of Indian revolutionaries around the world.

Har Dayal, later to be the spearhead of Ghadar, came into contact with Savarkar at India House. He was inducted by Savarkar into his Abhinav Bharat group, which had been resurrected amidst foreign environs. This Young India group was a cohort of chosen individuals from the larger Free India Society, initially formed by Savarkar upon his arrival. Well versed in the art of operating such revolutionary groups, he laid special emphasis on secrecy and covert operations. Har Dayal too was administered those oaths. From England, Har Dayal picked up the know-how and later on would use these experiences in forming his own party.

Once Krishnavarma left, Savarkar became the undisputed leader of India House.[16] He was experienced, he had the knack of doing things, he commanded respect and was popular amongst his followers and friends. Under his tutelage, the working of India House sharpened its teeth by acquiring an extreme edge. The Sunday meetings held on the premises of India House now raged with talks about bombs and revolvers. Extracts from Savarkar's book, *The Indian War of Independence* were read and the bravery of those who led this war was extolled. Savarkar also embraced Bankim Chandra Chatterji's *Bande Mataram* (Hail Motherland) as the 'national hymn', making it a greeting like the salute of staunch nationalists.

Savarkar had been building support for the Indian cause outside England. He had found support in the radical press all over the world, which not only sympathized with his determined efforts but also espoused them by translating his political articles into German, French, Italian, Russian and Portuguese. Irish agitators extended their arms in welcome and were soon imbued with the cause of the Indian struggle. The Irish mouthpiece *Gaelic American* would find mention multiple times not only for help but a whole-hearted acceptance of the Indian cause, which was unique and rare to find.

For quite some time, Indian revolutionaries were keen to learn how to make a bomb. Once this knowledge was obtained, some of the highly spirited ones even wrote a bomb-making manual. Copies were made of such manuals and sent to revolutionaries back home. Savarkar sent Browning pistols procured from Paris to his brother, who was undergoing a trial. Ganesh Savarkar's crime was the publication of his alleged seditious verses under the title 'Laghu Abhinav Bharat Mela'[17]. He was convicted for the alleged crime on 9 June 1909. The judge pronouncing his sentence said, 'The writer's main object is to preach war against the present government in the names of certain gods of the Hindus and certain warriors such as Shivaji. These names are a mere pretext for the text, which is, take up the sword and destroy the government because it is foreign and oppressive.'[18] Ganesh Savarkar was sentenced to prison in the Andaman Islands.

Arthur Mason Tippett Jackson, the collector of Nasik, was shot dead by seventeen-year-old Ananta Laxman Kanhere in December 1909 while he was watching a play. Kanhere belonged to the Abhinav Bharat Gupta Samaj, a revolutionary group formed by Vinayak Damodar Savarkar. The pistol used for the murder was one amongst the twenty that were sent by Savarkar from Paris. The boy had intended to poison himself but was caught by the police and handed a death sentence. Jackson was killed because he had committed Ganesh Savarkar to trial. This sensational murder came to be known as the Nasik Conspiracy Case.

This case brought to light the weaponry, including arms, gunpowder and pistols, being collected by Savarkar and his men for the greater goal of overthrowing the British Empire. The case involved the trial of thirty-eight men, most of whom were Chitpavan Brahmins from Poona. They were found guilty of seditious writings and inducting men in Abhinav Bharat, and organizing Mitra Melas with the intent of waging war against the king.

Meanwhile in England, Savarkar had decided to up the ante of his activities against the British. He gave rousing speeches exhorting Indians to spill English blood and wreak havoc on their person by all means. These speeches made an impact right away as there was one killing that elevated his credentials of being an extremist leader.

Madanlal Dhingra, an engineering student in England, shot Sir Curzon Wyllie of the India Office at a friendly get-together at the Imperial Institute, London, on 1 July 1909. Dhingra was sentenced to death for this crime. His last words before his death illuminated the ultimate sacrifice he undertook:

I admit, the other day, I attempted to shed English blood as a humble revenge for the inhuman hangings and deportations of patriotic Indian youths. In this attempt I have consulted none but my own conscience; I have conspired with none but my own duty. I believe that a nation held in bondage with the help of foreign bayonets is in perpetual state of war. Since open battle is rendered impossible to a disarmed race, I attacked by surprise; since guns were denied to me, I drew forth my pistol and fired. As a Hindu, I feel that a wrong done to my country is an insult to God. Poor in health and intellect, a son like myself has nothing to offer to the Mother but his own blood, and so I have sacrificed the same on her altar. Her cause is the cause of Shri Rama. Her services are the services of Shri Krishna. This War of Independence will continue between India and England so long as the Hindu and the English races last (if this present unnatural relation does not cease). The only lesson required in India at present is to learn how to die and the only way to teach it is by dying ourselves. Therefore I die and glory to my martyrdom. My only prayer to God is: may I be reborn of the same Mother and may I re-die in the same sacred cause till the cause is successful and she stands free for the good of humanity and the glory of God. Vande Mataram![19]

Savarkar's movements were being watched and when it appeared that he would be arrested for his activities, he had no way out but to escape to Paris where he had joined Krishnavarma and other revolutionaries. In Paris, Savarkar started a new journal *Talwar* (Dagger), which was being published from Berlin earlier and edited by another revolutionary, Virendranath Chattopadhyaya, the younger brother of Sarojini Naidu, fondly known as Chatto.

In Paris, Savarkar was getting desperate to come out of his self-imposed exile. He knew he would be implicated in the Jackson murder case if caught. Taking the risk, he returned to England and was arrested the moment he stepped out of Victoria Station. He was soon deported to India where he was sentenced to rigorous imprisonment in the Andamans in 1910. In between, he made an unsuccessful attempt to escape at Marseilles when the India-bound ship halted there for a short while.

Madam Bhikaji Rustom Cama

Known as the 'Mother of the Indian Revolution', she was the daughter of a rich Parsi businessman. Born in 1861, she was the epitome of revolutionary grit for European revolutionaries.[20] She was their guiding spirit.

She left India in 1902 after witnessing the plague epidemic of 1896. She was incensed by the oppressive measures instituted by the then British plague commissioner, Rand, an event that dominated the minds of ordinary men and women, turning them into revolutionaries for a lifetime. His actions affected Indian sensibilities. Cama was moved by the plight of the sufferers as she would harp on this emotion, transmitting it through her writings in the two journals she edited later in her life.

Cama, after travelling through Scotland, France, England and America, finally settled down in Paris in May 1909 where she started her radical propaganda on the lines of the teachings of

Savarkar. Both of them advocated the use of force in their methods to achieve freedom. Cama firmly believed in the importance of revolutionary literature as part of the freedom struggle. She was not wrong in saying that because of the restrictive measures of the government, the action had shifted from Calcutta, Poona and Lahore to Paris, Geneva, Berlin, London and New York. These views were published in her journal, *Bande Mataram*, which was on similar lines as *Indian Sociologist* by Krishnavarma, the only difference being that the voice of *Bande Mataram* was more crisp and full of rhetoric, intending to inflict damage and create a whirlpool of revolutionary activity that would threaten the British government.

Bande Mataram was initially edited by Har Dayal but later on, he passed on the editorship to Cama when he moved away from Paris. Similarly, the journal *Talwar* was initially published in Berlin under the editorship of Virendranath Chattopadhyaya but later, it came under Cama's aegis. Along with Cama was her faithful comrade S.R. Rana.

Madam Cama was very vociferous in her opinions when it came to castigating the British for their actions. The deportation of Lajpat Rai and Ajit Singh to Mandalay[21] on 9 May and 3 June 1907,[22] respectively, elicited some harsh words from her:

> If we all speak bravely like Lajpat Rai, how many forts and prisons must the government build before it can deport or confine us all. We are three hundred million strong. If Hindus and Muslims, Parsis and Christians would realize that they were as much Indians as Lajpat Rai this would provide the unity we require. Let us make his cause and his suffering as our own.[23]

Both these ideas of filling up the jails and non-cooperation with the government were taken up by Mahatma Gandhi to be part of his freedom struggle. Her views, which were made as an appeal to Indian populace, were published in Cama's journal *Bande Mataram* as well.

Cama represented India at multiple foreign forums. Everywhere, she captivated people with her roaring voice bellowing grave warnings of doom for the British and at the same time pleading for help from the international community. At the meeting of the London Indian Society held on 20 February 1909 at Essex Hall, Strand, she took out her self-designed silk Indian flag from her pocket on which were inscribed the words 'Swadesh' and 'Bande Mataram', asking all present to let her unfurl the flag over her head for she was only in the habit of speaking under its shadow.[24] Similarly, in Stuttgart where the International Socialist Congress was held on 18 August 1907, she represented India in front of a thousand attendees. She defied the protests of the British delegation to bring an unofficial resolution condemning British imperialism in India.[25]

Cama was well connected with French socialists and Irish freedom fighters who ran their own magazine, *Gaelic American*. Her writings not only helped the cause of the Indian revolution but she was also generous with her monetary support. Her journal gave Har Dayal an opportunity to learn all about the management of a journal. This knowledge would come in handy when he would bring out his own voice on paper in the form of a weekly newspaper that would be grander and more verbose in its attack. It would create a 'Ghadar' with its name and its approach.

Ramnath Puri

A bank clerk from Lahore, Puri came under the scanner of the government when he was caught publishing seditious pamphlets and a highly objectionable cartoon making fun of the British-Indian regime in 1905.[26] He chose to leave rather than get arrested and arrived in America sometime in 1906 as a political exile.

He is credited as the first person who ignited the flame of Indian freedom on Canadian and American shores. Before his arrival, the men had been listless, enduring their fate and had shown no spark for a cause they had no idea existed before them. But with the arrival of Puri, new avenues opened up, new associations were founded. He formed an association called 'Hindustan Association' in San Francisco and later on in Astoria and Vancouver.

The objectives of the association included making people politically volatile and active and training them in the use of guns and weapons, and making the American populace sensitive to the cause of the Indian freedom struggle.

He was the first on the Pacific coast to start a journal in Urdu called *Circular-i-Azadi* (Circular of Freedom) from 3700, California Street, San Francisco.[27] And after his journal came many more, emulating its success, following its footsteps.

In one of its issues, he wrote: 'We are no longer immersed in Asiatic ignorance. The king is no longer to us the representation of God in the country. We have come to know that people possess the right of appointing and dethroning kings.'[28]

Apart from the journal, he published seditious pamphlets and sent them to India to be circulated. He also lent support to the Swadeshi movement in Bengal.

He went into oblivion soon after igniting this flame. Amidst charges of forgery and looting his own gullible people in 1906, his role ended too soon, but he definitely was one of the earliest torchbearers.

Taraknath Das

He was born in Kathanpara, near Calcutta on 15 June 1884.[29] A recruit of the original Anushilan Samiti since 1903, he was also instrumental in forming its Dacca branch in 1905.

He was one amongst the first batch of students to be sent abroad with a specific mission. These students were to master the art of revolution and equip themselves with state-of-the-art knowledge by learning about the struggles undertaken against despotic regimes by revolutionaries around the world. They had to learn how to incorporate the same practices in their warfare. He was chosen with a careful eye by Jatindra Mukherjee, the 'Tiger of Bengal', also known as Jatin Bagha.

At the young age of twenty-three, he travelled from India to Japan and later to New York and then to Seattle where he earned a college degree and took up a job as an interpreter for Vancouver's US immigration office.[30] In Vancouver, he was joined by his comrades Guru Dutt Kumar and Surendramohan Bose, who worked in close association with him.

He started his political propaganda in Vancouver for which he had been trained in India despite holding a government position.

In January 1908, he opened a school for immigrant Sikhs near Millside, New Westminster.[31] Along with Bose, he launched an Indo-Vancouver Indian association and was designated as its treasurer. He started the publication of an eight-page English language bi-monthly journal, the much-acclaimed *Free Hindustan*, which was inspired by Krishnavarma's *Indian Sociologist*.[32]

The tone of this journal was severely anti-British and it preached extremism. It frequently published open calls to Indians, especially Sikhs, to leave their jobs in the army and side with the revolutionaries. The first issue of this paper highlighted the restrictions placed on the passengers of the ship, SS *Monteagle*.[33] It hinted at the upcoming law of placing legal restrictions on Indian passengers, which Taraknath suspected were in the making.

While in Vancouver, he and Bose created awareness amongst the Sikh population that was struggling as they were being branded 'outsiders', and were facing racial discrimination. Though the Sikhs were wary of Bengalis, they did accept their help in forming a committee for the management of Sikh gurdwaras.[34]

The political activities of Das and the seditious tone of *Free Hindustan* led to the loss of his job. To avoid prosecution on this account, he moved to Seattle from where he carried on with the publication of his paper. He used the printing press facilities of the American paper, *Western Clarion*. American liberals came to his help and with their support, he founded the Association for Promotion of Education for the People of India. He also formed an organization titled the United India House in Seattle with the help of the local Bengali population. He used to visit the camps of Sikh labourers in and around Seattle to preach the cause of revolution.

But Das was not to remain in Seattle for long. He moved to New York and started publishing his paper by forming a close association with *Gaelic American*, in whose folds it often travelled disguised to escape the notice of the Canadian government. New York was the hotbed of Irish revolutionaries, who were fighting for their own freedom. They were sympathetic to the cause of the Indian struggle. George Freeman, the proprietor of the Irish paper, was influential and a big help to many Indian revolutionaries.[35]

The journal was funded by Taraknath's own money and it changed places of publication based on his own movement.[36] Finally, in 1910, the curtains closed *for Free Hindustan* when Das ran out of money.[37]

He moved to Norwich, Vermont, and enrolled himself in the prestigious military school, but he could not get through to the advanced training because of his nationality and his background.[38] Das would later earn advanced degrees from the universities of Washington and California.[39]

Guru Dutt Kumar

He belonged to Bannu in the North-West Frontier Province.[40] He got sucked up in the revolutionary spirit prevailing in Calcutta when the partition of West Bengal was announced in 1905. He used to teach Urdu at National College, Calcutta, when he came into contact with Taraknath Das. When Das moved to Canada, Kumar followed him and reached British Columbia around 1907 where he opened a grocery store.[41]

Under the tutelage of Das, Kumar became secretary of the Hindustan Association in 1909. The organization boasted of some 250 members who were mainly students and the educated class of British Columbia.[42] The aim of the association was self-governance and the promulgation of domestic goods, education, industry, trade and agriculture.

Kumar was instrumental in opening the Swadesh Sewak Home in Vancouver in 1910 along with his associates.[43] The model was the same as that of the famed India House being run in London. This place doubled up as a school for immigrants' children but was also used by the Pacific coast revolutionaries, who were better trained and aware of their activities being intercepted than their eastern counterparts, where the movement so far had not generated much of a buzz. While Das was publishing *Free Hindustan* in English, Kumar started bringing out its counterpart in Gurmukhi titled *Swadesh Sewak*. Both the papers were using articles printed in *Indian Sociologist* and *Bande Mataram*.[44]

Kumar, along with Harnam Singh Sahri, also took up the initiative of involving the local Punjabi populace in his initiative, who had been unconnected with Das and his activities. There was a deep Punjabi-Bengali divide that Kumar tried to breach by meeting the Punjabi labourers frequently. He was always on the lookout for potential revolutionary material in the newcomers arriving on the shores of Canada. He would rope in the young and the bright, imparting them military training.[45] His activities attracted the attention of the Canadian authorities, which, unlike the American government, took strict notice of the militarism brewing in their land.

Colin S. Campbell, chief constable of Vancouver, wrote to the superintendent of police on 23 January 1908 stating, 'There existed in Vancouver, an organization of Indians which preached sedition under the cover of religious pretexts and that it collected money, ostensibly for the purpose of Gurudwara, but actually for purchasing arms and making other preparations for a violent uprising in India.'

Kumar had to shut down the paper as well as his organization and take cover in Seattle in June 1911 where Das had already migrated. In Seattle, Kumar started a journal called *Span of Life* for some time.

Both Das and Kumar once again returned to Vancouver and joined hands by forming a brand-new organization called the United India House, which was initially formed in Seattle. In the meantime, the Sikhs of Vancouver had organized themselves into the Khalsa Diwan Society. They allowed Das and Kumar to use the premises of the gurdwara. Now two parallel organizations were running from a common point of origin whose agenda was the same. A stark divide persisted between the educated Bengalis and the uneducated Punjabi labourers.

This must have troubled Kumar because he had always preached reforms in society. Despite the deep divides, he frequented the camps of Punjabi labourers and advocated to them the evils of alcohol, the consumption of which was rampant in their quarters. He encouraged them to rise above caste differences and participate in the spirit of community welfare.

This breach would only be filled by the formation of a common front later, representing all sections of Indians. But this would only happen after the arrival of Har Dayal.

Abdul Hafiz Mohammed Barakatullah 'Bhopali'

Born on 7 July 1854 in Itwara, Mohalla Bhopal in Madhya Pradesh, he was the son of a government employee. A meritorious and intelligent student, he was quick to learn Arabic, Persian, Urdu, Turkish, English, German and Japanese.[46] He left his home to serve as a tutor in Khandwa and Bombay.[47] From there he moved to England in 1895 to teach Arabic in Oriental College at Liverpool University.[48]

While in England he came into contact with Har Dayal, Krishnavarma and Raja Mahendra Pratap, son of the Raja of

Hathras, among others. It was in England that he began his revolutionary activities. His first consisted of writing a weekly newsletter on England's affairs. In London, he also got in touch with an association called the Muslim Patriotic League and helped them in editing a newspaper called the *Crescent* and a magazine the *Islamic World*.[49]

From England, he travelled to New York and became a pioneer in opening the revolutionary front on the East Coast. The Pan-Aryan association was established in New York in the autumn of 1906. A house was rented in New York in January 1908 and it was named India House. The much-acclaimed set-up of Krishnavarma in London was the guiding spirit. The place not only provided cheap lodging to the few Indian students studying in New York, it became the meeting point of the revolutionaries beginning to get active on the eastern front. Soon branches were opened in Chicago and Detroit, replicating the success of New York, and the membership of this society rose to a few hundred.

Valuable contacts were formed with George Freeman, the editor of *Gaelic American*. He also assisted Freeman with the publication of Taraknath's paper *Free Hindustan*.[50]

Barakatullah was a great advocate of Hindu-Muslim unity and placed the cause of the nation above the narrow confines of region, religion and caste identities. Perhaps this was the reason that later he identified himself with the Ghadar Movement started by Sikh peasants, nurtured by their Bengali counterparts, incorporating people of different states but one nation. A modern thinker, his efforts were always concentrated on the bigger picture and that was the freedom of his motherland.

From New York he moved to Tokyo, Japan, in February 1909 and joined the school of foreign languages as a teacher in Urdu.[51] Those were the times when the anti-British feeling in Japan was high, which helped in garnering support for the cause of a free Hindustan. Barakatullah started editing a paper, *Islamic Fraternity*, in which he espoused the cause of Indian revolutionaries.[52]

He remained in constant touch with Krishnavarma and other revolutionary friends from London and France. He became a crucial interface in this war where the pen became a substitute for the gun and the written word ruled the roost.

His literary interests grew manifold and the decibel level of sedition increased in Tokyo as he published an Urdu pamphlet, *An-Nazir al-Uryan* in May 1912.[53] Two more revolutionary pamphlets came out in early 1913—*Akher al-Helal Saif* in Urdu and *Proclamation of Liberty* in English.[54] This was the time when the Japanese were thawing towards the British. A new warmth between the two nations, which were to be allies soon in a war, spelled doom for all the magazines and papers preaching against England. Barakatullah's activities too came to an end amidst such circumstances, when the Japanese government under duress banned all such newspapers and magazines carrying an air of sedition.

He once again moved to New York and from there to Constantinople (present-day Istanbul) where he got influenced by a strong Pan-Islamic movement brewing under the caliphate. In between all this, he would become a part of the historic Ghadar Party.

Pandurang Khankhoje

Born on 7 November 1886 in Palakhwadi village, Wardha, in Maharashtra, Pandurang Khankhoje was an ardent disciple of Bal Gangadhar Tilak, the extremist leader from the Vidarbha region.[55]

As a young boy, he formed his own society called Bal Samaj.[56] Though his activities were not supported by his family, Khankhoje grew up with a strong inclination to learn military warfare.

He soon developed links with the famed Anushilan Samiti in Bengal and under the guidance of Tilak, proceeded to Saigon, Vietnam to fulfil his objectives.[57] He was disappointed to see the lack of political vision amongst Indian students in Japan, who were mainly concerned with their studies. He was credited with the formation of the first branch of the Indian Independence League, which would further proliferate in America.

Khankhoje not only advocated freedom for India, his vision even encompassed the rise and growth of the nation as a provider that fulfilled the needs of her populace. He was enamoured with the study of agriculture, which he believed was the key to improve the crop yield and thus the fortunes of a nation.

He joined the Mount Tamalpais Military Academy in San Rafael, California, to keep himself motivated while working on petty jobs to sustain himself and pay his tuition fee.[58] The Irish professors were supportive of his cause and identified with the long and arduous struggle to freedom. While Khankhoje gained help for his cause and the sympathy of his teachers, he was in for a shock when he was not able to apply for an advanced course in military academics because of being Indian.

He made his way to the west coast of America where the Punjabi peasant population worked in large numbers in the states of Washington, Oregon and California. After establishing another branch of the Indian Independence League in San Francisco, a city that would play a crucial role in amalgamating the collective woes of Indians and providing them a direction and a place of action, Khankhoje moved to Oregon where he came in touch with Kanshi Ram.

The two connected well and from here, Khankhoje's Indian Independence League grew in number of members and branches. He opened centres in Portland, Astoria and Sacramento. Kanshi Ram connected Khankhoje to the peasants working in lumber mills in the Oregon region where he was not acknowledged and taken to kindly because of the distrust manifested by Punjabi peasants towards the educated. They had encountered many English-educated babus who had duped them of their money.

Kanshi Ram had warned Khankhoje of their disapproval but nevertheless he went ahead. Language became a big hurdle as Khankhoje fumbled with words. How was a Marathi-speaking man to communicate with Punjabi-speaking peasants, who were hesitant to learn a foreign tongue and professed their faith in their own language? Khankhoje not only learnt a smattering of Punjabi and Urdu to communicate with them, he also spent time with them making himself useful. He would help them with writing letters, buying medicines and raising their awareness by talking about their exploitation where the natives worked in a far better environment and were well guarded with their rights and their demands.

The Sunday communions yielded fruit as Khankhoje was able to garner the trust of the workers, especially their leader and granthi Sohan Singh Bhakna, who had been vocal about his dislike of Khankhoje's intrusion. He had resented Khankhoje's help and took it as an affront for he was taking up a leadership role in the community of peasants.

Bhakna finally let down his guard and accepted this Marathi man as their own and in a gesture of goodwill, Khankhoje espoused his name for the presidency of the Portland branch of the Indian Independence League. Bhakna was managing one of the branches in Portland while the other was being managed by Kanshi Ram, while Khankhoje started looking after the work in Astoria.

* * *

Thus, these revolutionaries whose voice was throttled in their own motherland, who were banished from their own country, were on fertile ground on foreign shores where they proliferated. With their work they associated with more young people, and the voices of these dissidents rose, the clamour soon reaching a crescendo. The peasants, the bearers of the uniforms and the revolutionaries exiled from their homeland traced their entwined paths, circumambulating around a common emotion. They connected the dots and moved towards a common destination, freedom for their nation.

Chapter 5

The Lure of Studying Abroad

Historically, Indian education was mainly of a classical and spiritual nature and less practical in intent. It was mainly taught in Sanskrit, Arabic and Persian.[1] It was not meant to inculcate a scientific aptitude in students. At the village level, Brahmins gathered students and taught them. The teachers received no fee and the onus for providing accommodation for the students rested with them. The course duration extended for fifteen to twenty years with long and severe hours of teaching.[2] The Muslim seats of learning were called madrasas. They were few in number and were primarily meant for the training of law officers.[3]

The village-level elementary schools, where studies were conducted in the regional language, were called *pathshalas* and *maktabs*.[4] These schools existed because of people's generosity. Girls were not encouraged to be part of these schools because of superstition and regressive social mores and customs. A survey conducted by Thomas Munro in 1826, the then Governor of Madras Presidency, recorded there were 12,498 schools with 1,88,650 pupils in the province and a similar survey in the Bombay Presidency by the governor recorded the existence of 1705 such schools accommodating 35,153 pupils.[5] With roughly two schools for every three villages, this mode of education was very popular, serving the needs of the zamindars, trading communities and well-to-do farmers. The students were taught reading, writing and arithmetic. Although there were no printed books, students used slates and pencils. They could join the school at any time and leave when they had gained enough knowledge.[6]

This classical system of learning was patronized by some officials of the East India Company. When they came, the British wanted to spread English education with a view to propagating Christianity in India. They tried to substitute English for Persian as the official language so that Indians would take an active interest in learning it and be acquainted with the vast gamut of European knowledge. They thought that a common language would be beneficial to form a close contact between the ruler and the ruled and would also cure the Indian nature of superstition and false beliefs, promoting an aptitude for scientific knowledge.[7] A general committee of public instruction was formed for that purpose but the educational policy of this committee was not successful; they had a series of failed experiments between 1823 and 1826. The Serampore College was started in Bengal to train Indians in arts and sciences. Similar schools were established in Calcutta, Burdwan, Khulna and Krishnanagar in Bengal and at Agra, Chunar and Meerut.[8] Schools for teaching English came into existence in Hughli, Burdwan, Midnapur, Dacca, Barisal, Santipur, Murshidabad, Rangpur, Allahabad, Agra and Delhi.[9]

While steps were taken to bring the English language into official usage, it was suggested that schools of oriental learning be closed down as they were not serving any useful purpose.

Also the approach of bringing education to the masses was being fervently snubbed. The new approach was to give higher education to a select few in preference to a common education to many.[10]

Soon, dissent arose against the educational policies of the British. The Hindus and Muslims who were in favour of English education started sending petitions around 1835 to the government to stop the anglicization and conversion of their people. The decision to bring English to the forefront was not acceptable to them any more. Scholarships in schools were abolished and once again, the vernacular was accepted as the method of teaching to placate the orthodox Indians. The British did not want to extend any kind of help to the indigenous village schools, which they thought were impractical and expensive. They wanted education to remain the prerogative of upper- and middle-class Indians.

To act on their plan, funds were directed to the construction of some central colleges in Dacca, Patna, Benares, Allahabad, Agra and Bareilly.[11] No funds were allocated to the village-level schools while money was directed to the few Central colleges that were well-populated and their location was convenient. The study of jurisprudence, government and morals was encouraged in these institutes. One of the aims of these colleges was to raise a class of inferior schoolmasters.[12]

In the subsequent years, higher education was given credence and many universities were established, the first three being in Calcutta, Bombay and Madras. Punjab University was established in 1882 and Allahabad University in 1887.[13] Though higher education under the British showed phenomenal growth, these university-educated Indians were not incorporated into the system and were often left jobless, raising the rate of unemployment. Moreover, the nature of courses being taught in these Indian universities limited the career choices of the students, making them unable to find a job for themselves. More emphasis was given on literature and philosophy, while courses offering practical instruction were not being offered.[14]

These students could not be absorbed in the army and politics and to get into manufacturing and skilled employment, they had to compete against European industry, which was not feasible for they did not have the required expertise, the money to invest and were not treated at par with their European counterparts.

Agriculture was not lucrative and was rather mundane to the educated Indian; the civil service exam had to be given in England[15] and there was reluctance on the part of the British government to admit Indians. The only jobs available to Indians were low-paying with no promotion channels and poor service conditions. A few ventured into independent professions, such as teaching, law, journalism and medicine.[16]

The US had interests in a growing India, which was a burgeoning market to be harvested and sold things to. A few wealthy and visionary Americans in collaboration with Indians in the US formed an Indo-American National Association,[17] whose role was to encourage and motivate Indian students to consider the US for education. This alliance played a crucial role in generating a buzz amongst students in India, who started moving towards America for higher education. It was not able to generate a market for American goods in India because of the repressive policies of the British that did not allow any other country to have stakes in the market in which they were the only player. But the association was able to create a sympathetic view towards Indians among Americans, who were open to Indian students and goaded them to work against the British and the oppression they inflicted upon a populace of such a large magnitude.

Jawala Singh Thatthiyan[18], a prosperous potato farmer and an agricultural entrepreneur who lived near Stockton, California,[19] ran a farm in Holtville where Indian students were employed in their summer break. His desire to do something for people back home prompted him to initiate the Guru Gobind Singh scholarships[20] for desirous and meritorious students in 1912.[21] The scholarship was to be split into eight parts over a period of one year. It would take care of their tuition, textbooks, lab, fees, room and board, second-class return passages to India and provide a $50 monthly stipend.[22] There were certain conditions these students had to comply with. They would have to work and earn their own money and take care of their expenses in the summer break. They would be given an option either to work at Jawala Singh's farm or to choose any other place of their liking.

The sponsors of the scholarships would have the power to withdraw or cancel the scholarship if any of these conditions were circumvented. With the acquiescence of Lala Har Dayal, Prof. Teja Singh[23] and others, six deserving students were chosen for the academic year 1912–13,[24] of which two were Gobind Behari Lal[25] and Darisi Chenchiah. Kartar Singh Sarabha too joined them later when a chance meeting took place between him and Jawala Singh in California at a farm where Sarabha was working. He accepted Jawala Singh's generous offer of a scholarship and joined the University of Berkeley along with others in the summer of 1912.[26]

The beginning of 1912 witnessed a slump in Jawala Singh's potato business. This was the year of recession and it garnered no income for the potato king.[27] The students had come at their own expense with an assurance that the scholarship would cover their expenditure as promised.[28]

The constant calls from Berkeley for money went unheeded. It was not only the lack of income that was giving Jawala Singh sleepless nights, it was also the firm opposition from the extremist factions of the Sikh clergy that was demoralizing for him. People like Teja Singh wanted students to serve their faith by installing the Guru Granth Sahib in their rented accommodation. He wanted them to make regular prayers and reading of the scriptures a part and parcel of their student life along with university studies.

Jawala Singh disagreed with their proposal because he wanted the students to maximize their time for study-related activities. He thought that religion should be their personal choice and should not be foisted upon them. He considered it a waste of their precious time. His stand was not appreciated by his brethren, who took it as an offence and started a campaign of firm opposition against him. Singh was delisted from the post of vice president of the gurdwara committee.

Later, he was unable to fund the scholarships once his business hit a rough patch. The students invited under his scholarship programme were left to fend for themselves. They were able to manage their expenses on their own by calling for family help and by working at Jawala Singh's farm during their summer break. This farm became a meeting point for Indian students and the Punjabi peasants working as labourers. It was also frequented by revolutionaries in exile, such as Taraknath Das and Khankhoje. The disunited factions were now coming together.

Kartar Singh Sarabha

Born on 24 May 1896, Sarabha lost his father early in his life and his grandfather became his guardian.[29] The aged grandfather adored Sarabha and though he himself was tilling his forefathers' land, he detested the thought of the young boy doing labour. He wanted him to get educated and be like his uncles, who were pursuing government jobs.[30]

Sarabha completed his primary education in Sarabha village. He moved to Gujranwala to complete his middle school and later to Ludhiana for high school. He was an ever-smiling, witty and helpful pupil whose company was sought after by his classmates. He was called 'the flying snake' by his friends for being agile, nimble and for dreaming the impossible and coming up with the most innovative means to achieve it.

For college education, Sarabha was sent to Orissa and enrolled in Ravenshaw College, Cuttack. Orissa, along with Bihar, was then a part of the Bengal province that had been divided on religious lines in 1905 by Lord Curzon. Sarabha arrived in Cuttack amidst the charged atmosphere of anti-British sentiments. Being a highly receptive youth, he imbibed the resentment of people around him and ended up internalizing it. The magnitude of his thoughts and ideas grew manifold under these circumstances.

Apart from his academic texts, Sarabha started reading books and magazines to grasp more about life beyond his reach. The idea of going to America for higher education sprouted inside him amidst the turmoil. Receiving his family's support, this sixteen-year-old set sail for San Francisco and landed on American soil on 1 January 1912.[31]

Sarabha was deeply disappointed by the behaviour of immigration officials at the port. He and other immigrants were referred to as 'black men' and 'slave Hindus' again and again. Deeply troubled by this segregation and inferior treatment, he started working in the San Francisco area, availing job opportunities beckoning Punjabis. He attended a conference of labourers that saw the participation of Sohan Singh Bhakna, Harnam Singh Tundilat and Pandit Kanshi Ram. Here, Sarabha met Jawala Singh Thatthiyan, who motivated him to join Berkeley University in California. This university would become the hub of Indian students who would be revolutionized in mind and spirit.

Sarabha soon resumed his studies and joined the department of chemistry in Berkeley University.

Darisi Chenchiah

Born in 1890, in Nellore district of Andhra Pradesh, Chenchiah was one amongst the six students selected for scholarship.[32] He settled for BSc agriculture in California University, Berkeley.[33]

Around thirty students were living in the university campus and the hostel was divided into two camps: Punjabi and non-Punjabi.[34] Chenchiah experienced the divide between north and south. He observed that though both factions of students were politically motivated, the Punjabi students were seemingly more radicalized in their means to achieve their cause while the non-

Punjabis, who were mainly Bengalis, were more restrained in their approach.[35] The Bengali students were more inclined towards study and wanted to go back home to pursue government jobs, and they believed non-violence was the best strategy.[36] Perhaps it was this nature of thought that divided the students.

Chenchiah was deeply disappointed when he was shooed away from the Punjabi hostel. But the uniting force between these two factions appeared in the form of an adhesive known as Lala Har Dayal. He roused the students and gave them a much-needed direction. He would often address the students in the Punjabi hostel where Chenchiah would sit mesmerized, invigorated by the infusion of this new spirit of nationalism.[37]

Har Dayal would lay the foundation of Nalanda Hostel at Berkeley, which would unite the Punjabis and non-Punjabis for a common aim, the freedom of their motherland. Both Sarabha and Chenchiah moved to this hostel to be part of the like-minded group. Har Dayal, who taught at Stanford University, often spent his weekends at this hostel. In 1912, when he resigned from his job, he made this hostel his permanent abode.

Jatinder Nath Lahiri

Hailing from Bengal was another student in the scholarship scheme: Jatinder Nath Lahiri. He had moved to Nalanda Hostel along with Chenchiah and Sarabha.[38] A graduate from the University of Calcutta, he was pursuing research on explosives. He had been sent by a revolutionary group from Bengal to learn the art of making explosives. Clearly, not all the students from Bengal went in for the safety of government jobs. Students like Lahiri were revolutionaries back home and were firmly entrenched in their purpose. He was a well-read man who was not oblivious to the struggles of people of other nations who had fought or were still fighting the scourge of slavery. He made his peers read biographies of famous revolutionaries, such as Mazzini, Rousseau, Sun Yat Sen, Prince Kropotkin and Guru Gobind Singh. Chenchiah was enamoured by the restless spirit of Lahiri, who would teach them the tricks employed by Bengali revolutionaries back home and encouraged them to be physically strong and mentally balanced to handle any situation.

Vishnu Ganesh Pingle

Born in January 1888 in a village, Talegaon Dhamdhere, near Poona, in a Brahmin family,[39] Pingle enrolled himself in a Poona college for higher education in 1905. Pingle had become involved in the freedom struggle much before his association with the Ghadar Movement. He was deeply associated with Savarkar.[40]

In 1910, Pingle left Poona and moved to Mahim in Mumbai. He started working at an alkali unit in Mahim owned by Gobindrao Potdar, who was a nationalist and expert in bomb-making.[41] Under his tutelage, Pingle was exposed to a more nationalist framework of revolutionaries. Later on, Pingle also set up his own workshop at Latur though he always wanted to be an engineer.

His desire to study in America was fulfilled when he secured admission in Washington State University in 1912 and started studying engineering there. Pingle would later come in contact with Sarabha and the others.

These students who went to foreign shores to light themselves up with the flame of education ended up igniting themselves with a revolutionary fervour. Their motive to create a better life for themselves did get jeopardized when they found out that the conditions for them in these foreign lands were not so conducive. But, their interaction with the peasants and the revolutionaries would change the course of their lives.

Chapter 6

The Face of Ghadar: Lala Har Dayal

Born in an educated Kayastha family in October 1884, Har Dayal was the youngest of four sons of Lala Gauri Lal.[1] His father, a government employee, worked as a reader and the sons, by default, were expected to follow in the footsteps of the father.[2] His elder brothers ended up becoming lawyers. The eldest, Manohar Lal, practised at Meerut while the two youngest, Bhairo Dayal and Kishan Lal, practised in Muzaffarnagar and Delhi, respectively.[3] Har Dayal was the ideal type for a government job—hardworking, studious, sensitive and receptive to changes around him, with a family that was flourishing under the shadow of British rule. Nothing less was expected of him but loyalty to the *sarkar*.

Har Dayal was a prodigy and he proved his mettle very early in childhood. He not only read extensively but he could commit the words to memory with ease, reproducing each and everything that had passed in front of his eyes precisely, in a neatly defined order.[4] His memory was phenomenal and left people speechless.

He attended Christian mission schools in Delhi and was awarded the bachelor of arts degree by St Stephen's College.[5] He stood first in every examination he ever took in his life until his graduation. His English was so good that his papers were retained in schools and colleges as model test papers, the paragons of perfection.[6] He won numerous awards and scholarships during his school and college years.

It was only in his graduation that he came second overall, his marks dragging him down from the pedestal to which he was so used to. The man who surpassed him was from Lahore and this influenced Har Dayal to go to Lahore for his master's degree.[7]

Lahore was the place that gave shape to new beliefs and ideologies that were hitherto unknown to Har Dayal. It was burgeoning with new voices and ideas that were subdued in Delhi. Lahore would turn him conscientious and invoke in him a keen eye to understand his troubled nation better. He enrolled himself as a member of the Rational Society of the city and gained prominence with his involvement in their various activities.

The first and foremost person to influence him was the 'Lion of Punjab', Lala Lajpat Rai. The leader, who was associated with the Pagri Sambhal Jatta movement with Ajit Singh, had been imprisoned in Mandalay but was now back on the scene. He was connected with the Dayanand Anglo-Vedic (DAV) College, an Arya Samajist, a leader of national importance, an influencer of a new creed of extremist revolutionaries and had served as a lecturer in history at DAV College.[8] Later, he took on the occupation of a full-time leader, leaving his teaching post.

Bhai Parmanand became a close confidant of Har Dayal during his Lahore days. Their paths would intersect many times in their lifetime. Born in 1875, a native of Jhelum, raised in Chakwal in the Punjab province, Bhai Parmanand started practising the tenets of the Arya Samaj from a young age.[9] While Har Dayal was studying, Bhai Parmanand, after receiving his Master of Arts degree at the Punjab University had started teaching history and political science at DAV College.[10] He would later on become a preacher of the Arya Samaj.

Both the Arya Samaj and Brahmo Samaj movements had their influence on Har Dayal. While the Arya Samaj led by Swami Dayananda Saraswati advocated the slogan, 'Back to the

Vedas', the Brahmo Samaj founded by Raja Ram Mohan Roy was a reformist movement with westernized ideals. It advocated against the regressive practices of *sati*, child marriage and the dowry system.

The British government had instituted scholarships for promising Indian scholars and till that date, scholars from the coastal universities of Calcutta, Bombay and Madras had won them. Krishnavarma too had been the recipient of one such scholarship. But no one from North India had ever won this honour. Har Dayal became the first north Indian ever to achieve this feat.[11] Despite the fact that Har Dayal was indulging in anti-government activities and a criminal report was filed against him by the British Criminal Investigation department while he was still a student at Lahore Government College in 1904, he sailed to England in 1905. 'A firebrand in politics' was what he was called by James Campbell Ker of the British Police before he left India at the impressionable age of twenty-one.[12]

The scholarship included 200 pounds sterling each year for three years and a round-trip passage.[13] A penalty of Rs 3400 would be levied if the conditions of the scholarship remained unfulfilled but it was only perfunctory because no one had ever refused a scholarship abroad.[14] It was the dream of every young Indian and was regarded as the perfect opportunity to join a prestigious government service. The well-wishers of young Har Dayal too expected him to toe the same line.

Har Dayal enrolled at St John's College, University of Oxford in the School of Modern History. His special study included the latter period of European history and British India.[15] Har Dayal was the privileged Aitchison-Ramrattan Sanskrit scholar in Punjab University and he continued his studies in Sanskrit in Oxford where he was made a Boden Sanskrit Scholar.[16] Har Dayal soon found his footing in the foreign land. The sharpness of his intellect impressed everyone and soon he became the favourite of his teachers and peers.

It was in England that the conflict inside him began to burgeon, clearly manifesting itself in his ways. He had reduced his wants to a minimum and lived in a small lodging, permitting himself no luxuries.[17] He had started frequenting India House where he came into contact with Krishnavarma and worked under the tutelage of Savarkar. He attended the meetings of the Indian Home Rule Society and was inducted into Abhinav Bharat, Savarkar's core group.

Har Dayal's political manifesto, which he made during those times and submitted to Krishnavarma, was a little far-fetched but a marvellous product of his prodigious mind. It was the sketch of a complete political movement and emancipation of India. It included three phases of action:

1) Educational and academic
2) Destructive, meaning criticism of the British regime
3) Constructive, involving actual preparation for the inevitable struggle whether diplomatic, military or other[18]

He clearly demarcated four classes of members for this movement:

- The 'Dedicators' and the 'Missionaries', who could take part in all three phases of the programme
- The 'Enthusiastic' and the 'Ordinary', who would only be part of phases 1 and 2[19]

In a letter published in the *Indian Sociologist*, he wrote about the kind of men who should be chosen for this movement. The young, recruited men, he said, should put their country first, abandoning the vulgar craving for wealth, social rank and physical comfort, undertaking their work in a religious spirit with earnestness and self-denial as their guiding principles. He wanted to start a college with the name of 'India Sanyas Services' and emphasized the virtues of celibacy. He called it the highest ideal.[20]

Har Dayal had been married at a young age even before he arrived at Oxford, but his wife was not allowed to accompany him by the family, who considered it inauspicious for a young woman to travel beyond the sanctum sanctorum of home and motherland. He did not care much for this dictum from his family nor about the conservative society that did not allow a married woman to travel with her husband. He came back to India on an impromptu trip after the completion of his first term of Oxford. He kidnapped his own wife, put her on a ship bound for England and sailed to happy matrimony despite the firm objections of the family.[21]

While he was in England, the arrest of Lajpat Rai, who had been a great influence on him, back home in 1907[22] affected him deeply. It was then that the tenor of his voice became sharper. His writings in *Indian Sociologist* started gathering notice. His open association with Savarkar's extremist movement led him to write a letter to his brother, which was intercepted by the British government. The letter, dated 31 May 1907, gives a peek into the mind of the man troubled by heightened passions and the will to do much for the country.[23] The change that was brewing in his mind found an outlet in the following words:

> Our business is to prepare for that struggle quietly and rapidly and thus strike the blow when we are sure of success. Never bark till you can bite and never bite until you can make your teeth meet.[24]

He believed in creating and spreading propaganda and said:

> At present I think this propagandism is necessary. To spread literature broadcast and to affiliate new members to the organizations are the only things required. Literature is a great requisite. There is not only a single text book which represents the propaganda. It will be my first task to compose short manuals of political thought on my return to India. Personal work and not mass meetings will bring you success.

Men to be first contacted should be

1) Clever students
2) Sons of landlords
3) Sons of rich merchants
4) Sons of priests having a large clientele

If each man tries to instill some sort of patriotism into even three or four other young men the organization will spread like lightning. I have a scheme of organization which I wish to tell you of on my return to India. If you read books on Russia and Ireland you will find that we need not be frightened at the present situation.

. . . We should prepare six or seven short books in Urdu and Hindi and print them by lakhs. Let us turn out, say, ten lakhs at one time. Give each schoolboy and college student at least one. Then our work may be said to begin. That is the minimum. Some of our zealous men should lay aside some definite percentage of their income for political work as father used to have gulta for religious rites.

. . . When it is a living force among many, the time for action will come. Supposing you undertake to devote an hour every day in the evening and two hours on Sundays to the work of talking to some big college students and on political matters and discuss with them the books they read, and supposing you give two pieces out of every rupee you earn, will it be too great a burden? I think not. How many college students have in their possession even a few books on Indian politics? You cannot expect them to buy books. Some are poor, others are ignorant. Then take the entrance department boys. They should be provided for. You can take two or three college boys or sons of rajas (eminent people) for a drive every evening. Then treat them to fruits, etc. on Sundays. You will find that you have converted about twelve or more in a year. This is solid work. Man making, not speech making, is the thing.[25]

Before the British government could take any conclusive action, Har Dayal dropped a bombshell. He resigned the government scholarship in the fall of 1907.[26] This move perplexed the British for they did not have any mechanism to cancel the scholarship as no one had ever done that! It was hailed by Indian revolutionary circles as the ultimate sacrifice.

Har Dayal wrote to Oxford officials, 'I am unable to continue my studies for the final examination. I request the favour of your allowing me to withdraw from the college. I am sincerely sorry that I find myself unable to finish my course of studies. I hope you will kindly excuse me.'[27]

Shyamaji lauded him in *Indian Sociologist*, 'No Indian who really loves his country ought to compromise his principles and barter his rectitude of conduct for any favour whatsoever at the hands of the alien oppressive rulers of India.'[28]

And from there on, the fanatic traits of Har Dayal that were masked under a veneer of false pretensions started showing up. He gave up the English way of living by first renouncing English dress and took up dhoti and kurta.[29] The traditional Indian clothing was not suitable for inclement British weather. He caught a terrible cold leading to a severe bronchial disease from which he was to suffer for the rest of his life.[30] He stopped eating with his English friends and also did not accept English food if served. He reverted to a strict vegetarian diet.[31] Such extreme measures made Lala Lajpat Rai call him a man of strong impulse. Savarkar commented, 'We were helpless before the fanatic obstinacy of young Har Dayal.'[32]

Amidst this turmoil, Har Dayal returned to India in January 1908 with his wife, who was expecting.[33] He left her with her parents. His in-laws saw him as a big disappointment while his own family just did not know what to make of this self-styled political missionary.[34] Once back, Har Dayal met Tilak, who was impressed with him and regarded him as a tower of strength of the nationalist movement.

Har Dayal's hatred for Christianity and Christians and everything foreign became his way of life. His Lahore residence was pasted with a sign, 'No admission to Europeans or Christians'.[35] They say that he turned his one-time friend and foreign master, the principal of St Stephen's College, out of his home.[36] He had the mats and floor of the house thoroughly washed after this incident.[37] While this was only one aspect of his personality in which he resorted to extremes, he was extremely sensitive and balanced when he talked of Indian youth.

Har Dayal impressed upon young people to work hard. He said, 'A nation of thousands of millions cannot be conquered even by the whole world unless it has been first attacked by avarice, laziness, selfishness and cowardice. It is the vices which sap the vitality of a nation and leave it an easy prey for conquerors.'[38]

This was the rational Har Dayal with a sound reasoning and an argument ready for his detractors. He was profoundly dedicated to the cause of education. His writings in Lajpat Rai's *Punjabee* were turned into a book titled *Our Educational Problem*.[39] He emphasized that the ethical aspect of education should not be ignored.

Amidst this diatribe against the British and the changed scenario with an uncertain economic future threatening to overpower him, he returned to England at the beginning of September 1908 sans his wife this time. He had given the scholarship away, he had to pay the penalty fee, he had no source of income and thus no means to support a wife in an alien land.

When Har Dayal reached England, Krishnavarma had left for Paris leaving Savarkar as the controller of India House. Dayal continued writing for Lahore newspapers, his tone as scathing as ever against the English.

Har Dayal stayed in England from September 1908 to February 1909 in extreme poverty.[40] His health deteriorated. It was then that his friends in Paris persuaded him to join them and so he moved to Paris. Madam Cama was the biggest push behind this move. She gave him a new lease of life when she offered him the editorship of her magazine, *Bande Mataram*, which would be published from Geneva. This was a marvellous opportunity for Har Dayal. It was the beginning of a bigger responsibility that awaited him. While in Paris, he also started contributing to a Calcutta-based periodical, *Modern Review*, in which he would write for a long time.

Har Dayal kicked off his new responsibility with a bang. In the first issue of *Bande Mataram* that appeared on 10 September 1909, he wrote:

> We issue this journal with the object of continuing, commemorating and consolidating the good work that was inaugurated by that redoubtable champion of Indian freedom, Bande Mataram of Calcutta. The glorious campaign against foreign oppression that was initiated by our brave and wise leaders in Bengal through the medium of Bande Mataram shall be carried on with equal vigour and persistency by us at present.[41]

Har Dayal was in Paris when Madan Lal Dhingra assassinated Sir Curzon Wyllie and was hanged to death. Har Dayal curated a special issue with a bold headline, 'Dhingra, the immortal, whose words and deeds shall be cherished by the whole world for centuries to come'.

When Har Dayal joined *Bande Mataram* as an editor, Savarkar had his own journal *Talwar* published from Berlin with Chatto as the editor. Har Dayal was ebullient over this new venture by Savarkar and appreciated him in *Bande Mataram*'s pages.

He believed that the journals being published outside Indian soil were doing a great job in raising the consciousness and sympathy towards the Indian cause.

But Har Dayal, as was his temperament, did not stay put in Paris for a long time. Once Savarkar was arrested, he moved away from Paris, relinquishing the editorship of *Bande Mataram* to Madam Cama and moved to the North African city of Algiers.

The capital city of Algeria was a Muslim-dominated province where Har Dayal arrived with grand plans of spending his life in poverty, as an ascetic. He was unable to live in Algiers for a long time. He moved back to Paris, resumed editorial work but again got disenchanted and made his way towards the French island of Martinique.

Bhai Paramanand got in touch with Har Dayal at Martinique. Har Dayal wanted to found a new religion like the Buddha.[42] A votary of world peace and brotherhood, he was back to his ascetic lifestyle. He was sleeping on the floor, eating bland food and though he told Paramanand that a man can survive on fruits alone, his meal consisted of potatoes. When Bhai Parmanand added some chillies for taste, Har Dayal pleasantly remarked that Bhai Parmanand was definitely a better cook.[43] Har Dayal was spending his days in meditation and reading, unaware of his calling. The time had not yet come.

Bhai Parmanand was able to persuade Har Dayal to come out of his self-imposed exile and head to Harvard where he himself was planning to go. Finally, after a lot of coaxing, Har Dayal landed at Cambridge in Massachusetts, USA, in February 1911. He intended to join Harvard University for the study of Buddhism. But he did not stay put at Harvard. He moved to Berkeley in April 1911 after he met Teja Singh, who brought to his attention stories of Punjabi immigrant labour organizing themselves sans a leader. Har Dayal did not become their knight in shining armour immediately upon his arrival. He loved the free air of America and he extolled the virtues of being in a democratic set-up in an article that was published in *Modern Review*. He wrote, 'United States is perhaps the only country in the world from which a solitary wandering Hindu can send a message of hope and encouragement to his countrymen. America is the master of the future.'[44]

Har Dayal seemed to have got his mojo back but then again he became a traveller.

This time, Har Dayal moved to Hawaii and once again, his ascetic lifestyle drove him to renounce the so-called privileges he deemed unnecessary and frivolous. He started living in a cave in front of the Waikiki beach in Honolulu.[45] His food consisted of wholemeal bread, boiled potatoes and raw vegetables. He developed new friendships amidst new environs, engaging Japanese Buddhists in long conversations about religion. He began to read Karl Marx whose autobiography he would later translate.[46]

Despite the change of places and his moods, one consistency that perhaps kept him grounded and earned him many fans amongst young Indians was his dedicated flow of articles to Calcutta's *Modern Review*. His outpourings from every corner of the world were published and lapped up by his idolaters, who loved his writing sans any kind of censorship.

Har Dayal soon returned to Berkeley. By now, he was well known in the literary and revolutionary circles of Indians and Americans. When he was offered a position in Stanford University to teach philosophy, he readily accepted but without any monetary allowance accompanying it. Controversy's favourite child, he could not be anything but himself—highly volatile, energetic, expressing himself to the hilt.

Two things happened during that time, which created difficulties for his Stanford position, forcing him to resign:

1) A couple in California entered into a contract of free marriage without the obligatory vows of a religious ceremony. The move was hailed by Har Dayal as progressive and when he started publicly voicing his opinions, there were complaints that his statements encouraged immorality.[47]

2) His lecture to the Industrial Workers of the World[48] in the summer of 1912 titled 'The Future of the Labour Movement' was taken note of and some of his utterances,

which he considered his 'frank confession of faith', caused much heartburn amongst elite circles and the British police, who had been keeping tabs on him.[49]

A word-by-word account of his speech was published in an Irish-American paper, *Bulletin,* on 8 July 1912. Har Dayal talked about a few things that were needed for workers' and labour unions to win the war against the capitalists.

- Solidarity: Labour must think in terms of the whole world. Should one nation acquire freedom, the rich of another nation will crush it. For moral and practical reasons, the labour movement should be universal.
- A complete ideal: The desire should not only be for economic emancipation, but moral and intellectual emancipation as well. No man will lay down his life for a partial ideal.
- Good workers and leaders: The rich and respectable cannot lead the workers. They will have two kinds of leaders. First, the ascetics who have renounced riches and respectability for the love of the working man. Secondly, the sons of toil themselves, who must take up their own cross and lead their brothers on.
- Co-operation between the labour movement and the woman's movement: Workers and women are two enslaved classes and must fight their battles together.
- A feeling of actual brotherhood: The poor must love the poor. The shame of labour is that the poor must accept charity from the rich. The feeling must arise that workers are not so poor and can care for their own poor.[50]

This was Har Dayal, whose words were misunderstood by some, roused many and filled them with enthusiasm, the kind of energy that had never been experienced before.

Done with the responsibility of a formal job, Har Dayal formed a radical club at Stanford to keep up with the propaganda of his ideas.[51] He also formed an organization called the William Morris Circle[52] and a monthly meeting was held at Berkeley or Oakland at the home of one of its members. He continued with his ascetic lifestyle; he slept on a board and hardly ate anything except fruit. He denied himself the good things of life, including a full diet. His aim was to concentrate his physical and mental powers on his ambition, which was to mould more and more people to his ideals and thus overthrow the existing order of society.

Har Dayal came in touch with Jawala Singh Thatthiyan, the potato king, and gave his approval for his scholarship scheme that also involved Taraknath Das and Teja Singh.[53] One amongst the chosen ones was Gobind Behari Lal, a cousin of Har Dayal's wife.[54] Har Dayal would frequent their hostel earlier also but now after resigning from his teaching duties, he started living with them as well. They were charmed by his simplicity. He used to receive a little money from his wife, Sunder, who was living with her parents, and had birthed a daughter, Shanti, whom Har Dayal had not yet met. But there was something peculiar about him. The money that he received would soon be given in alms or to the needy and he would be without anything at all.

He wore one brown tweed suit with holes in it. After incessant efforts by the students, he was persuaded to buy a new one. Chenchiah was disgusted with his shoes and he wanted him to have a new pair. He hid them but Sarabha knew that if discovered, Har Dayal would use them again. He threw them in the dustbin.[55] Such an austere lifestyle could only be perfected by a saint. To the young boys, he was nothing less than a modern rishi.[56]

The association with young blood rejuvenated Har Dayal, who had grown morose after Savarkar's arrest. Another incident that provided lifeblood to him was the assassination attempt on Lord Hardinge by one of his associates. He was jubilant at this feat and though the new viceroy had escaped unhurt, the attack was reason enough to celebrate.

Har Dayal turned to the power of his pen once more and wrote a circular titled '*Yugantar*' (New Era), his heartfelt tribute to Madanlal Dhingra, who dared to challenge the British power, which got published in *Indian Sociologist*.

Perhaps the bomb was the omen Har Dayal had been waiting for to start something new, a path-breaking journey that would motivate men to cross the seas and wage a war for their homeland. Something had stirred inside Har Dayal. It would not die down before shaking the foundations of the British regime.

Chapter 7

Racism in Canada and the USA

Life in Canada and the USA was not easy for early settlers from India. They faced discrimination and bias, and though the countries were flush with opportunities, there were many instances of racism and prejudice against them.

The early settlers, especially the Sikhs, were not able to assimilate themselves with the local populace for various reasons. Firstly, they were illiterate Punjabi farmers and they could neither read, write nor speak English. This created a big communication gap between them and the natives.[1] They were not able to communicate outside their own community and were at a loss for words. They never addressed the natives despite working for them and could not establish any kind of personal relationship with them.

Secondly, they looked odd with their large *pagris* (turbans) and their peculiar dressing sense, inviting ridicule. They had long flowing beards, their skin was dark and their voices loud.[2]

Thirdly, their lack of education had created a lack of finesse in them. They were harmless and ignorant. They failed to understand that staring at people was considered rude in polite society. They were just mesmerized by the freedom of women, their colourful attire, their presence in parks and roads as if it were the most natural thing in the world.[3] Women back home did not have such liberties. They thought about their children living in penury when they saw the rosy cheeks of well-fed children and smiling, happy families with an air of contentment around them. Coming from a land lacking resources, they were in awe of the plentiful opportunities in the West and the kind of lifestyle enjoyed by the natives. And it all came as a shock to their senses.

Fourthly, they found it difficult to get rid of their ingrained habits. Some of them spat on the ground, told lies over trivial things, walked in large groups or gathered downtown to socialize and talked loudly to each other.[4]

While those with an army background had seen the world and assimilated well with the local populace, the ignorant Punjabi peasants lacked this sophistication.

The times in Canada when recession overpowered the economy were very tough for the immigrants. Sometime between 1904 and 1906, the immigrants who had been living in shacks in the South Vancouver province had been reported to authorities, who descended on them and threw them out of the city limits. They had been brought to Canada by the Canadian Pacific Railways (CPR) and they were directed to stay within the area of the company's property before they were taken to their work locations. But despite repeated warnings, they would come into the city, invoking the ire of local people.

On one occasion, the mayor of Vancouver got so infuriated by their constant aggression that he had bundled them all up and moved them to the condemned buildings of the city, housing them at their own expense, which amounted to $3 per month. These buildings had no running water and the stoves and lights had only been fixed recently to accommodate them. No one cared about them.[5] When the recession of 1907 arrived, those with no jobs and the new arrivals lived in pitiable conditions. Those were the times when these people begged for food, knocking on the doors of city people late at night. It was only after the recession of 1907 died down that things began to improve for them.

By 1908, their numbers increased to around 6000 and they started getting comfortable in their jobs and earning decently. No charitable organization from home or abroad and no government had come to their rescue during the recession. Their situation improved because of their own efforts and their inherent strength to support each other. They had formed a self-supporting ecosystem. New arrivals were supported, provided food and shelter by the men already living in Canada, as if they were members of their own families.

They built gurdwaras for themselves, which were to serve not only as places of religious congregation but also became their meeting points. The first gurdwara was built in Vancouver in 1908 and in Victoria in 1912.

The hardworking nature of these 'Hindus', as they were referred to, at the farms, was another reason for which they were despised. They had limited needs, spent very little and worked extra hours. They often worked as a unit, supporting each other. They lived together, their communal kitchens reducing their expenses to the minimum. Their motive was to earn money and send it back home for the maintenance of their families. Some of them were using their savings, which amounted to as high as $3000 to $5000 to buy land. They were intent on making this place their home.

They were tireless workers and for this very reason they were preferred by the employers in the ensuing years, who sometimes went to the ports where they arrived and took them to their farms right away. Their popularity graph was rising and this made the native worker worried about his job.[6]

The uneducated Punjabis did not know their rights. They were earning more than double of what they could earn at home. This was enough to keep them content and became a reason for differences to arise between the two classes of workers (natives and immigrants), which grew to the point of no return.

The local American worker was a citizen of a free country. His ancestors had fought to unshackle the manacles of dependence and he was fighting now for his rights. He would not work for low wages, would not agree to the unjust demands of his boss and would always ask for better working conditions. This consciousness was missing altogether in Punjabi workers. The local worker in Canada, which was a British dominion, was as aware as his counterpart in America. The bargaining power of the native worker was being weakened by the constant influx of cheap labour from Asia.

Before the arrival of the Indians, the Chinese and Japanese labour force had made inroads into the market, giving jitters to the native worker, who found the going difficult. An anti-Asiatic league came into existence in California, which aimed at excluding the Chinese and Japanese workers from entering the North American market. The rise of the turbaned Sardar was another addition to its list.[7] In 1907, the Vancouver Asiatic League came into existence, following the footsteps of its American counterpart. Wild allegations were made against Indians to tarnish them not only on the professional front but at a personal level as well. They were considered to be the worst slaves of the world. Little children would often greet them with the words, 'Hello, Hindu slave.' They were considered polygamous and their daughters were referred to as their wives in disguise. They were said to be unclean, disease-ridden and filthy. The ill-informed press gave them negative publicity.

'Indians and dogs are not allowed' was a common refrain. Life for the immigrants was a daily test. It was not about proving their worth; the conditions by themselves were not favourable for their survival.

This hatred towards Indians led to anti-Asiatic riots during the recession years of 1907 and 1908. The natives were left without jobs as employers preferred to employ Indians at lower wages, which led to an unprovoked attack on the Asian labour force. The first attack was at Bellingham on 5 September 1907 in Washington near the Canada border.[8] This was a pre-planned and organized attack on Japanese and Chinese labour by 600 armed native labourers. Since the Punjabi labourers too were working at this site, they suffered the ire of the miscreants as well. The Canadian labour force had armed itself on the other side of the border and it did not let in the Japanese and Chinese labour on their side of the border but they did let the Indians come in. However, in the following days, such favours would not be granted to Indians as their numbers would swell in both the countries. Foreign labourers were badly beaten, pushed towards the Canadian border with some of them losing their lives as they drowned in the ocean. Industrial Workers of the World, a labour union of America, was said to be behind these attacks.[9]

This attack was firmly criticized by the governments of China and Japan. It led to an increase in the imposition of a head tax of $500 from $100[10] by the Dominion of Canada on Chinese labourers to discourage their arrival. A gentleman's agreement was also made with Japan, which limited the number of labourers to 400 per year.[11] The dwindling number of Chinese and Japanese labourers resulted in the rise of the number of Indian workers coming in.

The attacks did not end. They were witnessed in the Wilamette Valley region of Oregon in the following years. In 1908, when the local labourers working on the Dukuma railway line went on strike, the owners recruited Indians to work, keeping them in the dark about the ground realities. This led to another deadly attack on them by the locals. The Indians were subjected to a double whammy in such circumstances: they were hated by the local labour force for taking their jobs and exploited by the owners because they were naïve. Later, when they realized their folly, they would stop taking up work on such disputed sites.

The situation improved in 1909, but the anti-Indian feelings stayed. The attacks did not cease but got more violent and brutal, leading to the immigrants gearing up for a fight. When they were attacked on 21 March 1910[12] at St John near Portland, they decided to meet the British councillor in Canada to complain about this ill-treatment. With no action being initiated against the perpetrators of the attacks, the Indians grouped together to fight for themselves. Several meetings were held among Punjabi labourers in Monark Mill, Portland, St John, Bridal Villa and Astoria.

In later attacks, they gave a sound thrashing to the local miscreants, making them run for their lives. It was only when they gave a befitting reply that the attacks died down. They realized their collective strength, but the opposition did not end here. Soon, it would be their families who would face stiff resistance when they attempted to join the men.

The Dominion of Canada wrote to the British government in India that they should stop the immigration of the Punjabi community but Lord Curzon[13] and then Lord Minto[14] were not in favour of passing any such regulation.[15] The mayor of Vancouver did not allow a ship carrying Indians to dock at Vancouver harbour in October 1906.[16] The ship was diverted to Victoria harbour. A mass meeting held in Vancouver Town Hall on 18 October 1906 passed resolutions against further immigration of Indians.[17] The politicians and labour leaders in British Columbia were against the influx of immigrants but the prime minister of Canada, Sir Wilfred Laurier,[18] was against the exclusion of British subjects of any kind or race from entering their territory.[19]

'The city of Vancouver will not stand for any further dumping of East Indians,' they wrote to the prime minister.[20]

In the beginning of 1907, the British government finally decided to get into action by putting some restrictions on the number of Indians leaving for foreign shores without passing any formal regulation. And this happened when the Indians were making plans to bring their wives and families to Canada.

It was not only the rustic peasants who suffered the barbs of racism. Educated Indian youth who were studying in prestigious universities too suffered the same fate. Boarding homes and restaurants refused them entry. They were not granted access or served at many places. These students were considered ineligible for membership of clubs because of their nationality.[21] This ridicule in everyday life cemented the bond between the educated and uneducated factions of Indians.

The feeling of white superiority amongst the natives of Canada and America was largely the cause of the spread of racial prejudice. The song 'White Canada Forever' became the chant, forcing the narrative of segregation based on skin colour:

This was the voice of the West and it speaks to the world
The rights that our fathers have given
We will hold by right and maintain by might
Till the foe is backward driven
We welcome as brothers all white still,
But the shifty yellow race,
Whose word is vain, who oppress the weak,
Must find another place.

Then let us stand united all
And show our father's might,
That won the home we call our own,
For white man's land, we fight.
To oriental grasp and greed.
We will surrender, no never.
Our watchword be 'God Save the King'
White Canada forever.[22]

It was not only the workers of the US and Canada who spoke with malice; lawmakers too suffered from a feeling of distrust and spread hatred against Indians. One of them was H.H. Stevens, who was a member of Parliament from Vancouver. His angry words would often provoke his compatriots to act against the immigrants with a firm hand. He often made statements like, 'Indians in their own country have no rights whatsoever. They cannot be allowed to become citizens here.'[23]

Soon, the incessant racism resulted in the creation of a consciousness among the Indian immigrants. They realized they were the stepchildren of the British government. Their own sarkar, the love for whom they carried around their necks like a garland of rubies, was nothing more than an illusion. The sarkar would not come to their rescue against any sort of discrimination being meted out to them in other countries. A little window had opened up giving them a fresh perspective and this was all they needed.

Chapter 8

British Honduras as a Potential Destination?

There were only 258 Indians in Canada in 1904.[1] Their numbers rose to 1500 in 1906 and around 5000 in 1908.[2]

The fear of a tide of turbaned men overwhelming the natives seemed to grow real for Canadians and Americans. There was also a core group of Indians that had established themselves. From being labourers, they had moved on to buying land, becoming landowners and diversifying into other professions. Several companies came up that established their identity and showcased their enterprise. Guru Nanak Mining and Trust Company, Canadian Indian Supply and Trust Company and Canadian Home Builders were some of these ventures. These success stories soon translated into hope back home and sent a message beckoning them to come and settle in the wake of prosperity.

If the Punjabis were proliferating and growing, the discontent against their rise was growing strong in the higher echelons of government. At one of the Imperial Conferences, in which all the prime ministers of British Dominions participated, it was decided that Indians did not have the right to travel freely in all the British colonies. The heads of the individual countries were bestowed with powers to decide upon this issue. This was contradictory to the Queen's statement, which mentioned that there would be no discrimination against the natives of countries governed by her.

In the British Dominions of South Africa, West Africa, Australia and New Zealand where Indians were thriving, such discriminatory laws had come into practice. In Honduras, Malaya and the islands of Fiji and New Guinea where they were being taken as indentured labourers, such laws and issues had never cropped up. In Canada, Indians went as independent labourers but began making inroads into the economy of the country and hence, these restrictions were bound to stop their progress.

The Indian government was not ready to impose any kind of restrictions on Punjabi emigrants. These emigrants mainly belonged to the five populous districts of Jalandhar, Hoshiarpur, Lahore, Ambala and Ludhiana. The people of Punjab were battling landlessness, increased revenue demands and diseases like the plague devastating families. Their flight was a blessing for the British, who feared that riots might erupt any time under such terrible living conditions. They did not want the emigrants to come back but neither did they want them to be treated as equals in British colonies, giving them ideas of freedom and liberty. But the people who were the first to emigrate from Punjab had definitely gained exposure and taking them back would spread the restlessness of an enlightened mind.

Therefore, the Indian government neither took up the case of Indian emigrants, like the Chinese and Japanese governments, nor did it give a complete nod to restrict emigration. The onus was on the Canadian government to settle things on its own without disturbing the equilibrium of the Indian government, which wanted peace in its territory on all accounts.[3] It only agreed to get rid of the emigrant sitting at the Calcutta port to board a ship to the land of dreams. Yet, this was not enough to discourage the people looking for an escape.

The Canadian Pacific Company was the largest stakeholder in the development work being undertaken in Canada with interests in roads, railways and waterways. It employed agents in Calcutta, Singapore and Shanghai, who encouraged and sold tickets to Indians and also paid the head tax of Chinese labourers that had been raised from $100 to $500. Despite reminders to stop issuing tickets to Indians, there was no stopping the influx of the community. These men were sturdy workers and were preferred over white labour for being hardy and resilient. The gentle reminders did not yield any effort as the immigration went on unchecked.

In 1907, J.B. Harkin, secretary to the home department, prepared a report on the poor conditions of Indians in British Columbia. The cold weather, food shortages and the lack of livelihood opportunities were some of the difficulties cited.[4] He proposed to move the colonies of the immigrants to a more favourable and opportune place—British Honduras.[5]

A decision was taken by the Canadian government in cognizance with the British government to take the recommendations of this report forward. There was an uproar in the Indian community when they came to know about their removal from British Columbia. They wrote to the Indian government condemning this move and about being kept in dark about the situation.

Finally, after talks with the community, it was decided that a delegation comprising the secretary J.B. Harkin, an Anglo-Indian police officer William Charles Hopkinson and two Indian representatives, a Hindu and a Muslim, would go to Belize (British Honduras).[6]

Hopkinson, born in 1880, was the progeny of an Indian mother and an English father, who worked as a sergeant instructor of volunteers at Allahabad. Hopkinson grew up being multilingual with parents belonging to two different ethnicities.[7]

He started working with the Calcutta Police in 1904 and was with them for four years before moving to Vancouver.[8] He was a quiet, intelligent and shrewd man who had a good command over Hindi and knew a smattering of Punjabi. He incorporated himself into the Canadian Police when he started sending confidential reports on Indian immigrants whose activities might be of interest to the government. As a result, he was hired by the Canadian government as an immigration inspector in 1909.[9] The government too was in need of a translator who could help them communicate with the Punjabi immigrants. Hopkinson would fit into many roles. He was a translator, an informer as well as an immigration official. His help was sought by the American government as well. He was drawing a salary from the Canadian government, the India Office as well as the American immigration authorities.[10]

Hopkinson's job was to keep tabs on the Indian community.[11] And he accomplished this task very well as he made inroads into the Indian community by having his own group of informers, like Bela Singh and Ganga Ram, who would report to him about every development happening in Indian circles. He kept the Canadian government up to date about the meetings in the gurdwara where the majority of the action took place—from incendiary speeches to general talk.

Hopkinson particularly reported about the paper, *Free Hindustan*, being run by Taraknath Das, which of late had acquired a seditious tone and was causing ripples amongst the readers because of its volatile content. His information had led to Das stopping the circulation of his paper and fleeing to Seattle. Joining him was G.D. Kumar whose own paper, *Swadesh Sewak*, too met with the same fate.

Hopkinson thus made himself indispensable to the government with this plethora of information, which it used to make dossiers against men like Das and Kumar. There was no one quite like him in America and Canada. His special language skills made him unique and sought after in regard to Indian immigrants in the North American continent.[12]

The delegation of members reached Belize on 25 October 1908. They stayed there for a few days before returning to Vancouver on 7 November 1908. Before the members could converse with their community leaders, Harkin and Hopkinson had prepared a favourable report for this move to progress smoothly. They encouraged the members of the Indian delegation to write positively about their experiences in Honduras even though they were non-committal about their decision. The Indians refused to write what they were asked to and did not succumb to the lure of bribes either.

The Indian community called for an open house, inviting all its members to the meeting hall in the gurdwara. They decided to make their report open, inviting Harkin and Hopkinson to do the same. When the Indian representatives spoke about the reality, the community was stunned to speechlessness with their eye-opening account. One account declared:

> The British Honduras is uninhabitable and inhospitable with all kind of diseases like malaria and yellow fever inflicting the inhabitants. The indentured Indian labor is being paid very little, meagre if we compare it to wages in Canada. Once arrived they are treated shabbily and never sent back home because they die under the scourge of diseases, bad food and back-breaking work. It would be a disaster for us to move there. They wanted us to speak in favor of this move but we cannot commit this treachery with our community. Our generations would be ruined, our honor soiled if we had lied about this whole thing.[13]

Harkin and Hopkinson never attended this meeting. They turned back from the gates of the gurdwara, lacking the courage to face the truth.

The decision of the Indian community was communicated to the Ottawa government. They would stay put and would not move out of Canada. And if they had to, they would fight till their death to oppose such restrictive measures. This matter was closed but it left a big blot on the credentials of the Ottawa government, which faced criticism from all quarters and from the Governor of Honduras, E.J. Swayne, who was sent to talk to the community and convince them about this move.

Chapter 9

Restrictions on Immigration

That the Canadian government wanted to close its doors to Indians was no secret, but it did not want to antagonize the Indian population back home by making it appear as racial prejudice, which would put the British Raj in a tight spot. That every Indian who reached the shores of this part of the American continent took pride in being a British national was a known fact. And this very attribute was the reason that restrictions by the Canadian government could not be manifested in a straightforward way. British imperial interests had to be considered. So, the regulations, when they came into existence in the early spring of 1908, were a result of talks between Ottawa, Delhi and London.[1]

The Indian government had realized that the growing numbers of Indians on Canadian soil were easing the burdens on the land in Punjab and were also creating a kind of political consciousness back home. They did not want ideas of self-governance and racial equality to make inroads into Indian minds.[2]

It also feared that these people in close contact with the white race would see the flimsy and dark side of their men and women, leading to a loss of respect in their minds. And this loss of prestige could have derogatory implications, for they thought it was only with prestige that they were ruling India and not with force.[3] For the English and the whites to maintain their position on the pedestal, it was necessary for race segregation to be implicit with less or no contact between the people of both nationalities.

The Indian government announced measures that included bringing into action the Indian Emigration Act (XXI of 1883),[4] making it an offence for Indians to travel from their country to anywhere but Ceylon (Sri Lanka) or the Straits settlements (Malaysia).[5] Emigration was thus made unlawful, but this did not deter Indians from making their way out of the country. This law had hardly any negative impact on the will and determination of the people who were being lured by the success stories of their brethren.

The British Indian government then put the onus on their Canadian counterparts. The British Imperial government passed the orders making emigration to Canada unlawful without questioning Canada's right to close the doors.

The report by Mackenzie King, deputy minister of labour, Ottawa, in 1908 stated:

> That Canada should desire to restrict immigration from the orient is regarded as natural, that Canada should remain a white man's country is believed to be not only desirable for economic and social reasons, but highly necessary on political and national grounds. Canada is the best judge of the course to be adopted and that as a self-governing dominion she cannot be expected to refrain from enacting such measures in the way of restriction as in the discretion of her people are deemed most expedient.[6]

After getting a go-ahead from the British government, the Canadian government raised the amount of money that an immigrant had to have on arrival to $200 from $25.[7] Most of the men arriving were penniless peasants who had bought the ticket amounting to $65, the fare to Vancouver, after selling or mortgaging their lands. They were in possession of a few dollars on their arrival but to raise such a large sum of money was an obligation they found difficult to fulfil. This law was a clear ploy to stop the arrival of women and children who followed the man of the family. It would inflict a double blow on the immigrants.

The second clause was specifically introduced to debar Indians. It stated that a person who would not travel on a single ticket or through a continuous journey from his or her home country to the port of arrival in Canada would not be allowed to enter Canadian territory.[8] No steamship company ran a direct shipping line from India to Canada. Even companies like Canadian Pacific Railways (CPR) took a detour through Hong Kong or Shanghai invoking disqualification, but the passengers did journey on a single ticket.

Hong Kong was the port that was serving as an intermediate link from which ships travelled towards the Indian and Pacific Ocean. Men and luggage were deposited at this port city from where they made their journeys onwards. The stricture of these laws strangled the hopes of those embarking at Hong Kong. The Canadian government snubbed the CPR, the monopoly carrier that was not heeding their instructions. Though CPR was not offering a direct passage, they were issuing single tickets to Indians and now the travel laws created an embarrassing position for their own government.

In February 1908, when the *SS* Monteagle was heading towards Canadian waters with a load of Japanese passengers along with Indians, the Canadian government put its order into practice to deport the passengers from its soil. CPR was miffed by this hurriedly passed regulation and challenged it in court. The court overruled the government and the passengers of this ship were allowed to de-board. This was a huge victory in the eyes of the Indians who saw the power of Canadian courts, which had the ability to circumvent the decisions of the government. This verdict gave them hope that all was not lost.

Another judgment made in favour of *Panama Maru*, a Japanese ship carrying thirty-nine Indian passengers in 1913, reaffirmed this notion that the courts in Canada were sympathetic to the cause of immigrants.[9] The immigrants were given entry despite non-fulfilment of both the clauses scripted by the government, but with the addition of another clause in the law. Within a fortnight, a new 'order-in-council' was passed, forbidding the entry of artisans or labourers, skilled or unskilled, at any port of British Columbia.[10]

From 1908 onwards, CPR did stop issuing tickets to Indian passengers. Despite the success of *SS* Monteagle, they did not want to be in direct conflict with their own government. With their refusal, it was almost impossible to fulfil the clause of journeying on a single ticket. The rest of the liners only issued tickets from Calcutta to Hong Kong from where passengers had to get fresh tickets and change their carrier. The pressure of the Canadian government was such that even these intermediate carriers at one point in time stopped issuing tickets to Indian passengers.

After 1908, the number of Indians entering Canadian borders decreased drastically. The hopeful emigrants got into a line to gain entry into the US now. By the end of 1913, there were three times as many Sikhs in America than in Canada. As their numbers started swelling in America, they were seen as competition by the strong labour union that was determined to protect the rights of the locals at any cost. The American government began considering proposals to limit the intake of Indians, especially Sikhs. They were under pressure to keep them out.

The first act of stemming the flow was to relook at the policy of issuing passports to the hopeful arrivals. Later on, it refused passports to the labourers. It also dissuaded shipping companies from selling tickets to Indians, following in the footsteps of the Canadian government.

That anti-British activities were burgeoning under the freedom imparted by the American government was no secret. Many freedom struggles had found a home in the US. If the Irish had waged their own battle of revolt, the Russians too had led their peasant revolt from this land, which perpetuated ideas of communism. America was a free ground for socialism and democratic ideals. For these very reasons though, curbs on any kind of anti-British activities did not meet with approval, but the disapproval of the local populace did bring restrictions to the fore.

Punjabi Sikh immigrants had acquired vast tracts of land in California with their hard-earned money. They had toiled hard, earned, saved and used the money to build their own little empires in this arid land, which had been turned fertile with their efforts.[11] The government in 1913 passed the Alien Land Law Act, which banned them from acquiring any land in some parts of California, leading to much heartburn amongst the immigrants.

More heavy restrictions would come later when President Woodrow Wilson would pledge support to the British, joining the First World War as an ally strengthening the British, French and Russian forces. It was then that the anti-British activities came to a halt. Also, the creation of an Asiatic Barred Zone[12] directly restricted entry from the Indian subcontinent.

Chapter 10

The Struggle to Bring Families
to Canada

When strict immigration rules came into existence, they created uncertainty in the minds of Indians who wanted to make Canada their permanent home. These people had been living in Canada for more than three years now, had been granted citizenship and were eligible to call their wives and children to be with them. However, the change in laws made the future of their families uncertain. But they were not giving it all away without a fight.

That the decision of the government was biased, but that it could be overruled by the courts in Canada, gave hope to Indians. They pleaded their case by writing to newspapers, and sending petitions to governments both in Canada and India. One article in *Saturday Sunset* published on 27 May 1911 was heavily in favour of their cause and stated,

> That the Indians as subjects of British government have the right to travel anywhere in British colonies along with their families. Those who are settled in Canada should be allowed to bring their wives and children. The Canada government allowed them entry, they have lands and property, they are well off to support their kith and kin. Why the government is not allowing them to fulfill their

duties towards their families? Let them not come but let those who
are already here be reunited with their families.[1]

The government paid scant attention to such passionate pleas.
There were others who vociferously applauded the anti-Indian
stand. The Women's National Council, which had a sizeable
following, did not want wives to join their husbands in Canada.
They feared that the community would grow if such measures
were allowed. On the contrary, it might dwindle and perish on its
own if the men were kept away from their families. Such attitudes
of the general populace supported the high-handedness of the
government and this was not helping the Indian cause of trying
to get the laws amended by making enough noise. Their voices
would be lost in the din but nevertheless, they were gearing up
for a fight.

Heera Singh was the first immigrant who decided to challenge
the draconian laws. He brought his family to Canada in early 1911.
They were not given clearance because they had not travelled on a
single ticket from their country of origin. He was, however, able to
get his family to shore by offering a guarantee. Later, he challenged
the decision in court, which went in his favour. This win upped
the morale of the Indians who wanted to test the waters once
again. They wanted to challenge the norms to see if the courts
would grant them immunity from such restrictive laws.

The Khalsa Diwan Society and the Hindustan Association
joined hands for this cause and held several meetings to plan their
strategy.[2] Bhag Singh Bhikhiwind, the secretary of the society who
later went on to become the president, along with Balwant Singh
Khurdpur, the granthi of Vancouver Gurdwara took the lead to
follow up on this ambitious cause.[3] Both of them had been active
for the cause of Sikh migrants since their arrival in Canada.

Bhag Singh belonged to Bhikhiwind village in present-day
Tarn Taran district while Balwant Singh belonged to Khurdpur
village in Jalandhar district. Both of them had gone to India and

were now on their way back when the restrictive laws were passed. Bhikhiwind and Khurdpur with their wives and Khurdpur's two minor daughters started their journey from India in 1911. They were not issued direct tickets from Calcutta port as was the norm. On 17 May 1911 they sent a telegram to the Viceroy of India conveying their disappointment, to which they got a reply that the Indian government could do nothing about this particular concern.[4] The shipping companies did not come under their jurisdiction and they had to take up this matter with the Canadian government.

Not losing hope at such a disappointing reply, they managed to travel from Calcutta to Hong Kong but more disappointment awaited them. On reaching Hong Kong, they realized that none of the shipping companies were ready to sell them tickets for their journey to Canada.[5] They were stranded at the place for more than two months. The communication went to and fro between Hong Kong and Canada. The Indian community in Canada was being kept in the loop about the developments back home by Taraknath Das, who was keeping a close watch on them.

Das, along with Prof. Teja Singh, took a deputation to Ottawa for the settlement of this cause, where they were assured that the restrictions would be eased.[6] Meanwhile, Bhikhiwind was blessed with a son. They secured tickets on a ship travelling to San Francisco en route to Vancouver. They disembarked at Vancouver port but were not let in because they had not travelled on a single ticket.[7] The assurance of the higher authorities in Ottawa was only a side-stepping measure and their guarantees were false because now, firm measures were in place that would stop wives and children from entering Canadian territory. Both Bhikhiwind and Khurdpur were given permission to enter the territory because they were citizens but not their wives and children, who stood to be deported.[8]

This was a very precarious situation for the Indian community as well for the families who, after undertaking a tortuous journey of many months, now stared at an uncertain future. This was the beginning of a long court battle. Bhikhiwind and Khurdpur were soon let in, but their families were put under arrest. This triggered a wave of resentment and anger in the community for the anguish caused to the new arrivals. For them, it was a targeted move on their leaders to break their families and their spirit.[9]

This decision was a big letdown for the leaders as well as those who had led a deputation to the Ottawa government.[10] It had fetched them nothing but remorse. This incident led to the organization of an extremist faction amongst the Sikh community of Canada, which would soon come under surveillance for the promulgation of their anti-government activities. The petition soon went to court.

The decision of the court indicated only a temporary relief as it read, 'The orders of deportation served on the wives of two Indian residents of long-standing arriving to join their husbands were subsequently withdrawn as an act of grace and not because of any change of policy on the part of the dominion immigration authorities.'

The battle had been won amidst the shouts and cheers of the small Sikh population in an alien land. These small battles were counted amongst victories but were not enough to get them what they really aspired for. The restrictions still stood and the fight had to be continued to win the war to secure the rights of the immigrants. But these little wins gave hope to immigrants waiting in Hong Kong, Malaya and Shanghai. They too wanted to join their friends and relatives. They believed that the courts would favour them and they would always have an option to circumvent the laws in this case.

Chapter 11

The Hindi Association of the Pacific Coast

Punjabi immigration to the US was a spillover from Canada,[1] and from 1904 to 1906, about 600 Indians had crossed over.[2] The number of immigrants in the US increased from 1072 in 1907 to 1710 in 1908.[3] They found work as farmhands and lumber men in the states of Washington, Oregon and California.[4] In California, they could not get outdoor work, so they picked grapes and oranges, hoed beans and asparagus and thinned and topped beets.[5]

Since the situation was favourable for Punjabis in the US, the immigrants started to go directly to California instead of going through Canada.[6]

Since 1908, the American Bureau of Immigration was under pressure to close the doors to Sikhs. Loud protests and violent demonstrations by the Asiatic Exclusion League[7] of San Francisco led to a decrease in the number of Indians entering the US.[8] The local press termed this immigration of Sikhs as the 'turbaned tide', calling the immigrants 'ragheads'.[9]

The US government was more direct in its methods as compared to its Canadian counterpart. They simply refused to let immigrants in on account of one of the three reasons:

1. Liable to public charge
2. Suffering from dangerous contagious diseases
3. Violates alien contract labour law[10]

In the following months, more than 600 immigrants were refused admission to the US on one or more pretexts. With the doors of immigration closed from both Canada and the US, the only way out was to seek support from each other. To group together, to unite, became not only a necessity but a motive to achieve something more tangible.

The fear of deportation became a major reason for solidarity.[11]

The awakening of political consciousness in Indians residing in Canada and the US was the result of three factors:

1. Resentment and hostility against the white community for its prejudice and oppression
2. Development of an ethnic identity
3. Nationalism directed against British colonialism in India[12]

The immigrants in Canada started building gurdwaras for themselves to keep their own people intact. The Khalsa Diwan, Canada's first Sikh organization, was formed in 1906.[13] The first gurdwara was inaugurated in Vancouver[14] on 19 January 1908.[15]

The primary reason to build gurdwaras could be traced to the Singh Sabha Movement[16] back home, which had its influence on the immigrants who did not want to lose their men to the *mauna lehar*,[17] wherein many immigrants had taken off their turbans and shorn their hair in an effort to assimilate. They took it as a direct threat to their identity. Many had started wearing hats, ditching the turban, the pride of every Sikh.[18] This was not acceptable to those who were more rigid about their religion.

The gurdwaras were open to people of all religions. Soon they became meeting grounds of Indians of diverse backgrounds and cultures. The peasants, the students and the revolutionaries were all getting together at one place and exchanging ideas.

Apart from discussing religious, educational and philanthropic issues, these religious institutes became grounds of discussion about the prejudice being faced by the immigrant community.[19]

The presence of gurdwaras erased the class and caste divides amongst Indians on the basis of which they had been segregated in their home country. It had started with Hindus, Sikhs and Muslims getting united and defending themselves against attacks. The narrow lines of religion that were battlegrounds back home were losing their essence as people of all castes were shacking up together, living and eating together and jointly professing the desire to stay united.

In gurdwaras, they vented their anger and discussed how the Chinese and Japanese governments had taken up the issues of safety of their citizens and spoken for their welfare, but their government did not care for them. They realized that their government was indifferent to their plight.[20] Also, back home, even the Chief Khalsa Diwan promoted loyalty to the government.[21]

The Sikhs had been given preference in the army as compared to the Hindus and Muslims since the events of 1857. Their caste identity, the five symbols, *kesh, kangha, kaccha, kara, kirpan* (unshorn hair, comb, breeches, bangle and sword) had been made mandatory for the Sikh regiment.[22] While the Sikh community was made to feel privileged and superior back home, the same community was the victim of racial discrimination in a foreign land. Most of the peasant immigrants were Sikhs, but no one took up their cause.

Such feelings of dismay amongst Sikh immigrants and their meetings with people, especially the revolutionaries who openly attacked British rules, turned the gurdwaras into centres of political activity.

Apart from gurdwaras, their workplaces were the common meeting grounds where they discussed their issues and aired their grievances.

The likes of Sohan Singh Bhakna and Harnam Singh Tundilat frequently met at the lumber mill at St John owned by Kanshi Ram[23] or at Jawala Singh's farm in California. This consciousness of being different, along with the motivation given by politically active messengers such as Taraknath Das, Harnam Singh Sahri and G.D. Kumar, who often toured these meeting points, made them sterner in their resolve to adhere to their association and give it a firm shape.

Indian students had formed their own organization in New York in 1906 with the assistance of Irish nationalists, particularly George Fitzgerald Freeman, editor of the Irish paper *Gaelic American*.[24] The United India League in Vancouver[25] and the Hindustan Association of the United States of America[26] were other organizations that worked for the betterment of Indian immigrants.[27]

The Punjabi peasants, revolutionaries in exile and the students joined hands and collectively formed an association at Portland in 1912.[28] The association was named the Hindi Association of the Pacific Coast.[29]

Sohan Singh Bhakna was chosen as the president, G.D. Kumar as the secretary and Kanshi Ram was designated as the treasurer. Later, a similar association was formed in Astoria with different office-bearers. Meanwhile, G.D. Kumar, afflicted with a stomach ailment, was unable to work for this organization and resigned from the post.[30] Now the hunt began for a new secretary who was ambitious and capable enough to help the spread of this organization and would take up the mantle with aplomb.

The name of Ajit Singh[31] had been doing the rounds. Living in self-imposed exile in Paris at that time, doing revolutionary work with other expatriates, he was the face of peasant agitation along with Lala Lajpat Rai. And while the correspondence with him went on, Lala Har Dayal's name cropped up like a beacon, promising to guide the ship of Indian freedom through the choppy waters of slavery. And Har Dayal did arrive, conquering their fears and reinstating in them the courage and power they needed to see things with a fresh perspective. He did set things in order and carried on from where they handed him the baton to lead them.

Har Dayal, when he arrived, brought along his close aide and confidant, Bhai Parmanand, who was now on a mission to profess the Samaj ideology in the faraway lands of Africa. He had become a preacher and travelled to different countries to propagate the beliefs of the Samaj. He was charged with sedition when on his person was found the incriminating manual of making bombs, similar to the one found with V.D. Savarkar in the Maniktola Bomb case. The raid was conducted on Bharat Mata Book Agency owned by Ajit Singh. The premises after Ajit Singh's deportation were occupied by Bhai Parmanand. To evade arrest, he subjected himself to self-imposed exile, which would lead him to Berkeley, California with his close friend, Har Dayal.

When contacted, Har Dayal promised to arrive in St John, California, in December 1912 but eventually arrived in March 1913 with Bhai Parmanand, who was likely instrumental in leading Har Dayal to a concrete course of action.[32] Har Dayal's first meeting with the peasant folk of Oregon and Washington proved fruitful. He was bursting with energy, his talk full of contempt for the British and his words carried the gravity that weighed heavily on the minds of his listeners. They were thoroughly impressed with his simple yet firm talk and wanted him to lead them on to this path of advocated revolution. Har Dayal was completely smitten by their dedication, their bare minds, perceptible, ready like fresh slates to be written on, their persona accepting enough to be moulded into whatever cast he would choose. They wanted to be led and Har Dayal had taken on the mantle to do so.

When Har Dayal addressed them at Astoria, his voice was loud and clear and made a strong impact. These were the words no one had ever uttered to them and deep down they could fathom the connect. Har Dayal stated:

> You have come to America and seen with your own eyes the prosperity of this country. What is the cause of this prosperity? Why nothing more than this, that America is ruled by its own

people. In India on the other hand, the people have no voice in the administration of the country. The British are mindful of their own personal interests. As an agricultural country India is infinitely richer than any other country in the world, and yet we see famine ravaging our country. The reason for this is that wheat is grown in India merely to be exported to England by the government. From the official statistics of the last sixteen years it is seen that two crores of people have died from hunger alone in India. Again, during the last decade, eighty lakhs of people have succumbed to plague. Government has been totally unaffected by this enormous loss of life.[33]

He further added that the British brought along famines and made plague a frequent phenomenon. He wanted the immigrants to rise above the narrow constraints of their religious divisions. He wanted them to turn themselves into tireless workers for their country. He wanted the youth to get educated in America and go back to serve their own country. He wanted them to turn themselves into an epitome of sacrifice and work for the salvation of the country.

In the meeting at St John, one individual at the gathering got up and laid a few crisp dollars lovingly at his feet, revering him like a guru, genuflecting before him and the others followed. They gave their precious savings, whatever they had for this cause but Har Dayal refused to accept this money for himself. He decided to let all of it go for the cause of the larger good.[34] His gesture delighted Bhakna, who had always castigated the educated babus for giving them false hopes.[35] A few such incidents that had occurred in the past, when some well-read men had preached amongst them, collected donations for the cause of the nation and never showed up again, made their distrust inevitable for such pretentious men. But Har Dayal was honest, simple, dedicated and determined. He had never once made a show of his intelligence before them, which could have created a strong wedge. Everything went off amicably and the association that was rendered redundant after the illness of G.D. Kumar was given a new lease of life.

The spring of 1913 augured a brand-new start for the Hindi Association of the Pacific Coast. Har Dayal proposed an office in San Francisco at 436, Hill Street.[36] An isolated, grey-coloured house reflecting the sombreness of the purpose, perched on top of a hill like an eagle ready to soar high with the wind of charged emotions under its wing, it was a mighty warrior. This house was a survivor like them. It was inured to earthquake and fire, and would now house the brave spirits who would bear a semblance to its own qualities. There was a will to survive bursting through the seams of this house. The front was bedecked with plants whose colourful flowers heralded the arrival of a new spring in their lives. The backyard too had a garden with a few shady trees, a pool of pristine water and an aura that could turn an ordinary man into a philosopher. It was called Yugantar Ashram. Rhyming with *Jugantar*, the fearless Bengali paper, which was banned by the government, Yugantar Ashram symbolized freedom in the free land of America.

The organizational set-up of the Hindi Association of the Pacific Coast remained the same with Har Dayal now appointed as the general secretary. Bhakna, Har Dayal and Kanshi Ram would be the three people who would carry on the secret work of this association.[37] There were no secret vows though, no rituals, and all who were present or those who would come in contact with them would become like an extended arm of this movement. But right at the start, they made some rules and regulations.

1) There was a definite objective, an aim that was the overpowering factor for the initiation of this struggle—the end of British rule.

2) There would be no salary instituted for those who would work for the party's cause. The work was to be considered

religion, above all, and given importance but without the lure of monetary benefits.

3) Religious beliefs were to be personal. They were not Sikhs, Hindus or Mussalmans; they were all one. They were all Ghadarites, which they would call themselves later. The party would be called the Ghadar Party (*Ghadar* is an Arabic-Persian word that means 'mutiny' or 'rebellion' and Ghadarites were the eternal rebels).

4) They shunned casteism. They did not indulge in any kind of ritualism. No oaths were to be undertaken.

5) Those who would work on the premises of Yugantar Ashram would be provided food and clothing from the party fund.

6) A membership fee of one dollar was instituted.

7) It was a fight against slavery and every member had to continue this work on an individual front as well along with others.[38]

And this was how it all began—on a positive note.

Now they had to spread their word to the uninitiated. They needed a mouthpiece, a newspaper that would resonate with their values and carry their mission forward, wage the Ghadar.

Chapter 12

The Launch of the Ghadar Newspaper

Je tau prem khelan ka chao
Sir dhar tali gali meri aao

(Should thou seek to engage in the game of love
step into my street with thy head placed on your palm)[1]

The Publication of *Ghadar*

Once the Hindi Association of the Pacific Coast was formed, it
was decided to spread the ideology of the party far and wide in
print by bringing out a newspaper that would help the cause. But
it did not happen immediately after the formation of the party.
Har Dayal went back, leaving his followers assured of quick action
and a ready response to their enthusiasm and determination. But
after the passage of few months when nothing happened on this
front, party workers approached Bhakna wanting to know what
was the cause of this delay. Once again, the apprehensions of being
cheated and the large sum of money collected for party work
being misused perturbed their minds. Probably, Har Dayal might
have found another occupation with his restless mind looking for
change. But he had been taken sick and with no earning prospects,
he was unable to get himself treated.

Once again, the recruits of the Ghadar Party raised funds and sent it to San Francisco for the benefit of Har Dayal. After the arrival of funds and being constantly goaded to show results, the day finally came when the first issue of the newspaper, called *Ghadar*, arrived. The first issue, printed in immaculate Urdu, handwritten by Har Dayal and cyclostyled manually by Sarabha came out on 1 November 1913.[2]

It got a magnificent reception amongst its circles. After a few weeks came the edition in Gurmukhi on 9 December 1913 and later, some editions were translated into Gujarati, Bengali, Pashto and Hindi.[3] It was going to be a weekly paper.[4] Handwritten and cyclostyled, the paper was a lot of work for Har Dayal, Tundilat and Sarabha, who worked, ate and slept on the premises of the Yugantar Ashram. When the workload increased, they were joined by Pingle and Khankhoje. Lahiri and Chenchiah arrived from Berkeley every weekend to help them as well.

Initially, around 2500 copies were being printed in Gurmukhi and 2200 in Urdu and the demand kept on rising.[5] It was no longer possible for Sarabha and others to cyclostyle it by hand. They then bought a litho machine and shifted their premises to a more spacious location.[6] Publication of the paper was a full-time occupation for these tireless Ghadarites, who were engrossed day and night in this work, their minds preoccupied with writing and gathering information to make *Ghadar* a huge success.[7]

Ghadar was not only a weekly newspaper; it soon became a cause and they used it to exhort those still in deep slumber. And for those who read it, this became their chant, 'If you talk, talk of Ghadar, if you dream, dream of Ghadar. If you eat, eat for the sake of Ghadar.'[8] Everything else can wait. Bring on the Ghadar and bring it now.

The first issue was released in Shattuck Hotel in Berkeley amidst farmers, students, labourers and intellectuals as well as eminent Americans. In his address, Har Dayal, as usual in his peculiar style, waxed eloquent about his creation: 'In the history of today's India, a new era is set in motion. The power of "PEN" will explode like a cannonball. This newspaper is like the staunch enemy of English Empire, and a bugle of challenge for the Indian youth. Wake up, take up the arms and fight for the independence of India.'

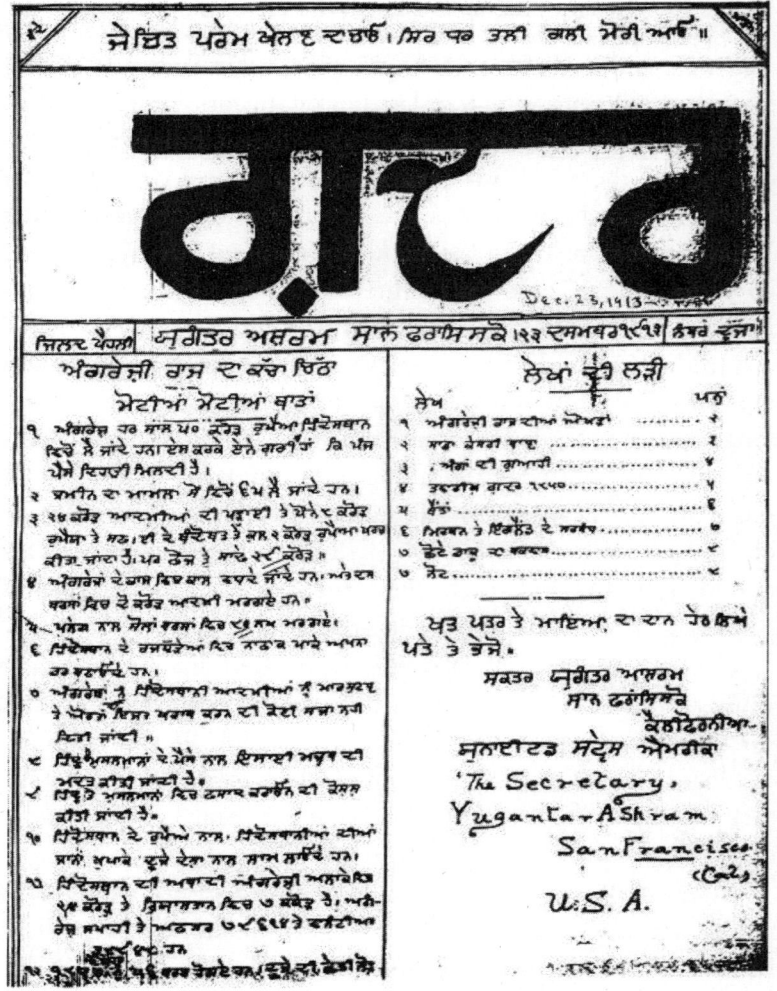

The 23 December 1913 issue of *Ghadar*

The Content

Har Dayal firmly believed that no literature unless written in one's own language could be the harbinger of revolution.

The very first issue of *Ghadar* opened with these lines by Har Dayal under the heading 'Our name and our work': 'A new epoch in the history of India opens today, 1 November 1913 because today there begins in foreign lands but our country's language a war against the British Raj.'

Later on, it read:

'What is our name? Ghadar (mutiny)

What does our work consist of? In bringing an uprising

Where will the uprising break out? In India

When will it break out? In a few years

Why? Because the people can no longer bear the oppression and tyranny under British rule and are ready to fight and die for freedom.'[9]

The first issue carried the following articles: 'Evidence of Statistics', 'Sikhs and the Government', 'History of the Ghadar–1857', 'What do the Americans say?', besides others.

The regular features of the weekly included the 'Exposure Sheet', 'Evidence of Statistics' and 'History of the Ghadar–1857'.

Angrezi Raj Ka Kacha Chittha (A Balance Sheet of English Rule) consisted of fourteen points printed on the front page. It emphasized that the British were taking Rs 50 crore to England every year, leaving the Indian people poor with their average per capita daily income as only 5 paise. The land tax was above 65 per cent. The famines, plagues and hunger had killed millions of Indians under British rule. They were allocating less for health and more on military and were using the same to commit aggression on neighbouring countries. The last point was the need to have a mutiny like 1857, reminding people that fifty-six years had elapsed since they revolted against the British and they needed to do it again. These arguments highlighting the atrocities committed by the British became a regular feature of the weekly paper.

Translation of books was also undertaken by the Ghadar press. The highly contentious book (in British eyes) of V.D. Savarkar, *The Indian War of Independence 1857*, was translated into Urdu and Punjabi and serialized from 8 December 1915 in the Urdu edition and from 23 December 1915 in Gurmukhi. Bhai Parmanand's *Tarikh-i-Hind*, a book on Indian history banned by the British government, too was published in the paper.[10]

A special edition was reserved for the anniversary of 1857 along with a picture of the Rani of Jhansi. The Gurmukhi edition, printed on red paper, on 10 May 1914, was called the 'Ghadar in Saffron' and exhorted people to follow in the footsteps of the warriors of 1857.[11] The paper printed frequent articles on Bengali revolutionary groups like the Anushilan Samiti and others. The heroes of Bombay and Bengal—Lokmanya Tilak, Aurobindo Ghosh and V.D. Savarkar—were lauded and their deeds mentioned as worthy of emulation.[12] The doings of revolutionaries living in exile, such as Shyamaji Krishnavarma, Madam Cama, Lajpat Rai, Sufi Amba Prasad and Ajit Singh too, were brought to the attention of readers.[13] Their sacrifices were painted with words of valour reflecting their inherent contradiction of being away from the motherland and yet espousing its cause with firm determination. The paper wrote about the restrictions they faced in their homeland.

Revolutionary literature from around the world was also published. *Roosi Baghiyon Ki Dastan* (The Tale of Russian Revolutionaries) along with Irish, French and Egyptian tales of valour highlighted their determined efforts and daring exploits with their martyrdom stories.[14] The paper wrote about George Washington's struggle against the British as well as the French revolutions, and emphasized Bismarck's efforts to unify Germany.

The photographs of Indian martyrs were published regularly and a plea was made to readers to donate more such photos for publication. It planned to reproduce thousands of such photos and often asked the people, 'Those brethren who wish to hang them in their houses, will please let the Ghadar know by postcard. This is most necessary.'[15]

Har Dayal wrote about the necessity to guard themselves from the spies of the British government.[16] He was very vocal about such men, who targeted the nationalists and reported their activities to the government. While he was writing all this, he was being watched by Hopkinson, who till now had been confused by the multiple and various interests of Har Dayal and was not able to pinpoint one single thing to build up his case.

But Har Dayal with *Ghadar* was very loud and his voice was being amplified through the publication. In any case, since the resignation of his scholarship, neither Har Dayal's words nor his amazing intellect had sounded like a melody to British ears. But now his existence in America had become a jarring noise.

In one of his articles, he motivated Indians to rise above temporary comforts, shed sluggishness and serve their country with *tan, man, dhan* (body, mind and wealth). This was the appeal in an article titled 'The Voice of India': 'My heroes! O, lions, O, brave men! Recover your senses. How long will you continue to sleep? How long will you consent to being shoe-beaten by others and put up with their tyrannies.'

The anniversary of the bomb thrown on Lord Hardinge received special mention in an article 'Our Saffron Attire' (*Hamara Kesari Labas/Sada Kesari Bana*) in the *Ghadar* issue of 23 December 1913.

Har Dayal always carried a pamphlet titled *Shabash!* (Bravo!) to commemorate the bombing attempt on Lord Hardinge. It carried this inscription in bold at the top: 'Price per copy: Head of an Englishman'.[17] He sang paeans to the cult of the bomb because he thought that governments were frightened of the bomb and that was the only way to earn one's rights. Individual pamphlets written by Har Dayal in a dramatic and instigating tone were also being circulated along with the paper.

In its 'Wanted' columns, it appealed to the patriotism of Indians by advertising the requirement of the chosen few who would not hesitate to take the call to serve the motherland. It read something like this:

> 'Wanted—Heroic and enthusiastic soldiers for mutiny
> Remuneration—Death
> Reward—Martyrdom
> Pension—Freedom
> Field of work—Hindustan'.[18]

Har Dayal would organize meetings, resurrecting the custom of India House. Such meetings were organized in public places and notices of forthcoming meetings would be printed in *Ghadar*.

The Reach of *Ghadar*

Ghadar reached every nook and corner where Indians were residing. No place was too far away and unapproachable when it came to preaching sedition. It was being circulated in the North American continent and in Egypt, South Africa, Fiji, Canada, British East Africa, British Guiana, the Philippines, Hong Kong, Thailand, Burma, the Dutch East Indies, Mexico, Panama and Brazil. It was intercepted in Trinidad, Sudan, Aden, Morocco, Manila, Java, Madagascar and Réunion, Canton, Johannesburg, Nairobi, Australia, Japan, Hankow, Tientsin, Singapore, the Malay States and Honduras.

The world was its home. *Ghadar* was reaching places and soon became a cause of worry for the Indian government. The first issue of *Ghadar* arrived in India on 7 December 1913 addressed to one

Gajjan Singh of Ludhiana.[19] It was immediately reported to the higher officials and from there on, the paper was termed seditious and placed under prohibition, and its importation was made a crime.

On 24 January 1914, twenty-four copies of *Ghadar* were intercepted at the Lahore Post Office.[20] Once Yugantar Ashram came to know about this development, they started sending the paper in simple envelopes, giving it the appearance of private letters. Despite this, a large consignment of these harmless-looking envelopes were intercepted in Bombay.[21] Now they needed novel ways to make their voice heard, which was being throttled by the Indian government. Indians all over the world were getting inspired but in the land itself, for whose freedom they were preaching, the sound of it was being boxed.

They asked their readers for help. And help did pour in from all quarters. To enable its reach in India became a challenge, but they were game for such challenges. The newspaper, instead of being sent as such was copied by hand in letters, its content written on slips that were disguised and sent with private letters. People were asked to pass along issues of *Ghadar*, if it evaded detection, for others to read. A chain was thus formed. From one hand to another, by word of mouth, *Ghadar* was being read aloud in private assemblies, discussed and then passed on to other readers for their perusal. It was being sent to army people discreetly to awaken their better sense.

Despite the heightened government security and the interception of the paper again and again, it was reaching Punjabi villages where it was stirring souls. It was being sent to Manila and Hong Kong and posted from there to India in business envelopes while cuttings of *Ghadar* were sent in ordinary envelopes.

Some seditious letters were intercepted by the government, which had the essence of *Ghadar* rubbed on them. These letters made a passionate plea and each of them espoused the cause of freedom. Thousands of such letters escaped their notice, yet many were seized, their contents dissected with a viciousness and alerting the government about the plans being hatched against them in a foreign land.

Ghadar Dian Goonjan (The Resounding Echoes of Revolution)

Through a sprinkle on the withered hearts
The Ghadar fired a new life into the dead
The pen has done the work of a cannon
Shaken the foundation of the tyrannous government.[22]

—Written by an anonymous Ghadar poet

Har Dayal knew the importance of the vernacular. It was language that played an important role in the spread and conflagration of the fire that had been smouldering invisibly, causing the British heartburn. And now with the encouragement of Har Dayal, the uninitiated were being inducted into the art of writing. A few rustic poems had been contributed by first-time writers in Gurmukhi. And the editor had given them space, encouraging others to pen their heart's anguish. More such pieces followed. They decided to publish them separately in a booklet called *Ghadar Dian Goonjan*. The booklet was free for distribution along with the newspaper.

The poems were raw, their language a little rustic, unedited and passed on as such for the consumption of the readers. Har Dayal called them organic and was criticized for encouraging such an outburst of emotions. If *Ghadar* was well tailored and full of scholarly articles, *Ghadar Dian Goonjan* was the complete opposite. These were the outpourings of an embittered heart given vent to in a language they knew by heart and were comfortable enough to write in. The first issue of these poems was in April 1914, a few months after the publication of *Ghadar* had begun.[23] It turned out to be a huge success. If the paper was awaited with bated breath, the poems were lapped up with an eagerness hitherto unknown. If the first issue sold 10,000 copies, the demand soared in further issues.

The poems generated a huge frenzy when read aloud in meetings, get-togethers and gurdwaras. They often did not carry any names to protect the privacy of the writer. And even if they did, these were pseudonyms. The newspaper followed the policy of carrying only the name of the editor on the front page. They had decided that if any action was called upon in the future, the editor would bear the brunt, a single person who would then be replaced by a new one. One at a time! People like Sarabha and Tundilat, who were the real workers behind the scene and often contributed poems as well, were never mentioned in the paper for the same reason.

Dabbling in diverse topics from socio-economic issues to the adversities faced by the immigrants to questioning the unguarded loyalty of the Indians back home, the paper contained it all. The desire for a free motherland, the ignominy of being called slaves, the life away from home and loved ones—the poems were written with the invisible blood that seeped out of their veins all the time, painting their surroundings red. The poems spoke to those who read them. How could anyone not be affected by this true display of emotion and courage? It was infectious!

The first issue carried a poem that depicted the pain of being called names in a foreign country. It conveyed the pain of being called slaves because the country was enslaved. It read as follows:

The world calls us coolie.
Why doesn't our flag fly anywhere?
How shall we survive, are we slaves forever?
Why aren't we involved in politics?
From the beginning, we have been yoked to thralldom.
Why don't we even dream of freedom?
Only a handful of oppressors have taken our fields.
Why has no Indian cultivator risen and protected our lands?

Our children cry for want of education.
Why don't we open science colleges?[24]

More of this was to follow in future poems.

Why do you disgrace the name of Singhs
How come you have forgotten the majesty of 'lions'
How could the Singhs have been taunted?
People say that the Singhs are no good.
Why did you turn the tides during the Delhi mutiny?
Cry aloud: 'Let us kill the whites'
Why do you sit quiet shamelessly?
Let the earth give way so we may drown
To what good were those thirty crores born.[25]

These people might not have been educated, but they were aware of the game of divide and rule being played back home. In one of the poems, they tried to spread this word of caution to their brothers and sisters.

They sought the unity of different religions. They had the foresight that nothing but one nation, one soul and a collective religion would give them hope. They wrote against the narrow divisions trying to subvert their cause.

The Impact of *Ghadar*

Ghadar was fearless in its writing and in its approach. The first look of the paper could be described as nothing less than nationalistic, seditious and anti-British. It had a deep effect on the consciousness of ordinary people who were yet to come to terms with any sort of political expediency. Uninitiated, raw minds would soon acquire a political will and consciousness new to them. Such would be the impact of *Ghadar* on the people who would read it. Like the Pied Piper of Hamelin, it goaded them to follow it into the mystique of revolution.

The usage of Urdu and Gurmukhi endeared this paper to the masses. It was being read by the uneducated peasants with enthusiasm and by the educated men with panache. Language barriers were demolished by its arrival.

Ghadar raised the consciousness of the ordinary man who had no idea about the Russian, Irish and Chinese revolutions taking place around the world. It made them realize that their struggle was not unique and not wrong. It was the same struggle that was being undertaken by oppressed people all over the world. It was their right to fight. Acceptance of slavery in any form was something that was meant to be fought. Revolutionaries in other countries became their compatriots and their struggle their own. Reading about the struggles of other people enhanced their political acumen.

This newspaper gave rise to self-operating Ghadar groups all over the world that had no connection with the main centre in Yugantar Ashram, San Francisco. These self-appointed leaders did not need any guidance of leaders, nor did they adhere themselves to the centre. Ghadar was their guru and they were getting their sustenance from the Ghadar literature. Never had the written word made so much impact in the revolutionary history of the world.

Soon the demand for the paper rose so high that they had to make alternate arrangements to make more copies. They needed more hands to help, a larger area and more press facilities. They were getting donations from all corners. Money was not an issue although the paper was being delivered free of charge. Readers were contributing on their own.

Perhaps this kind of response was unexpected even for Har Dayal, who was by now a seasoned editor and writer. But what *Ghadar* did to him was something more proverbial and the pressure was building upon the government to make a case against him. Now they did not need any pretext. This time, the damage was immense and beyond repair and Har Dayal was the price they would have to pay.

Chapter 13

The Arrest of Har Dayal

That Har Dayal's activities were under the scanner was no secret even to him. The Canadian-British secret agent Hopkinson had been following him for quite a while now and building a case against him.[1] The charges had to be framed in such a manner to give the case weightage to secure conviction in an American court. After all, Har Dayal was no ordinary man now. His presence in America and his party, along with its publication, were giving nightmares to the British officials. And they were constantly putting pressure on their American counterparts to arrest him as soon as possible.

Meanwhile, even before his arrest took place, the meetings that he organized in the different cities of the West Coast were becoming a cause for concern. Announcements of upcoming meetings were published beforehand in *Ghadar* and reports on these meetings were published later.

The *Ghadar* issue of 23 December 1913 carried a notice that a meeting would be held at Sacramento on 31 December 1913. An account of this meeting was later published in the *Ghadar* issue of January 1914.[2] In this meeting, Har Dayal was unstoppable even though he must have known that the British were closing in and every word he uttered would be used against him. He said:

> As the story goes, the jackal, when he gets bad luck, goes to the city; the same way the English Government has moved their capital from Calcutta to Delhi. They cannot save themselves now because they are between the Punjabis, Rajputs and Mohammedans. Everyone remembers the mutiny of 1857 at Delhi, and we hope the people of Delhi will do their duty. It is our own fault if we are under the power of the government. If we try we can easily be free. Those hearing the unfairness of the government should be fired with anger and readily sacrifice their lives and not sit down and become careless. If the patriots are captured, it is the fault of the countrymen who are not ready to fight for them.
>
> We ought to be ashamed of ourselves and hate the government servants who are oppressors of our countrymen. We ought to give the police trouble all the time, and we should always be ready to start the mutiny. If we are always prepared you will not become afraid. It is the duty of all our countrymen to join the soldiers' mutiny. Help the paper and be ready to start a revolution as soon as you can return to India. There is nothing greater than this at present and it is everyone's duty to join in.[3]

The die was cast! This was open sedition. The revolutionaries thought the American government was neutral and would espouse their cause. But not any more.

Ernest Scott, the British embassy first secretary, filed a complaint against Har Dayal and a warrant was issued against his name 'on charges of being a member of excluded classes, an anarchist or advocating the overthrow of the United States government by force'.[4] Though the warrant was issued in Washington, Har Dayal was arrested in San Francisco on 25 March 1914.[5]

The case that was finally built up against him levelled charges that he gave a speech against the Russian Czar about two years previously and this gave the US authorities a reason to charge him with being an anarchist. The context of the speech was something like this: The speech was made on 31 October 1913 during the time when the Ghadar Party came into existence. The speech emphasized and discussed the importance of the Russian Revolution. The authorities construed Har Dayal to be a disciple and sympathizer of the revolution and used it against him.

The other case that the British embassy with the help of Hopkinson and some American officials were building up against Har Dayal was of his stay being less than three years[6] since his arrival, which made him liable to deportation. But the actual warrants were served a little late and by that time, Har Dayal had completed more than three years of his stay and he could not be transported on that account. Though Har Dayal had well-wishers in the American government, they were unable to help him. The pressure on the American government from their British counterparts was too much to handle and it led to his arrest, which Har Dayal, as if anticipating, graciously accepted. After his arrest, he was granted bail on the deposition of $1000 and was asked to appear before the court on 10 April 1914.

The news of his arrest was splashed in newspapers all over the world in bold letters. The San Francisco newspapers ran it as the lead story. The leaders of the Ghadar Party poured in from all quarters to Yugantar Ashram. The free press of America that sympathized with the radical elements spoke against it. Intellectuals deemed it as a conspiracy. They started raising money against this move and soon $800 were raised to fight a strong case against his deportation. Har Dayal's friends were equally vociferous on this move targeting a particular individual who had raised the bar for his countrymen and had given them dreams and the conviction to fight for them.

The Friends of Russian Freedom[7] sent a letter to the commissioner general of immigration defending Har Dayal's right of asylum, which stated, 'It seems preposterous that in this, of all countries, it was proposed to surrender this Hindu who has been doing for his people what we revere the "fathers" here for having done for us.'[8] Madam Cama rallied for Har Dayal all the way from Paris. She cabled the secretary of state requesting him to free the distinguished Hindu scholar and democrat.[9]

The despair was evident in the next issue of *Ghadar*. That the Ghadar Party would lose Har Dayal sounded like a painful blow to them. Thus read the last poem of the *Ghadar Dian Goonjan* published in the edition of 31 March 1914:

When he broke the news of the warrant of arrest
It set our hearts ablaze
It poured oil on the burning fire
The already burning fire was fanned all the more[10]

Har Dayal issued a public statement in the *Ghadar* issue of 27 March to the American press, his anger against the British and American governments palpable:

My arrest calls public attention to the despicable pro-British subservience of the United States government which is so vivid a feature of President Wilson's foreign policy. The democratic administration is licking the boots of England as anyone can see who observes the administration's attitude towards Great Britain. For many months, I have been spied upon by the British secret service operatives, but have gone about my affairs openly and have not tuned my statement or modulated my declarations because of their presence. My arrest was not a surprise. I have been expecting it for a long time.[11]

Har Dayal did not want to be deported to India. He was a suspect in the Lord Hardinge bomb attack case.[12] He had publicly applauded the act then. It was not only deportation he feared, it was the fear of being sent back to India like Savarkar, who had been extradited from France and later on sentenced to a long spell of imprisonment in the Andamans.

The only way to avoid it was to jump bail, leave everything midway and go. It must have been painful for him to leave his newspaper, the party he had helped in binding itself together, but it was now or never. And just like that, Har Dayal left America and moved to Switzerland with the help of friends who knew how dangerous it could prove for him to remain on US soil.

The main motive of targeting Har Dayal was not only to stop the ongoing Indian freedom movement in America, it was also to stop the publication of *Ghadar*, which was seen as the most seditious newspaper ever to be published from foreign soil. The British had a presumptuous understanding that proved to be wrong.

Once Har Dayal left, Yugantar officials reorganized themselves. Har Dayal's confidant Ram Chandra took over his editorial duties.

Ram Chandra, son of Mathra Mal, was from Kalu Khan, Peshawar. He was associated with Ajit Singh and the Pagri Sambhal Jatta movement. He was the editor of two journals back home: *India*, which was published from Gujranwala, and *Akash* from Delhi.[13] He had left India in 1911 and arrived in Washington sometime in 1913. Here, he got in touch with Har Dayal and had been with him while he toured the West Coast of the US, creating societies in different cities before the formation of the Ghadar Party in Astoria.

On 7 April 1914, Ram Chandra took over as the editor of *Ghadar*, which would from now be known as *Hindustan Ghadar*.[14] Barakatullah arrived from Japan and was made in-charge of the Urdu edition of the *Ghadar*.

Har Dayal was not only managing the paper but he was the general secretary of the party as well. Bhai Santokh Singh stepped up to take up that responsibility.

Bhai Santokh Singh was born in Singapore where his father was working with the British army as an orderly. After his father's retirement, the family went back to Punjab where he received his education at Khalsa College, Amritsar. As a student, he moved to California where he became involved with the Ghadar Party. Now, he was in a prime position as the party general secretary.

After Har Dayal left, duties were delineated. Har Dayal was a one-man army juggling multiple responsibilities. As a result of his departure, the work of the paper and the party was done with a new zeal, for there was the fear that the paper and the work would suffer since Har Dayal had left. Also, Bhakna, who had now started residing on the premises of Yugantar Ashram, doubled up his reserves. New people were being added to the party and the circulation of the paper increased manifold.

Har Dayal, though not physically present, kept up with his articles, a moral support to boost their spirits. He kept on sending articles to be published in *Ghadar*, one of which spoke of the need for Ghadar and guns.[15]

The Ghadarites heeded Har Dayal's advice. The party attempted to strengthen its military wing by making them undergo training. Jawala Singh opened his farm for such training camps, imparting knowledge of guns and bombs. Master Udham Singh, a retired army man, was appointed as the instructor for this specialized training. Sarabha was sent to Europe to learn the art of flying planes, which his seniors thought might come in handy.

They prepared themselves on a war footing for the battle they would wage upon the British. But something was coming up on Canadian shores to jolt their attention. That something would turn the tide of events. The battles they had waged in their minds were now going to get real.

Chapter 14

A Ship Called *Komagata Maru*

'150 Indian Sikhs have chartered steamer from here to British Columbia, are not on through ticket from India. Am advised that local emigration clauses do not apply to other than Chinese emigration. Please telegraph whether in the circumstances they will be permitted to land in Canada,' read a cable sent from the Governor of Hong Kong, F.W. May, to the Canadian government on 30 March 1914.[1] The saga of the steamer known as the *Komagata Maru* would soon become a story heard around the world.

The *Komagata Maru* was a vessel built in Glasgow in 1890 for a German company, Dampfschiff Rederei Hansa of Hamburg, registered under the name Stubbenhuk.[2] About 100 metres long and 13 metres wide, it was powered by a 265-horsepower steam engine.[3] There were a few cabins on the upper deck and nothing much apart from that to boast about. Basically a cargo ship, it was not meant for carrying people and lacked the basic facilities for that altogether. It was owned by Shinyei Kisen Goshi Kaisa, a small Japanese company consisting of only four or five people, which had in its possession only one more ship apart from the *Komagata Maru*.[4] In 1914, in a peculiar turn of circumstances, it was christened *Guru Nanak Jahaaz* and set sail for Canada on 28 March 1914.

'The main purpose of every Sikh was to fight for independence because Guru Gobind Singh died for his country.'[5] Gurdit Singh's voice resonated, making a deep impression on his audience. The man from Sirhali in Amritsar was not a meek person. An entrepreneur, he had lived and worked in different parts of the world—Malaya, Singapore, Taiping, and here he was in Hong Kong addressing the men in the gurdwara on the occasion of Gurpurab, spreading the spirit of Ghadar.[6] Gurdit was not only a man of words; he also had a clear plan.

While in Hong Kong, Gurdit Singh noticed Indians waiting for a ship to take them to Canada, the land of their dreams. The government was changing the laws, the rules were being made inflexible but they had seen in the recent judgments that the Canadian courts had the power to overrule the government. They saw hope in the judgments. And Gurdit Singh thought the same. He was a born fighter. He chartered the *Komagata Maru* with the idea of sailing it to Canada.

These were the terms and condition for chartering the ship:

- HK$11,000 per month rent
- First term of rental to be paid on signing
- The second within a week
- The third and fourth within two weeks
- Remainder within two months of commencement
- Captain and crew would be provided but no wireless telegraphy would be affixed[7]

Tickets were sold at HK$210 by one of Singh's confidants.[8] Out of 500 hopefuls, only 165 chipped in as the rest of them were too scared to undertake this journey.[9] The ship would have sailed with more people if the Hong Kong police had not played spoilsport. They scared and shooed people away with the declaration that they would not be taken in by the Canadian government. The ship started its journey from Hong Kong on 28 March 1914. Hindus, Sikhs and Muslims were packed together on 533 wooden benches with no backs. The lower deck looked more or less like a third-class railway coach.

'If we are admitted, we will know that the Canadian government is just. If we are deported, we will sue the government and if we cannot obtain redress, we will go back and take up the matter with the Indian government,' said Gurdit Singh in Shanghai,[10] the first stop of the journey from where boarded another seventy-three hopefuls.[11] There, Gurdit Singh spoke to a press reporter with a certain nonchalance. Though the second instalment of the ship had still not been paid, the third was about to come and the count of passengers was still not to the ship's capacity, it did not deter him. He had brought Ghadar literature on board and raised the spirits of his men by readings from *Ghadar Dian Goonjan.*

The second stop of the ship came at Moji, a port 210 kilometres from Nagasaki in Japan.[12] Refuelling of coal was undertaken at Moji as the men on the ship explored Japan.[13] Eighty-five passengers had arrived from Manila at Nagasaki and boarded a train to Moji.[14] Thirty-eight were waiting at Moji itself. By now, Gurdit Singh was making exaggerated claims of starting a revolution by the Indian troops if the government opposed the sailing of the *Komagata Maru.*

In Moji came a high-profile visitor who lectured the men on board. This was Balwant Singh Khurdpur, the priest of the gurdwara of Vancouver, who, along with Bhag Singh Bhikhiwind, had secured his family's entry to Canada after a fierce court battle. His rousing speech revived their sagging spirits.[15]

The last and the final stop before the ship reached the North Pacific was Yokohama, a port city to the south of Tokyo. There, Bhagwan Singh, the man who had been bundled up forcibly and removed from Canada, spoke to the passengers. 'You will not get permission to land, the Canadian government will make sure of that,' said Bhagwan Singh to the passengers of the *Komagata Maru*.[16]

Bhagwan Singh had jumped out of the ship at Yokohama and was staying put with Barakatullah, devising his own plans to enter Canadian territory once again.

The curious case of Bhagwan Singh being deported deserves a mention. A man of passionate speeches, he commanded attention when he spoke. He was into anti-government activities when he left Punjab in 1907 to escape arrest. He landed in Hong Kong and became the granthi of the Hong Kong gurdwara where he carried on with his seditious activities. He finally made his way to Canada on a ship called *Empress of Russia* and was able to land with a forged identity. His activities came to the fore very soon as he was extremely vocal in his criticism of the British regime. He was shunted out of Canada and ended up becoming a living martyr for the local community.

After this last stop, the *Komagata Maru* was not going to permit entry to new passengers. For now, there was no land in sight.

The number of passengers stood at 376 now. Most of them (340) were Sikhs from Central Punjab (Amritsar, Patiala, Ferozepur, Ludhiana, Jalandhar and Lahore).[17] The majority of these Sikhs belonged to Gurdit Singh's district, Amritsar. The twenty-four Muslims were from Shahpur in west Punjab and the rest were Hindus.[18]

Gurdit Singh was the man in command and remained so till the end. Apart from the passengers, there was a doctor on board, Raghunath Singh, who was travelling with his wife and child. He was an employee of the 8th Rajput Battalion in Hong Kong and was currently on leave.[19] A granthi with the Guru Granth Sahib was accorded a special place on the ship where the passengers would recite hymns and pay obeisance regularly.

Even as the *Komagata Maru* sailed to Canada, on the Vancouver shore, hectic activities had begun to stall the entry of the ship into Canadian territory. When it arrived on 23 May 1915, it was anchored at Burrad inlet, the harbour that was a shallow cleft of the sea that separated the city of Vancouver from the mountainous region.

Local politicians were virulent in their opposition to the landing of the ship and this was dutifully carried by the British and Canadian press.

The arrival of the *Komagata Maru* was described as a second oriental invasion of Canada by *The Times*, London.[20] Similar emotions were expressed by the *Vancouver Sun* on 1 June 1914, when it wrote that Asia was knocking and knocking persistently at the door of Western America.[21] *The Times*, London also spoke disparagingly of the incident.[22]

The Canadian press was also waiting to get a glimpse of the passengers and report about their uncouth demeanour. As soon as the gangway was lowered, they hopped on to the ship. But they were pleasantly surprised to find the passengers nice and well turned out. This was something they had not expected. Indians were, perhaps, not savages, who amused them as they wrote in their columns.

The *Vancouver Daily News Advertiser* reported thus after interviewing the passengers on their arrival: 'They all seemed in good health and were certainly clean, well set-up and handsome men. Some of the old men in particular were magnificent specimens of humanity.'[23]

The *Victoria Times* reported:

The majority of men had served in the British army, and they are a tall handsome lot. They seem superior to the class of Hindus which have already come to this province. They stand very erect and move with an alert action. All their suits are well pressed, and their turbans spotlessly clean. Most of them know a little English and some of them converse in it remarkably well.[24]

The men happily posed for pictures, feeling elated at this reception. The kind words of the *Vancouver Daily News Advertiser* and *The Victoria Times* were not taken to, too kindly by the immigration people, who shooed the press away and did not allow anyone to embark on the ship. The men on the ship were bamboozled at this development. They had enjoyed the limelight even if only for a little while. They were unaware of the frenzy they had generated on the shores, the reverberations of which were soon to be felt in Ottawa and back home. For them, the second home was open and welcoming and it was going to be nowhere else but here in Canada.

By now, a firm opposition had begun to take shape amongst the local anti-immigration lobby and politicians of British Columbia. They would not tolerate another ship full of immigrants to land as it had happened in the past. The decision by Justice Hunter in the *Panama Maru* case and the liberties extended to the families of Bhikhiwind and Khurdpur had angered them.

Immigration officer Malcolm R.J. Reid, a Vancouver immigration agent, was the main face of the opposition. He was a man who made decisions on his own with the backing of the local MP, H.H. Stevens. He was the face of rabid nationalism and the strongest opponent of the Indian cause. A political appointee, he was an elementary school teacher until 1911 when the Conservative Party came to power.[25] Reid forbade anyone from going near the ship, which was put on watch and surrounded by government boats. He did not let the ship unload its cargo of coal and the request to reload the ship with Canadian lumber was outrightly rejected.[26]

H.H. Stevens, the local conservative MP, Reid and Hopkinson formed a strong trio who, with all their might, would try to keep the passengers of *Komagata Maru* on the ship itself, providing them no leverage or outlet to express their grievances and, most importantly, keeping them away from the courts.

The Indians on the shore had no illusions. They knew very well that this time it would not be an easy task to get their brothers down from the ship. They had in the past gone to the courts and won, but this time, the level of resentment had reached gargantuan proportions. Though they were ready to fight for the rights of their own people, Canada would not give them success on a platter.

The Indians in Canada were well prepared with a lawyer, J. Edward Bird, and had formed a Shore Committee of fifteen members who would represent the rights of all 376 men on board.[27] The important members of this Shore Committee were Hussain Rahim, Bhag Singh Bhikhiwind, Balwant Singh Khurdpur, Sohan Lal Pathak and Bhagwan Singh Jakh.[28]

Chagan Kairaj Verma, a Hindu from Porbandar, Gujarat came to Canada with an assumed Muslim name and identity, Hussain Rahim, took charge of the Shore Committee's affairs and managed them impeccably, becoming a connection between the people aboard and the authorities.

Before coming to Canada as a tourist in 1910, he had lived in Japan for a number of years. He had been deported from Canada nine months earlier after a search on his person led to the discovery of a formula depicting the making of nitroglycerine that was used in bomb-making.[29] But he had gone to court against this decision and had managed to gain entry back. Now, donning the role of an activist, he was ready to fight for his own people.

Rahim was bold in his comments whenever he addressed public meetings. He had been opposing the unjust rules and regulations of the Canadian government and vehemently castigated the press, which had been meek, lacking a voice of its own.

Meanwhile, back at the ship, ninety passengers of the total were declared medically unfit by the immigration department.[30] Then began the Board of Inquiry hearings, one passenger at a time being ferried to and from the boat to the office of Malcolm Reid. The head of the inquiry being Reid himself.[31] He was making inordinate delays, examining each passenger, leisurely withholding his decision. He was not only delaying the normally brisk procedure, he was also putting pressure on the agents of the ship to get it removed from Vancouver harbour.[32] The owner of the ship sent a cable to the agents to pay ¥8000 as charter expenses and coal hire, and if unpaid, send the ship back to Hong Kong.[33] The people on the ship were in a deplorable state. The wait seemed never-ending for them. Soon they were plagued with food and water shortages. Malcolm Reid dusted his hands off this responsibility, yet he indicated that it could be done if he was paid some money.[34]

Meetings were regularly being conducted by the Shore Committee and donations were being accumulated. In one such meeting, the lawyer, Edward Bird, spoke up against the thinly veiled motives of the immigration department, who were hell-bent upon delaying things. The physical examination of every passenger was being prolonged and no decision was being made, so they could not go to the courts and gain advantage or laxity. A few provisions had been supplied. The people on board were surviving from meal to meal. The Shore Committee tried to take proprietorship of the vessel by presenting a cheque of $11,000.[35] Gurdit Singh was relieved of one big task of arranging the money.

Meanwhile, a few of the passengers on the *Komagata Maru* who had been in Canada on earlier visits were given permission to disembark. Out of the 376 passengers, 355 were still on board, their future undecided. Finally, the Shore Committee gave in and agreed to the test cases, which would be representative of the rest of the passengers. Two people were chosen: Munshi Singh of Hoshiarpur and Narain Singh of Lahore and cases were filed on their behalf. They were questioned and their replies were found unsatisfactory.

A full bench of the Supreme Court sat to decide on these cases. Their unanimous decision was to refuse admission to the passengers of the *Komagata Maru* and as a result, deportation orders were issued for the 355 passengers on board.

This decision was a big blow for the passengers, who retaliated by proclaiming that they would not let the ship move and were ready to fight.

Indeed, they were not afraid. The gloominess of arriving and yet not being allowed to disembark, and not being allowed to set foot in the land of their dreams was unfathomable. The wait had humiliated them. Some of them had removed their three-piece suits and folded them neatly to be put in their trunks. And now they were back in their traditional clothing. There was no joy to be celebrated and soon the pain of rejection intensified into anger.

The *Komagata Maru* had to be driven out of Canadian waters now. The *Sea Lion*, a tug boat, was brought to take control of the ship but the passengers aboard retaliated by attacking the 120 policemen with coal, bricks and scrap iron.[36] Next, the warship *Rainbow* was brought, which was armed with war guns to threaten the ship. Finally, the men on the *Komagata Maru* accepted the offer of provisions by the Canadian government along with help from the Shore Committee and sailed back with their hopes dashed and dreams of a rosy future made redundant.

Chapter 15

The Long Journey Back Home

Even as the *Komagata Maru* was still sailing in the Pacific and had not reached its first stop, Yokohama, the political situation changed drastically. The allied powers—England, France, Russia, Italy, Romania and Japan—had declared war upon Germany, Austria, Hungary, Bulgaria and the Ottoman Empire, the central powers. The Ghadar Party had been waiting for this war and had kept their spirits high for they had their own plans. They wanted to wage their own war against England while it was busy battling the foreign powers. But that the war would come so early was unexpected.

In Yokohama, a special visitor awaited the ship. He carried 200 pistols and 2000 rounds of ammunition on his person.[1] This man was the president of the Ghadar Party, Sohan Singh Bhakna. He had been entrusted with this important task of meeting the passengers on the ship and giving them the ammunition. The ammunition had been arranged by Bhagwan Singh and Kartar Singh Sarabha. The thought of young Sarabha brought a smile to Bhakna's face. He was fond of the enthusiastic young recruit, who with his ever-smiling demeanour and his intensity had won the hearts of many. And now Bhakna was ready and would be the first to board the ship. The war had changed the game.

Even as he struggled with these thoughts, the arrival of the ship made him sigh with relief. Barakatullah took charge of the ammunition and with the help of the Japanese, it was hidden in the ship. No one knew about the ammunition but Gurdit Singh and some of his close associates. Bhakna aroused them with his encouraging words. Dejection writ large on their faces, the passengers listened dumbfounded to his diatribe against the British government. They had no strength to participate. It was the ignominy of going home empty-handed that weighed on their minds.

Another task on Bhakna's list was to save the ship from the *Emden*, the mighty German cruiser that was prowling the waters of the Indian Ocean. He met the German chancellor, fixed a code and conveyed the same to the *Komagata Maru*. It was necessary to save the ship from an accidental strike by the *Emden*, which might have mistaken it for an enemy ship.

Some of the men on the *Komagata Maru* disembarked at Yokohama and the rest of them sailed towards Kobe. Since the *Komagata Maru* was a Japanese ship, once in Kobe the owners started demanding possession of the ship. The payment of coal that was loaded on the ship while it was on its way to Canada was also due.

The Indian government released ¥19,000 to meet the demands of the coal payment and provisions of the passengers and without further ado, the ship was once again on the move.[2] They did this to assuage the hurt sentiments of the Indian populace who they feared might react in an unpleasant way if those on the ship were not sent back home safely.

Some of them left the ship at Kobe, and it then sailed towards Hong Kong. The government of Hong Kong was disinclined to receive this unexpected visitor and did not let anyone disembark from the ship. Those who had started their journey from Hong Kong also were not let out of the ship. Some provisions were provided to the passengers after a lot of hue and cry.

The ship reached Singapore on 16 September 1914 and on 19 September, it began the last leg of its journey. It was headed to Calcutta. No one was allowed to disembark at Singapore and no provisions were provided either. The passengers were tired of the apathetic attitude of governments at every port. For them, each and every morsel of food had been a struggle. And now they were reaching an end point where they would snap if even a little pressure were to be applied.

The passengers were not going to get any sympathy from the Indian government. On the contrary, they would have to face a trial of fire. Because, with the commencement of the war and with Hopkinson reporting about the plans of the Ghadar Party, the government had become concerned about the danger staring it in the face. The dreaded Ingress to India Ordinance Act came into effect on 5 September 1914.[3] The law accorded special powers to the viceroy to arrest anyone entering the country if it was judged necessary to protect the safety, interest or tranquillity of the state.

The *Komagata Maru* finally touched Indian waters on 29 September 1914. It was not allowed to reach Calcutta but was docked in Budge Budge harbour at the mouth of the Hooghly. The police made a thorough search of the baggage and could find nothing incriminating. The ammunition had long been dumped in the ocean. These men were not revolutionaries, they had gone to foreign shores only in the hope of earning a decent sum of money. They were wary of being caught off-guard with weapons.

Gurdit Singh, however, was ready with his list of grudges for he was hopeful that the Indian government would lend a sympathetic ear, but he was in for a disappointment when told to disembark at Budge Budge harbour. The government had plans for them and they were not given any choice. Trains were waiting for them at the station and all they had to do was occupy the empty seats and they would be taken to Punjab.

But they did not want to go to Punjab at all, Gurdit Singh argued. They wanted to go to Calcutta because at this time of the year, there was no work in Punjab. Also, everyone needed time to settle their affairs. The men owed money to him, to each other. In the six-month-long voyage, the men had formed friendships that had tethered them to each other. The uncoupling of these bonds needed time and a sympathetic attitude. Moreover, the ship contained 533 beds and other provisions that had been installed at Gurdit Singh's cost. He needed time to sort out his affairs with the shipping firm. And what about the cargo? The coal that he was not able to unload at Vancouver, he wanted to sell in Calcutta and make some money. After all, it was a business venture that had failed. And what little money could be made out of this failed venture should not be let go of easily.[4]

But the police were in no mood to listen. Gurdit Singh and his men were given no choice. Some got off on their own (about sixty-two) but there was a large group that stuck to Gurdit. Finally, Gurdit moved out of the ship carrying the Guru Granth Sahib on his head for it would be disrespectful for the holy book to be carried on a train. He wanted the Granth Sahib to be placed in a gurdwara in Calcutta before he could make up his mind about anything else.

This strong contingent of 250 under Gurdit Singh began a peaceful march, which was a silent form of protest against the high-handedness of the authorities. Now it was not only the Bengal Police alongside them but the Royal Fusiliers of the City of London Regiment and the reserve police as well. When the group finally stopped for a breather, the inevitable happened. Shots were fired, leading to the deaths of eighteen men and wounding twenty-five.[5]

Who fired the first shot? No one would ever know. But what was the need to impose heavy diktats on tired and broken men when all they wanted was to earn money and then go home? What could have happened, had they just let them go to the big city and do things their own way? The inquiry instituted by the Indian government laid the blame squarely on the passengers. While the moderate voice of Surendranath Banerjee in Bengal questioned the government, the leaders in Punjab province, who wanted to prove their loyalty to the British Indian government, poured vitriol on the passengers. And the government of Bengal too escaped their responsibility by issuing a formal statement, putting the onus on the hapless men.

Gurdit Singh fled the scene. His six-year-old son Balwant was lost amidst the fracas and later on arrested by the police.

Chapter 16

In the Aftermath of the *Komagata Maru*

Hopkinson, who was an informer of the immigration department, had recruited his own set of Punjabi informers. All of them were much hated men in the Indian community after the denial of permission to the *Komagata Maru* to land on Canadian shores. The anger and hurt was palpable in the populace, which spiralled to strong hatred against these men, who were passing on every bit of information regarding the Punjabi community to the immigration department, which was keeping tabs on them.

Harnam Singh, friend of the informer Bela Singh, had worked for the immigration department and was the first one to be murdered, on 31 August 1914.[1] The killing was gruesome with a slashed throat and his own turban found tied to his legs.[2]

The second reported death on 3 September 1914 was of Arjan Singh, another man of the Bela Singh faction.[3] He was shot down and the death was called accidental.

This was a challenge to Bela Singh's authority. For a long time, he had intimidated the Sikh community because of being a government informer. He was receiving a salary of $62.50 from the government and was a bully who had considerable influence in the immigration department. He used to harass the newcomers and extort money from them to clear their immigration papers.[4] He was once offered a return ticket to India and a plot of land by

Mewa Singh, a local immigrant, to stop his anti-Sikh, anti-Indian activities but there was no stopping Bela Singh.

On that ill-fated day, 5 September 1914, when Bela Singh reached the gurdwara to attend the after-death ceremonies of Arjan Singh, the inevitable happened. There was firing in the shrine. Bhag Singh Bhikhiwind and Battan Singh were killed while six were injured when Bela Singh fired shots to avenge the murder of his cronies.

A trial was initiated and Hopkinson agreed to testify in favour of his man. Mewa Singh, who was present at the time of the shooting, was also being pressurized by Hopkinson to testify in favour of Bela Singh.

Mewa Singh was born in 1880 in Amritsar in Lopoke village. He moved to Canada sometime in 1906 and began working in the Fraser Mills of New Westminster.[5] He was a deeply religious man, who spent most of his time in the gurdwara. He had been instrumental in collecting funds from the Sikh community and helped in building up the first gurdwara in Vancouver. This place became his sanctum sanctorum.

Mewa Singh was deeply disturbed by the killing of people inside the gurdwara. And now he was being forced to become an accomplice in this crime by giving false testimony.

This was not the only grievance he nursed against Hopkinson and his men. When he was caught on the American-Canadian border a few months previously with ammunition on his person, he was made to testify against his companions, the Ghadarites. He had broken down and given a softer and rather veiled version of events and they had let him go with a fine.

Hopkinson had tried to befriend him, to make an informer out of him at that time.

But this time he did not give in! He gave evidence against Bela Singh, placing one hand on his heart. He would not act according to their nefarious designs. He would not be a puppet any more.

After this testimony, his life was threatened. Mewa Singh then decided that if it was his turn to die, he should use his death for a purposeful cause.

He shot down William Hopkinson in court on 21 October 1914.[6] He surrendered to the court with a confession: 'My religion does not teach me to bear enmity with anybody, nor had I any enmity with Mr. Hopkinson. He was oppressing poor people very much. I, being a staunch Sikh, could no longer bear to see the wrong done both to my countrymen and the Dominion of Canada. This is what led me to take Hopkinson's life and sacrifice my own life.'[7]

Bela Singh was acquitted in the twin murder case while Mewa Singh was put on a quick trial and executed on 11 January 1915.[8]

Mewa Singh not only became a martyr, he became a respected name in the community. His death came to be celebrated. In 1917, Sikhs congregated for three days at the gurdwara in Fraser Mills where his cremation had taken place. The next year, this number rose to 500. For years to come, he would be remembered on his execution day by the Sikh community. His death brought an end to an inglorious chapter of Sikh struggle against oppressive diktats. The immigration department did not recruit another informer. The community could finally breathe free, though it was not able to break free of the mould of slavery back home.

Chapter 17

The Homecoming of the Warriors

Chalo, chaliye, deshnu yuddha karan
E, ho, akhiri vachan, te farman hogaye

(Come on! Join us, let us go to fight the battle of our freedom.
Why waste time, the final order is given, let us go!)

—Kartar Singh Sarabha[1]

The mailbox of the Khalsa Society of Stockton was full of letters, pleas and the registered deeds of lands.[2] As the employees sorted it out, they read every fervent request to sell land and do it as soon as possible. Some wanted the land to be sold at half rates, some just wanted to donate it to the gurdwara and some had already given possession of the little they had to someone else and were now waiting at the harbour to board the ship. These were not only scraps of paper they had left, these were their dreams that now lay scattered.

This was not the kind of homecoming they must have thought of! Under normal circumstances, they would have gone back loaded with presents for their kith and kin and the joy of being united with their family after a long spell. But now all they wanted to do was to sacrifice. Not even one amongst them was thinking about their family. Would they meet them at all? There was no trace of discontentment but a firm resolve etched on those taut faces. Those faces, merrier in happier times, had gone grim now, for these were men with a purpose.

'Your duty is clear. Go to India. Stir up rebellion in every corner of the country. Rob the wealthy and show mercy to the poor. In this way, gain universal sympathy. Arms will be provided for you on arrival in India. Failing this, you must ransack the police stations for rifles. Obey without hesitation the commands of your leaders,'[3] Ram Chandra addressed the gathering at San Francisco port. With him stood Barakatullah, Bhagwan Singh and Santokh Singh.[4] The men were preparing to board SS *Korea*, the first ship to leave the harbour with a batch of sixty Ghadarites.[5] The shoreline was full of ships. The scene was similar in Victoria.

'Go to India and incite the native troops. Preach mutiny openly. Take arms from the troops of the native States and whenever you see the British, kill them. If you do your work quickly and intelligently, there is hope that Germany will help you. Get help from Nepal and Afghanistan. Start the war quickly. Don't delay,' read a report in the *Hindustan Ghadar* dated 4 August 1914.

Before they had boarded the ship, the Ghadarites held meetings at Oxnard, Upland, Fresno, Los Angeles and Clairmont. *Ghadar* had put out a call to them to leave it all and gather. There was to be revolution in Punjab. The Emir of Afghanistan and the powers of Germany with arms and ammunition were supporting them so there was nothing to fear. Many newspapers reported about their flight back home.

HINDUS GO HOME TO FIGHT IN THE REVOLUTION
—*Portland Telegram*[6]

Astoria (Oregon) August 7th – Every train and boat for the south carries large numbers of Hindus from this city, and if the exodus keeps up much longer Astoria will be entirely deserted by the East Indians. The majority at the Hammond mills have gone and the balance are preparing to depart in the immediate future. It is alleged that the men are returning to India by way of San Francisco, where, it is said, a vessel has been chartered to aid in a revolution which is expected to break out in India as a result of England being occupied in the general European war. It is said that a Japanese steamer will carry the Hindus to their native land.[7]

Meanwhile, Bhakna, who never returned from Yokohama after depositing the arms on the *Komagata Maru*, was asked to move to India as well. He was joined by the energetic Sarabha. Sarabha had boarded the *Nippon Maru* from Yokohama and through Colombo, he had reached Madras, sometime in late 1914, from where he had made his way to Punjab. His impatience had been rewarded for he had escaped from the dreaded clutches of the new ordinance law, which came into existence after his arrival.

Bhakna had travelled from Yokohama to Shanghai and then to Hong Kong from where he had boarded the *Nam Sang*.[8] Amongst other major ships to arrive soon were the *Lai Sang* and the *Foo Sang*.

The *Nam Sang* was stopped at Penang for a day when the unfortunate killings at Budge Budge harbour took place. The ship carrying Bhakna was the first to arrive at Calcutta port after the *Komagata Maru*. All the passengers became casualties of the new law, Defence of India Regulations Act, which led to mass arrests though there was nothing incriminating on their person.

Under this new law, the government could arrest anyone on the basis of mere suspicion.[9]

Under this law, every Indian landing at the harbour was a suspect. And in the case of the Ghadarites, Hopkinson had supplied the details much earlier and the antecedents of Bhakna being the head of the Ghadar Party were enough to send him to the gallows. He was kept in Calcutta prison from where he was taken to Ludhiana and transferred to the district jail in Multan.

Sarabha was in Punjab at the time Bhakna was arrested, and the news reached him. While Bhakna was being taken from Ludhiana jail on a *tonga* to the station to be transferred to Multan, he followed him on a cycle. Bhakna implored him to go back.[10]

Sarabha had gone back with a heavy heart, full of remorse, but he was not defeated at all.

By now, the police were arresting those who had arrived with alacrity. The men were categorized into three groups:

1) The most dangerous: These were the leaders of the Ghadar Party whose name, village and entire manual of activities was at the disposal of the government. They were directly arrested and put behind bars.
2) The harmful ones, who were not to be let free and were interned in their respective villages.
3) The innocuous ones, who were expected to do no harm to the government and were set free.

The central inquiry officer, Michael O'Dwyer, had his office in Ludhiana. All the passengers to be categorized were presented before him for a final verdict.

Once the plan of the government was revealed, the Ghadarites became more conscious. They started avoiding British vessels because extensive searches were being undertaken at Hong Kong itself. They preferred Japanese vessels and divided themselves into equal groups and even changed their ways of dressing to avoid detection.[11] They began to come through Colombo and land at Madras, the strategy that had worked for Sarabha. They started grouping in China and would improvise on their plans to avoid arrest. Often, they came in small groups, posing as ordinary passengers.

SS *Korea* was a very important ship that arrived at Yokohama from San Francisco on 29 August and had on board sixty to seventy passengers. Amongst them were Jawala Singh Thatthiyan, the potato king, Ram Rakha and Nidhan Singh. The men on this ship were divided into gangs and this was understood to be the ship with the most 'dangerous' occupants. Ram Rakha and Amar Singh had got down from the ship at Yokohama to buy ammunition. Some had boarded from Kobe and others from Manilla.

SS *Siberia*, SS *Mashima Maru*, SS *Mexico Maru* and SS *Canada Maru* were the other important ships that had sailed with a number of Ghadarites. Ram Rakha and Amar Singh had boarded SS *Siberia* after purchasing arms from Yokohama. Eight thousand valiant men came back in the first two years after the *Komagata Maru* incident. Four hundred were pushed on to the gallows, 2500 were confined to their villages and the rest were sent to be imprisoned in their own homes.

The passengers from all these ships were the first batch of revolutionaries to arrive in India. The people who courted maximum arrests bore the brunt of an unjust law, which had the power to undo their confidence. It was able to shake the weak-willed who got scared and gave up the thought of Ghadar and became ensconced in the familiarity of their old ways of life. But for others, the cause was sacred.

For all those who had escaped the careful eyes of the government, it was time to wage a war.

Chapter 18

The Reorganization of the
Ghadar Party in Punjab

The Ghadar Party was devastated by the mass arrests of its men and especially its leaders, such as Bhakna, who had provided a strong framework to the party. Yet, those who managed to reach Punjab decided to regroup. Their dominant sentiment was that the cause that had brought them back home should not get lost. They were disappointed to see the lack of awakening back home. It was difficult for them to fathom the darkness that had pervaded the minds of the populace at home.

Sarabha covered 40 to 50 miles every day, interacting with people. Randhir Singh of Narangwal held *Akhand Paths* (continuous recitations of the Guru Granth Sahib) in different villages.[1] The congregation was briefed about the message of Ghadar. The Ghadarites spoke loud and clear at religious fairs in Tarn Taran, Amritsar, Nankana Sahib and Muktsar.[2]

Harnam Singh Tundilat, after arriving in Punjab, had donned saffron robes. He stayed with his family in the Kotla Naudh Singh village for a while but when the *zaildar* of the village asked him to accompany him to the police station, he was quick to assess the situation.[3] He feared arrest and so he moved to Sangwal village and joined Banta Singh, another Ghadarite. He and two of his comrades began addressing public meetings in Sangwal.[4]

Kanshi Ram arrived a little late, on 12 November 1914, for the party had entrusted him with the responsibility of taking along ammunition that he had shipped separately.[5] He was supposed to take possession of his parcel once he reached Punjab. But the ammunition was intercepted and it never reached the Ghadarites.[6] Now the Ghadarites were without ammunition and money. Before his arrival, Ghadarites had started to assemble together. They made committees and met at Khanna, Moga, Ludhiana and Amritsar. Kanshi Ram was designated as the head of the party in Ludhiana along with Sarabha and Nawab Khan. They had a rough plan ready with them:

1) Ammunition was foremost on their minds. They could not bring about a revolution without guns. The government arsenal would come in handy. Mian Mir cantonment in Lahore and Ferozepur cantonment would end up becoming their areas of activity. They also planned to loot guns and revolvers from police stations.

2) They needed money to buy more ammunition, for which they would commit planned robberies.

3) The men in the army had to be disaffected. The war between England and Germany meant that men would sooner or later be sent to the front to fight. The army men were peeved. Ghadarites were banking on this dissatisfaction in their minds. Ghadar literature would be used to provoke them as well as appeal to their better sense.

4) Sarabha was already cyclostyling Ghadar literature at Ludhiana. This material had to be circulated all over Punjab and used with maximum efficiency. A thousand copies of the seditious pamphlet 'Eilan-i-jung' were distributed in the barracks.

5) School students were to be involved in this battle. The message had to reach schools and colleges.

Several detachments in different regions were holding their own, but so far they lacked the cohesiveness and organization that would propel them forward. The arrival of Kanshi Ram had created a favourable impact and the message had been conveyed to the men, who held a meeting at Ladhowal on 17 November 1914.[7] The meeting was attended by the leaders of different detachments. Sarabha, Pandit Kanshi Ram, Nawab Khan, Nidhan Singh and others chalked out their future programme.[8] An attack on Mian Mir and Ferozepur cantonments was on the cards.

Sarabha had once been audacious enough to ask an army man about his reasons for serving the British when he knew that he would be sent to the front to face the cannons and become fodder for a war he had nothing to do with. This army man, a Sikh havildar, had promised to hand him the keys of the arsenal.[9] He had been impressed by the brave demeanour of this young man, who had openly spoken about his resolve without any fear of the sarkar. It was not only Sarabha. Others too spoke with no holds barred. This peculiar characteristic would result in their speaking about their plans before they materialized. These men were warriors, not conspirators. They were open and loud. They had been speaking against the *angrez* in foreign lands, on the ships and now, when they were so near, how could they choose to keep quiet? They had lit up the minds of the 26th Punjabi Regiment at Hong Kong and now they were igniting the minds of men back home.

One such meeting of all the men was held at Moga on 19 November 1914, in which they had discussed simultaneous plans to loot the district treasuries of Moga, Jagraon and Amritsar.[10] Along with ammunition, they were eyeing money as well. They were confident that everything would happen smoothly and they would be able to overthrow the powerful British empire.

To give firm shape to their plans, a further meeting on 23 November 1914 was called at Gurdwara Jhar Sahib in Amritsar to which they had invited the men of the 23rd Regiment who had been disaffected. On parallel lines, on the same day, Kanshi Ram had called a meeting at Badowal.[11] There were too many preoccupations and their energies were scattered on multiple fronts. The plan was to capture Lahore's Mian Mir cantonment and then take the Ferozepur cantonment on the same day, 25 November. Sarabha was put in charge of the Amritsar plan while Kanshi Ram would lead his men from Ferozepur.

The disaffected men did not participate in the meeting held at Amritsar on the 23rd. The army personnel who were enthusiastic to get associated with Ghadarites and thought of playing a historic role by siding with them had developed cold feet. While they were getting ready to go to Jhar Sahib, the granthi of the regiment, Moola Singh, had played spoilsport. He had warned them that their digression from the way of the sarkar would land them in trouble. He made them realize that they could never match the strength of the British Raj, that they would only end up making a mess of themselves and that they should think about their families and the fate they would suffer when they would be captured.

This gentle warning was not to be ignored, thought the men. They decided that it would be the Ghadarites who would take the first call. They would then come over and help them.

In the Badowal meeting on 23 November, Kanshi Ram addressed his men. The plan was made to charge on Ferozepur cantonment on the same day and same time when Mian Mir cantonment was being captured—25 November. This was then changed to 26 November.[12]

The jathas with their men reached Lahore on the night of 26 November. On the 26th night, none of the army men from Lahore cantonment reached the designated spot. The Ghadarites waited but the plan had failed. They were asked to disperse.

Chapter 19

The Rage at Ferozepur Shahr

The men in Ferozepur who were camping on the outskirts, around Jalalabad, were disappointed when they came to know of the failure of the Mian Mir plan. Kanshi Ram, with Nidhan Singh's faction, were a disappointed lot and now the day of action was further postponed to 30 November.[1] This inaction was troubling the men. They were losing precious time and their group was disintegrating. Most of them were departing. Would they return on the 30th? The plans were changing too frequently. They were longing to do something larger than life, which at present seemed a far-fetched thought.

Nidhan Singh decided to leave for Sursingh village in Lahore district to get help from emigrants as most of them belonged to that village.[2] The rest of them, twenty-two in number headed by Kanshi Ram, decided to loot the treasury of Moga and hire tongas to put their plan into action as the last train for Moga had already departed.[3] Near Ferozeshahr they were spotted by the local sub-inspector of police, Bisharat Ali, and Zaildar Jowala Singh, who were waiting for the superintendent of police.

The zaildar intimated Bisharat Ali about the suspicious nature of the men who signalled the tongas to stop. The Ghadarites, apprehending arrest, urged the drivers to drive the tongas faster but the police caught up with them and Bisharat Ali ordered

140

the men to identify themselves. An altercation between Bisharat Ali and one of the Ghadarites, Rehmat Ali, turned violent as the latter was slapped by the policeman. This infuriated Bhagat Singh of Kacharbhan village who shot Bisharat Ali and the zaildar point-blank.

Reinforcements from the police station chased the Ghadarites, who tried to hide themselves in the long reeds by the side of a canal, but they failed to camouflage themselves. They escaped the bullets but fell into the hands of the villagers from Misriwala, who handed them over to the police.

The police had advertised in the villages that the Ghadarites were robbers and dacoits. The impact of Ghadar was not yet apparent to the ordinary people, who believed the police's version. The lamentations of the Ghadarites escaped their notice and did not melt their hearts either. Rehmat Ali, Kanshi Ram and five others were arrested that day. The absconders too were caught by the police.

The arrest of Kanshi Ram, who was not only the treasurer of the Ghadar Party but also a towering figure and the guiding spirit for its men, was a huge blow. The men were dispirited by this other big loss after Bhakna. Kanshi Ram was imprisoned and hanged in February 1915.[4]

After this debacle, Sarabha gave things some consideration and decided that the Ghadarites should not act on their own. They needed a leader. The man they wanted was in Bengal, the one who had dared to plan an attempt on the life of Lord Hardinge. He and Har Dayal were the co-accused and were on the wanted list.

Sarabha would go to Bengal to get the man himself, Rash Behari Bose.[5]

But it was not easy to find Bose and persuade him to come to Punjab. His hideouts were guarded. His right-hand man, Shachindernath Sanyal, was the outlet through which information flowed to Bose. So now the scene moved to Kashi where Sanyal was hiding.[6] Bose, evading arrest, was safely ensconced there as well.

Chapter 20

Shachindernath Sanyal in Punjab

Rash Behari Bose, a Bengali revolutionary, had been living in Kashi after his implication in the bomb attack on Lord Hardinge and the subsequent arrest warrant. A sum of Rs 7500 was on his head, which prompted him to go into hiding.[1] He chose Kashi/Banaras (now known as Varanasi) because of the presence of his confidant Shachindernath Sanyal, who had been instrumental in starting a revolutionary unit in the city. The city, with its tight-knit residential community of Bengalis, provided the perfect cover.

On the face of it, the working of the Bengali revolutionaries and Ghadarites were completely opposite. The Bengalis were very particular about the men they recruited. Not everyone was allowed into the group and all their secrets were not spoken of in front of the new entrant. The Ghadarites did not have any kind of scanning policy; every person who was willing to work for the cause was let in and became privy to all secrets. The secrecy and caution with which the Bengali revolutionaries worked were exemplary. They were not loose cannons who kept on launching themselves in all directions; they harnessed their energy and launched an attack when they knew it would make the maximum impact. Perhaps that was the reason the Ghadarites thought about bringing a leader from amongst them, who could guide them better.

When Rash Behari Bose was invited to Punjab by the Ghadarites to become their leader, he decided to send Sanyal first to assess the situation.[2]

Sanyal had been visiting the barracks, interacting with the men in uniform. By now he knew that the problem of the Raj was two-fold. The war had made them employ the best of their men on the front fighting the Germans. The men who were left in India were newcomers, still learning the ropes. To take care of disaffection, they were not letting one regiment stay in one place for long.

Sanyal interacted with Sikh army personnel posted in Kashi and they seemed willing to go with the plans. The thought about men from Punjab motivating their fellow men in Kashi had also not escaped Sanyal's mind. But for that he would have to reach out to them. He would have to go to Punjab and understand the scenario.

Vishnu Ganesh Pingle, who arrived in Punjab late in 1914, met Sarabha and formed the link between them and the Bengalis. He knew Sarabha since his university days and they had been active under the leadership of Har Dayal. Pingle had met Jyotindranath Mukherjee in Bengal before meeting Sanyal. Jyotindranath Mukherjee, known as Jatin Bagha (Tiger Jatin), was the head of the Dacca Anushilan Samiti at that time.[3] He wrote a letter to Bose, following which Pingle reached Kashi after receiving the sanction from Bengal.

It was at this point that Bose decided that Sanyal could go to Punjab to assess the situation. He would make two visits before he would give the final approval to Bose to come to Punjab.

Sanyal took the Jalandhar-bound train and Sarabha joined him at Ludhiana.[4] He met other Ghadarites, gave them some explosives and returned to Kashi. In the next meeting, in which he was accompanied by Vishnu Ganesh Pingle, he was notified about the safe houses demarcated for Rash Behari Bose by the

Ghadarites. He also met Mula Singh, who belonged to Mirankot village in Amritsar and had previously worked in the Shanghai Police department, and was now in charge of Ghadar activities in Amritsar.[5] In one donation drive, Sanyal was disappointed to see the amount of money collected. He encouraged the revolutionaries to go in for dacoities to cover the cost of bombs.

His last visit to Punjab was sometime in December 1914 and he expressed satisfaction with the arrangements. The stage was all set for Rash Behari Bose's arrival in Punjab.

Chapter 21

Rash Behari Bose

Rash Behari Bose was born in the village of Parala-Bigati in Hooghly district, Bengal, on 25 May 1886.[1] Born in his maternal uncle's home, he received his education in Chandernagore.[2] At the time of his birth, his father was working with the government of Bengal but later moved to Simla. At the insistence of his mother, he got employed with his father at the government press in Simla.[3]

Bose was something of a difficult child, assertive and bold in his ways. An expert at wielding the lathi, he felt violence was the only way to counter British rule. His defiance made his mother worried. Although Bose had left Bengal, the revolutionary roots that had sprouted in his childhood and youth started anchoring him firmly. From Simla, he moved to Kasauli where he started working in the Pasteur Institute.[4] In Kasauli, he got in touch with Jatindernath Banerjee, who had links with Punjab revolutionaries such as Ajit Singh, Kissen Singh (Bhagat Singh's father) and Har Dayal.[5] Sometime in 1906, Banerjee travelled to Punjab and inculcated the idea of self-rule or Swaraj in Punjabi revolutionaries through violent methods.[6] The association between the revolutionaries of the two states had deep roots, for Punjab and the United Provinces were important centres for Bengali revolutionaries during those times, long before the idea of Ghadar was floated.[7]

Jitendra Mohan Chatterjee, the son of a government pleader, had formed a secret society in Dehradun and after his move to England to thwart a possible arrest, Rash Behari Bose, being a close confidant, was given the mantle of heading this society.[8] Bose became the connecting thread between Punjab and Bengal.

Later, when he moved to Dehradun, his home became a meeting point for the revolutionaries of Punjab and Bengal. He had been sneaking away acid from the lab in Kasauli for manufacturing explosives and now in Dehradun, he began purchasing second-hand revolvers from retired Gurkha officers.[9] While he was in Dehradun, Lord Hardinge had moved his durbar to Delhi from Calcutta in 1911 and also annulled the contentious division of Bengal. It was then the idea hit Bose to terrify the government with an outrageous act.[10]

The Delhi Bomb Outrage

'At Dehradun when driving in a car from the station to my bungalow I passed an Indian standing in front of the gate of his house with several others, all of whom were very demonstrative in their salaams. On my enquiring, I was told that the principal Indian there had presided two days before at a public meeting at Dehradun and had proposed and carried a vote of condolence with me on account of the attack on my life. It was proved later that it was this identical Indian who threw the bomb at me!!'— Lord Hardinge[11]

The Delhi bomb outrage on 23 December 1912 was a planned attack on Lord Hardinge carried out by Bose and his men in the capital city. The making of the bomb had been initiated in Bengal. Basanta Kumar Biswas was specially trained by Bose to carry out this task.[12] Bose had accompanied Biswas to Delhi to carry out the bomb-throwing on Hardinge who was to pass through Delhi on his elephant convoy. Though Hardinge defied death in this attack, the bomb had done the damage it intended to achieve. The revolutionaries wanted to strike terror in the heart of British bureaucrats and let the government know that repressing Indians and then appeasing them (dividing Bengal and then unifying it in this instance) was not going to yield them dividends.[13] Violence was also seen as a means of asserting the might of Indian revolutionaries. Biswas had stayed at the house of Amir Chand, an associate of Har Dayal from his Lahore days.[14] Both Bose and Har Dayal were on the government's wanted list after this attack.

Bose had left Delhi and fled to Dehradun with Biswas the same day. Reaching there, he organized a meeting of the employees of the Forest Research Institute and publicly condemned the attack on the viceroy (he was the one Lord Hardinge referred to).[15]

He had played the perfect part in Dehradun by taking a pro-government stance and giving speeches in their favour to prevent suspicion, but the authorities eventually found out about his role, which led him to become a proclaimed offender.

The searches they initiated made Bose turn towards Bengal and hide in Chandernagore, the place where he had spent his youth.

Bose left Chandernagore soon after but not before signing off the last letter to his father which read:

After crores of salutations, my submission is this that you have surely heard by this time that I am now entangled in a net of dangers of the most terrible nature. Though God knows that I am wholly innocent, yet through the influence of my stars, I am today in the eyes of all, an accused in the Delhi case. This is perhaps my last letter. But I trust you will never look upon me as faithless and guilty. I say in the name of God that I am wholly innocent. Be that as it may, everything is happening through the influence of stars and I too am being drifted along in their revolutions. What can I do? Man can never alter fate. Besides, when the most mighty Government is my antagonist, it will be extremely difficult to obtain justice in the Court. However, whatever is decreed by fate, will come to happen. I had been dreaming of how you might get happiness in the end of your life, when the terrible bolt from heaven fell. Don't waste money for nothing by engaging pleader for me, for it is almost an impossibility to fight against the Government . . . I resign everything into the hands of God; do pray to him for my welfare.[16]

Bose later left Chandernagore and made Kashi his home where he lived from April 1914 to January 1915 without being detected by the police.[17] While in Kashi he would come outdoors only at night to meet his men and plan his next course of action. He was never caught despite the fact that his pictures were distributed all over the city by the police with a hefty reward on his head. He was an excellent master of disguise. He stayed in constant touch with his rank and file and especially the man who commanded them, Jyotindranath Mukherjee. Before heading for Punjab, he held a meeting in which he designated men for a common cause to be launched from different locations: Damodar Swarup in Allahabad, Bibhuti and Preo Nath in Kashi and Nalin Mukherjee in Jabalpore. All of them were to engage the troops in talks for an uprising. Vinayak was dispatched to Cawnpore, Pingle was to supervise it all over India and Punjabi revolutionaries would do so in Ferozepur.[18]

Bose went to Punjab sometime in January 1915 after a go-ahead from Pingle and arrived in Amritsar. He was to reside at Mussamat Atri's house in Chauk Baba Atal in complete secrecy. But his arrival could not be kept a secret and Ghadarites soon started pouring in to pay their respects. Sant Gulab Singh's *dharamsala* (rest house) was another place that was designated for him to meet people.

The talk once again circumambulated towards two things that were needed the most—bombs and money. Bose possessed the know-how to make bombs. But the larger question was, where was the money going to come from?

Chapter 22

The Dacoities

The Ghadarites were not dacoits or robbers; they were revolutionaries in dire need of money. Time did not dissuade them from committing the follies that would end up being their nemesis. They were impelled to act and so they did! The dacoities they committed brought them some money but along with it, there was also a gradual loss of credibility.

The first plan was executed at Sahnewal near Ludhiana on 23 January 1915. The men who executed it included Sarabha, Jagat Singh and Ram Rakha.[1] Armed with pistols, they arrived at a residence, assuming it to be the household of a rich landlord but all they got was Rs 150 in cash and a few pieces of jewellery from a girl who was about to get married.[2] Sarabha had an altercation with one of his own men, who misbehaved with the girl, and he volunteered to return the money and jewellery. Touched by Sarabha's gesture, the lady of the house kept only some of her assets and willingly parted with the rest.[3]

The next dacoity was committed at Mansooran on the night of 27 and 28 January 1914.[4] Sarabha had gathered the villagers and gave them a heartfelt speech trying to make them understand that they were doing all this for the good of the country.[5] He stood before them on a raised pedestal recounting the terrors they faced in foreign lands and elucidating the reasons for their actions.

Most of the villagers, uninitiated in the concept of freedom, had no idea what these hot-headed men were doing. Their talk of love for their motherland was nothing but concocted stories for them.

The money the revolutionaries got from this dacoity amounted to Rs 23,700 but they had to use one of Mathura Singh's bombs to dispel the crowd.[6] The Jhunir village dacoity took place on 29 January 1914, in which a large amount of jewellery was collected.[7] In the Doaba region (Jalandhar and its neighbouring districts), Balwant Singh led from the front and robbed the wealthy, landing a booty of Rs 9130.[8] A dacoity was carried out at the house of a widow, Bibi Sharda Kaur, at Rabon Uchchi village on 3 February.[9]

The dacoity, which proved deadly to some of them and ended up being a huge mistake, was carried out in Chabba near Amritsar on the same night. The moneylender who was the target of this robbery used to charge a huge rate of interest and the Ghadarite who led his men to him was contacted by his relative who owed a debt to this man. This robbery was purely out of spite. Ordinary bandits, including a blacksmith, had joined hands with Ghadarites to commit this crime. They killed the moneylender and burnt his ledgers. The villagers heard the commotion and raced towards the moneylender's house. A bomb accidentally exploded, killing a Ghadarite and injuring another. The angry villagers attacked them with clubs and sticks. The Ghadarites retreated carrying the injured man. The blacksmith was captured and handed over to the police. He divulged the name of Mula Singh as their leader. And with this was opened the Pandora's box that would lead to the downfall of the nascent dream, which had yet to soar high.

Chapter 23

The Making of the Berlin Indian Independence Committee

The Germans exhibited no particular interest in India before 1886. That year, they established consular relations with India by opening their first-ever embassy in Calcutta (the capital of British India then).[1] Later, they sent only their best officers, adept at foreign dealings, to take care of affairs with India. They were in a strong position in Europe while Britain stood isolated despite its conquests, guarding its own, lacking the trust of its peers, amongst whom they failed to generate neither faith nor friendship.[2] Along with their suspicions about Russia, France and Japan, Britain was also wary about Turkey with its Pan-Islamism, which invoked the trust of the 85 million Muslims of India. The empire feared the Muslim community and had so far kept them out of the army, reposing its trust in Sikhs, who had not forsaken it in 1857, and the Gurkhas for their loyalty.

Muslims in India respected the caliphate and there had been reports of people from the Ottoman Empire instigating Indian Muslims to revolt against British rule. Turkey had just won the war against Greece with the Greeks accepting an armistice on 20 May 1897. The sound of celebrations had reverberated in India too. The Muslim majority in India was angry with the Queen for not supporting the caliphate in the war against Greece and later favouring the Armenians in another conflict. Britain did try a rapprochement of sorts by sending medical missions to Turkey and helping them out with financial aid. But whether this was enough for them to garner the sympathies of their Islamic counterparts would be seen later. It was a question of millions of Muslims who could be easily aroused and angered by outside influences.

There was another fear of Russia conquering Turkey and then taking along the Muslim population to invade India. The Germans were keeping a tab on these fears but not meddling with them or provoking them to raise the intensity.

Germany, at least on the face of it, did not seem as if they desired India's freedom. The emperor of Germany, Kaiser Wilhelm II, was always full of praise for Lord Curzon. He had a motive that would be revealed later. The idea of the white man's supremacy was not lost on the Kaiser and he firmly believed in it. The maintenance and expansion of the British Empire was a dream Curzon visualized with his eyes wide open. He would not let the Russians, the French, the Japanese or even the Germans have a share of what he deemed was the right of the empire. The Persian Gulf was one such area of his interest where he would not let others carry out operations. He had even extracted a secret agreement from Mubarak, the Sheikh of Kuwait, to not let any foreign power conduct operations in the Persian Gulf without British consent.

The Kaiser's praise for Lord Curzon, and his desire to have some kind of control over India, was known to Britain and they were wary of the Germans. They did not trust the Germans or their word. There was only an outward show of love and affection between the two nations.

The Germans, when they started with their expansionist programme, needed British help to create business in Indian territory. They did not want to antagonize the empire by working against them but on the contrary, they had extended a hand of help when India suffered a famine in early 1900. The Kaiser pledged a sum of half a million marks by sending a telegram to the Queen and Lord Curzon.

Lord Curzon too did not lose the opportunity to thank the Kaiser publicly for this generous offer, but this kindness did not wash away the distrust from the mind of the empire. And though the Kaiser wanted to erase this British antipathy at least from India, it was not successful.

Germany wanted Lord Curzon to allow Indian immigrant labour to settle in German East Africa, their African colony that was reeling from a labour shortage.[3] This area, spread around 3,85,000 square miles, amounted to twice the size of the German Empire in Europe. Here they had plans to grow rubber, sisal, cotton and coffee. The African wars had taken a toll on the men, leading to a crunch in manpower. The Germans wanted to employ Indian labour to change the prospects of this land, but their hopes could not materialize because the final approval from the viceroy never arrived.[4] They were able to establish illegal colonies of Indian labourers with the help of the Aga Khan, the influential Muslim religious figure. Lord Curzon was so firm in his disapproval that when he came to know about this proposed plan, the Aga Khan had to let it go because there were issues that could not be settled and Indian immigrants could not be accommodated in German East Africa at that time. In the coming years, Indians did follow the Germans and ended up making East Africa their home, adding to the economy by working as traders and artisans.[5]

The Kaiser also needed Curzon to approve the high-profile Baghdad Railway project in the Persian Gulf area, a possession very dear to Curzon where he wanted no intrusion despite the reservations of the British authorities in London, who deemed this obsession unnecessary. The Kaiser did get the nod for the Baghdad Railway in the area of the Persian Gulf, which now saw Russian activity as well, but this project would run into difficulties after the Entente powers[6] resolved their differences.

Britain, in 1905, included the safeguard of India in its already continuing treaty with Japan. The issues with Russia too were being sorted out as it no longer posed a threat and assured support against any infringement on Indian territory by the signing of a treaty. Thus, the trio of England, Russia and Japan grew strong, painting a grim picture for Germany, who felt that it was being targeted by them along with other European nations for being too ambitious and carrying on its expansionist policies. The Austro-Hungarians were the only ones it could count on as its friends.

In the later part of 1907, Germany's fears about this deliberate encirclement policy proved right when England raised fresh objections to the continuation of the Baghdad Railway project. Britain wanted the last stretch of the railways to be handed over to them because it feared that it posed a threat to Indian security. The Kaiser had objected and rebuked them for this folly.

The makings of war had begun.

Another German fear was the use of the railway for sending Turkish troops into Indian territory in the scenario of a conflict and Turkey lending support to England. That Pan-Islamic Turkey would seek the support of its ardent Muslim followers in India was feared by Britain as well as Russia.

The Germans were keeping a tab on the growing friendship between Britain and Russia after the opening of the Russian consulate in Calcutta and the favours being bestowed on them. Along with it, they saw the rise of Indian nationalism, which evoked a curious interest in them. Their prestige rose in the eyes of the Indian Muslim who connected the dots by placing Turkish-German friendliness on an exalted frame. In the Greco-Turkish War, when Turkey won, Kaiser Wilhelm supported them. He negotiated with Greece for the autonomy of one of their islands and refrained from working out an armistice, defying the diktats of Queen Victoria. This attitude of Germany was seen as a sympathetic gesture towards the Turks.

Different camps were in the making—the Entente powers or Allied powers versus the Central powers.[7]

If Germany had enjoyed the pre-war period with aplomb by making great strides into the Indian economy, garnering business of DM105 million in exports, now was the time to rethink its strategy. The Indian plight from which it had disengaged itself, being a votary of imperialism, suddenly began to haunt them. Educated Indians impressed them with their prowess and intelligence. Indian oppression was beginning to look real and their fight for rights appeared just. There was a sea change in German attitude as the clouds of war began hovering over the horizon, making them see an enemy's enemy as their friend. The Germans would eventually invest themselves in India's independence struggle. Now that war was on the cards, it wanted to weaken the defence of the enemy at all costs, hoping to win or at least expecting a rapprochement from the enemy side.

Indian revolutionaries working in London, Paris and other European cities were being hounded by British authorities putting a check on their activities. They drifted towards Berlin, which by now was ready to welcome them. Help from Germany was initially sought by Bengali revolutionaries and groups such as the Dacca Anushilan Samiti and Jugantar, but the right time for this association coupled with German interest only arrived after the initiation of the First World War in July 1914.

The Indian National Party, later known as the Berlin Indian Independence Committee, came into existence towards the end of 1914 with Virendranath Chattopadhyaya, who was studying in Germany in early 1914, as its architect. Virendranath Chattopadhyaya was closely involved with Shyamaji Krishnavarma's India House earlier and was a close friend of Savarkar.

The German foreign office started a search for Indian revolutionaries in Germany, Austro-Hungarian territories, Switzerland, America and the Ottoman Empire.[8]

Shyamaji Krishnavarma, who was living in Geneva, expressed his reluctance to join this committee, citing old age.[9] Madam Cama was confined in France. The most important revolutionary who lent support to the German ambition of invading India was Har Dayal, who arrived from Switzerland.[10] Pingle, Barakatullah, Taraknath Das, Lahiri, Khankhoje and other Indian revolutionaries also arrived in Berlin to lend support.

The Germans and the Indians listed out a three-pronged strategy to strengthen the fight for Indian independence. The first part involved sending forces to Afghanistan and, with the help of the Emir, launching an attack on India.[11]

The second part was to help the Indian cause with men, money and ammunition. A specific sum was pledged by German officials along with a promise to supply a cache of arms that was pledged for the Bengal revolutionary movement. Centres in Shanghai and Batavia would be set up to coordinate the arms operations as well as the dissemination of the news. Outside India, Siam (Thailand) was chosen to give military training by Germans to Indian revolutionaries.

Lastly, there would be the printing of propaganda literature and spreading it amongst the army, urging Indian army men not to fight the Germans. Spreading disaffection in the armies of France, provoking Indian pilgrims to Mecca, seeking the support of Indian students in foreign universities and bringing more revolutionaries to Berlin were other ideas that were put into action.

The Ghadarites under the leadership of Har Dayal had envisioned a twin strike on the British Army. The first through Afghanistan and the second through Kashmir where they believed that the distrust of the British was the highest amongst the local Muslim population, whom they believed would side with them when it came to a physical fight. Control over Kashmir was believed to be the first step towards gaining independence.

The tragedy of the *Komagata Maru* had done the inevitable. It had added the last drop of fuel in the burning hatred growing amongst Indian nationalists. While different kinds of preparations went on in Berlin where a cornered Germany was more or less trying to save its sinking ship in the troubled waters of war, the brave-hearts who had reached Punjab were making their own plans.

Chapter 24

The Uprising in Lahore and Ferozepur Cantonments

The fort of Lahore stood solemn, its minarets looming large on the horizon, unperturbed at a sudden surge of excitement in the guards' barracks as there were veiled talks about an attack on the Lahore fort. The 23rd Cavalry was back home after a short sojourn in Hong Kong. The Ghadarites preached sedition to this regiment, which had been contacted in Lahore as well. Dafeddar Lachman Singh shared the plans of the Ghadarites with his men. As they heard more about it, their eyes widened with excitement with clouds of doubt wavering in their minds, but they were also pragmatic. They told the *dafeddar* (sergeant) that they would not be the first ones to make the move. They were also unsure about the date, 21 February, for they did not know how long they would be putting up in Lahore. They could be called to the war front to fight the German any time now.

It was not only the 23rd Cavalry at the Mian Mir cantonment that was being taken into cognizance but the 26th Punjabis at Ferozepur too had joined in. Sarabha and Nidhan Singh had been in talks with them.[1] And along came the 128th Pioneers and 12th Cavalry regiment of Meerut and the 35th Regiment at Bannu.[2]

The Lahore cantonment was established in 1852 and was given the name Mian Mir in 1906. Mian Mir was a great Sufi

157

saint who had laid the first brick in the construction of the Golden Temple in Amritsar.

The plan was that Lahore and Ferozepur would initiate the chain of revolt followed by Naushera, Peshawar, Hoti Mardan, Jhelum, Rawalpindi, Kapurthala, Meerut, Agra, Banaras, Ferozabad and Lucknow. Starting from the north and extending towards Central India, a chain of revolts and disaffections was to take place. The regiments of Cawnpore, Allahabad and Agra did not pledge support but that did not deter the Ghadarites, for the majority of the regiments in north India had given them a go-ahead, siding with them and their plans.

While all this was happening on the field, about 100 men would be sent to the capital city, Delhi, to unfurl the Ghadar flag, which was to represent independent India. This particular flag, which was created at Yugantar Ashram, was a curious mix of three stripes of red, yellow and blue. Red signified revolution, the colour of blood, the colour chosen to designate the unwavering spirit of the Hindus. Next came the yellow, the colour of mustard flowers, the colour chosen for the Sikhs, for their courage and valour. And lastly the green for progress, the colour of nature.[3] This colour was indicative of the resilience of Muslims. Together, Hindus, Sikhs and Muslims formed the confluence of this movement, the Ghadar, they were going to wage on English forces. And in the middle of the flag were a pair of intersecting sickles representing the hardworking spirit of peasants and the dare that they had taken upon themselves to transform their working instruments into forces of agitation. This summed up the Ghadar flag, the force of courage and bravado and the ultimate revolt.

While north and central India prepared for the war, Bengal was still reluctant. They had their own plans of receiving help from the Germans. And they wanted to wait for two months. So, they did not become part of this grand plan.

The uniforms, the flags and the planning was all set. 21 February 1915 was going to be the grand day when it would all start. They were making bombs, collecting ammunition and printing *Eilan-i-Jung* in large numbers to be distributed amongst the disaffected units.[4] The instruments for destroying railways and telegraph wires were collected and stored.[5] The last telegraph would be the message of revolution. The looting of the *thanas* (police stations) of Lopoke and Sarhali villages was also on the agenda before the capture of Lahore fort was to take place. These attacks were to be carried out on the night of 19 February.

If these were plans in Lahore, the ones in Ferozepur were no less audacious. The attacks were to be carried out on arms depots and the arms and ammunition was to be taken control of and political prisoners released.[6] The spree of killing the British was to be carried on here as well.

But the British sabotaged their plans by introducing a mole amidst their network.

Balwant Singh, a Ghadarite, brought his cousin, Kirpal Singh, to the Rasulpur Haveli at Lahore in the presence of Tundilat, Amar Singh and Nidhan Singh. The latter knew him since his Shanghai days and had vouched for him.[7]

A few days previously, Mula Singh had been arrested and now that vacant space was easily filled by this mole, Kirpal Singh. This mistake of inculcating a man without checking his antecedents would prove detrimental to the Ghadarites.

The blacksmith who was caught in the Chabba dacoity had spilled the beans about the activities of the Ghadarites. Then the CID Deputy Superintendent Liaquat Hayat Khan had approached Zaildar Bela Singh of Madoke village to bring him a man who could penetrate the core of Ghadar leaders and get him all the information. He brought Kirpal Singh, who was incorporated as a raw Punjab Criminal Department police recruit and deputed for this job. His cousin Balwant Singh had joined the 23rd Cavalry to keep track of happenings at Mian Mir cantonment where they were planning an uprising. Kirpal had approached Balwant Singh, who was in the dark about his motives. Leave was granted to Balwant who then accompanied Kirpal to meet Mula Singh. In Lahore, they came to know about his arrest and perhaps the time was right for Kirpal to fill in the shoes of Mula Singh.[8]

The date of the uprising, 21 February, had been leaked by Kirpal Singh to the police. Before the uprising, the Ghadarites were preparing for the attack on Lopoke police station. Kirpal Singh's plan was to get them arrested as they raided the police station to secure ammunition on the night of 19 February.

Meanwhile the needle of suspicion was pointing towards him. If his incessant questioning bothered the Ghadarites, his presence at the Amritsar railway station while he was supposed to be in Lahore organizing preparations for the uprising made their doubts real.[9] Kirpal Singh was sent by Bose to Dadehar village with some ammunition but instead of going there, he had gone to Amritsar. He was spotted by Mathura Singh and Tundilat. The previous day, the men had gathered at the Mochi Gate residence in Lahore. With Bose were present Tundilat, Sarabha, Pingle, Dr Mathura Singh, Parmanand Jhansi and others. The matter involved the discussions around the preparations of the imminent uprising.

Sensing an opportunity, Kirpal Singh had telegraphed the Amritsar police, for he was their employee. He had not been able to establish a rapport with the Lahore police who would have acted promptly. The telegram was delayed and when it reached the Amritsar police, the men had dispersed. That day he had gone to Amritsar railway station to check for the arrival of the police and he was spotted by some Ghadarites, which deepened their suspicions further. When the police arrived in Lahore from Amritsar, there were only a few men in the Mochi Gate house. The bounty was far less than expected.

His sighting at the police station and his inquisitiveness about their plans made the Ghadarites doubt him. They would go quietly around him after the arrest of their men at the Mochi Gate house. The conversations would be stalled, brought to an abrupt halt. They did not question him but he had heard the whispers directed against him. Kirpal Singh knew that if he did not get them arrested, they would kill him.

Some of the Ghadarites held a meeting on 19 February morning and changed the date of the uprising to the evening of the same date. Kirpal Singh, who was present at the meeting, ran to the roof and gestured to the police who had been camping outside the Mochi Gate residence awaiting his signal.[10] The few men inside were captured.

The next day, more men who came to this safe house, their meeting place, were captured. Amongst the arrested was Parmanand Jhansi.

Since Kirpal Singh did not know the addresses of the other safe houses that were being used as meeting places, he was not able to get all of them arrested. But the damage had been done. The uprising had been laid bare and so was the plan to wage the Ghadar.

On the night of 19 February when the uprising was to take place, the 23rd Cavalry was asked to line up. Lance Daffedar Lachman Singh sensed something was wrong. He immediately asked Balwant Singh to alert the Ghadarites not to come inside. The audacious plan would have gone something like this:

When the men in the regiment would be called for roll call, one batch of Ghadarites would enter their barracks and seize their swords. Guns were only provided during combat training. The Ghadarites would have lined up along the railway line and waited for a signal. The other batch would attack the arsenal and the men who were guarding it would cooperate and let them have the ammunition. Then, the men in uniform, their accomplices, would join them.[11]

But what happened was not even close to their plan. The guards at the arsenal had been changed. A sea of white men emerged and they had occupied all the spaces. The gaps that were to be utilized were firmly caulked up. The uprising could not find a way through such tight seams.

Balwant Singh, afraid of being found absent from duty, did not go and alert his men waiting to launch an attack, but they had made out from a distance that something was amiss. Their hopes were dashed to the ground after a prolonged wait.

Meanwhile, in Ferozepur cantonment, the eight men who were to guide the Ghadarites were let off duty. Here, Sarabha and Bhagat Singh Kacharbhan had been waiting for the signal that never arrived. A group of fifty to sixty Ghadarites had arrived a day before to fortify the rank and file. When there was no movement on the other side, Sarabha sent Kirpa Singh, the man who had been discharged from service, to inquire but he had not returned.

Sarabha spotted a harmonium in their midst.[12] The Ghadarites who came to Ferozepur in the bus might have brought it along, he thought. He gestured to the others who took the clue and followed him. They disguised themselves as a wedding party. With loud chants and wedding songs being sung in an animated manner, they reached the cantonment from where they were shooed away. But Sarabha and the others learnt that their plans had been exposed.

Meanwhile, Kirpa Singh had been put under detention for his presence in the cantonment area when he was not in service any more. He was allowed to leave only when he convinced them that he had come to settle his accounts.

The uprising was quelled even before it raised its nascent head.

Chapter 25

The Arrest of Sarabha, Tundilat and Pingle

Sarabha arrived in Lahore on the same day the uprising in Ferozepur did not happen. Bose had received information prior to the arrival of Sarabha that things had not taken place as planned.

Bose had been lying on the cot in a stupor unable to move or think coherently and Sarabha joined him.[1] This was supposed to be a game changer. He had given it his all. He had left Kashi and come to Punjab and now it looked like a lost cause to him. And yet, he was not ready to believe it. Bose boarded a train to Kashi from Lahore disguised with a heavy turban.[2] The house where he had been staying was searched the very next day after he left.[3]

Sarabha, Jagat Singh and Tundilat decided to cross the Afghan border and meet the Emir. They went to Lyallpur where they met Harchand Singh, a loyalist who gave them Rs 100 and advised them to leave.

The trio took a bus for Peshawar from Lyallpur. After reaching there, they changed into Pathani suits and started towards Michni on foot.[4]

One of them purchased a newspaper at Peshawar, which mentioned that sixteen Indian students who had crossed the border had been arrested in Kabul and were handed over to the British. They changed their plan and decided to go to Sargodha instead where the 22nd Cavalry was put up, planning to take help from a friend of Jagat Singh who had promised them arms in the past.

They retraced their footsteps and reached the regiment where they were received with love and care. It gave them hope that all was not lost.

Jagat Singh's friend, Rajinder Singh, took them to the barracks and introduced them to the military men.[5] But though he had given word to Jagat Singh about help earlier, the tide and times had changed. The hint of an association with the revolutionaries meant a quick end to life now. The fear of death led him to inform Rasaldar Ganda Singh, who then called his men to arrest the trio.

Meanwhile Vishnu Ganesh Pingle had returned to Kashi where Bose was busy keeping his Kashi gang intact and saving them from any eventuality. Pingle had come back from Meerut to inform Bose that the 128th Pioneers and the 12th Cavalry, the regiments in which Pingle had worked with Sarabha earlier, were ready for revolt.[6]

Afghan Nadir Khan, the jamadar in one of the regiments, was ready to go along. He accompanied Pingle to Meerut and received the promised 300 bombs that were to be used to blow up the guards of the arsenal to secure ammunition and attack Delhi. The procedure of using the phosphorus solution to make slow fuses for the bombs was also explained to the jamadar.

Pingle was sleeping in one of the quarters of the 12th Regiment one night when he was arrested in Meerut cantonment. Someone had obviously leaked his plans.

Bose left India in April 1915 and travelled to Japan, posing as P.N. Tagore.[7] Rabindranath Tagore was about to visit Japan in those days. He posed as a relative of Tagore and as a member of the contingent that was leaving for Tokyo to make preparations for his visit. A bounty of Rs 1 lakh stood on his head at the time of his leaving. In Japan, his influential friends helped him against the government's move to deport him while the British government was pressurizing the Japanese government for his extradition.

He remained hidden in Japan until he was given Japanese citizenship in 1923.[8] He associated himself with many universities, imparting lectures on the Indian way of life, thus strengthening Indo-Japanese relations. He later formed the Indian Independence League in Japan and then handed over the reins of this organization to Subhas Chandra Bose on 4 July 1942, who christened it Azad Hind Fauj. He died in Tokyo on 21 January 1945.

Harnam Singh Tundilat was sentenced to capital punishment along with others in the First Lahore Conspiracy Case. Pandit Madan Mohan Malaviya had made a plea for clemency to the viceroy who had transmuted the death sentences of seventeen prisoners, including Tundilat, Bhakna and others. Tundilat reached the Cellular Jail on 12 December 1915 and was released on 15 September 1930. He started working for the Kirti Party and was arrested once again in 1941 and released in 1945. During the partition of the country, he was instrumental in saving the lives of Muslim men and women of his village. He suffered from cancer in the last years of his life and breathed his last on 18 September 1962.

Sarabha and Pingle were sentenced to be executed in the Lahore Conspiracy Trial.

Chapter 26

Banta Singh Sanghwal

Born in Sanghwal village in 1890, Banta Singh Sanghwal completed his matriculation from DAV College, Jalandhar.[1] A brave young man, he and a bunch of his classmates went to help the victims of an earthquake in Kangra in his student days.[2] Hailing from a wealthy background, his father being a rich moneylender, he moved to America after finishing school. Coming in touch with Bhakna and Har Dayal had a deep impact on him, which acted as a motivation for him to get associated with the Ghadar Party. He was the first one to get his name registered when the clarion call was given by the party for young men to return home to do a recce of the field conditions in Punjab.

He came to India in 1913 to assess the situation. On seeing the lackadaisical attitude of people back home, one of the students had written back, 'It is very cold here while it is very hot in America.'[3]

Sanghwal arrived in Punjab towards the end of 1913. His first act of defiance was to burn the moneylending books of his wealthy father and free the poor people from the vicious cycle of debt.[4] He led the Doaba side of the resistance from the front. To begin with, he regrouped the Ghadarites who had escaped arrest. After the failure of the Lahore and Ferozepur uprisings, he was part of many attempts to keep the fire ablaze. While he was fighting against the regime, he was indulging in philanthropic activities as well.

With Arur Singh, he started a panchayati raj system in Sanghwal.[5] He encouraged people to stay united and resist paying the heavy taxes levied on them. He collected donations from the people and started a veterinary hospital, a library and a school and encouraged the village populace to start dealing with their own affairs. The ordinary matters of dispute began to be resolved at the village level.

Sangwal's group were troublemakers in the eyes of the government for they were frequently cutting the telegraph lines, pulling up the railway lines and looting the government arsenal. Sanghwal became an important centre of Ghadar activities of the Doaba region. Such was the dread of him that the police termed him a 'terror to Punjab Police'.[6]

Banta Singh Sanghwal was badly injured after the attempt to blow up Walla Bridge (more about this later). The government declared a sum of Rs 2000 and land of 50 acres (2 murabbas) as a reward to anyone who would give a lead on him.[7] Banta Singh's brother-in-law got lured by this and took him to the police on the pretext of taking him to a doctor.

Banta Singh was shocked at this treachery by his relative. A sea of people gathered at the office of the deputy commissioner, Hoshiarpur to support him. He was charged in the Anarkali Murder Case, Walla Bridge Murder Case, Chanda Singh Murder Case and the Dynamite Case, sentenced to death and hanged on 12 August 1915.

Chapter 27

Attempts to Reignite the Revolutionary Fervour

The Anarkali Shoot-Out

After the failure of the Lahore and Ferozepur uprisings on 19 February, the Ghadarites were a disappointed lot. Amongst the arrested men, Mula Singh, Nawab Khan and Amar Singh had turned approvers and had given detailed information to the police about hideouts and the houses being used by them as meeting places. This information had proved crucial to the police, leading to mass arrests and increased patrolling in and around city borders. The only viable option the Ghadarites had was to escape somehow without being caught.

On the morning of 20 February, Ghadarites Arjan Singh of Khokhrana, Banta Singh Sanghwal and Harnam Singh of Sialkot district were on their way from the Lahore bus stand to the Anarkali Bazaar.[1]

The police, deeming them to be suspicious elements, stopped them for checking. Sub Inspector Muhammed Musa and Head Constable Mohsin Ali Shah were on special patrol duty.[2] On examination, the lathi that the three had in their possession turned out to be a sword stick and the policemen asked all three of them to accompany them to the police station.

On further questioning, they were asked to hand over any other incriminating articles they were carrying. Arjan Singh was hiding a revolver under a blanket and he shot the inspector in his right shoulder.[3] With another fatal shot, he laid the head constable to rest. There was commotion in the bazaar after the shoot-out as the three Ghadarites escaped.

Arjan Singh, who stopped for a water break, was caught by men in the bazaar and handed over to the police. He was sentenced to death in the Anarkali Murder Case while the other two escaped.[4]

Attempt to Blow Up Doraha Bridge

Fifteen Ghadarites had taken a trip to Doraha Bridge with the intention to blow it up on 21 February.[5] It happened after their failure to get things moving in Ferozepur. Harnam Singh and Banta Singh had escaped the Anarkali bazaar fiasco and now, with Anokh Singh, the orderly of Kartar Singh Sarabha and others, were ready to execute the deed. Bhagat Singh Kacharbhan was their leader, the man who had fired at the police and killed two at Ferozeshahr. He had evaded arrest while Rehmat Ali, Kanshi Ram and others had fallen into the hands of the police.

Blowing up bridges and railway lines, and cutting telegraph lines had been their line of targets. And though there had been feverish attempts from their side, they had not proved successful so far.

They had procured powerful bombs with large screw caps this time. These bombs were meant to cause maximum damage when their devastation-laden caps blew up. Kacharbhan was to be at the front and throw two bombs. They decided to approach the guards first and try to coerce them to take their side. The guards appeared unrelenting and so the Ghadarites buried the bombs, deciding to come back on a more favourable day. Before their arrival at the opportune time, the bombs were recovered by the police. This scheme too failed, bringing them more disappointment.

The Nangal Kalan Murder (Chanda Singh)

On 25 April 1915, the 15-mile stretch from Mahilpur to Hoshiarpur was cordoned off. Public announcements were made that no one should venture out of their homes. A caravan of policemen guarding a man on a cart, walking with cautious steps, could be seen on the empty road. His ankle was bleeding profusely as it was tied firmly with rope to the cart. The blood oozed out in spurts and dripped on the road. People defied the orders of the sarkar and gathered by the road to have a look at this man.

The man was Piara Singh Langeri, belonging to Langeri village of Mahilpur near Hoshiarpur. Guerrilla warfare tactics would become the hallmark of this village and the tehsil Garhshankar would be adjudged the most dangerous in the entire district. This was the village of Ghadarites that included Udham Singh Kasel, Darshan Singh Canadian and many more.

Langeri, a close friend of Sanghwal, enrolled in the army but soon left it and moved to Canada in 1906. In Canada, Langeri became associated with the United India League, ending up as its treasurer. He was an associate of Sunder Singh in his press and also brought out a magazine called *Sansar*. Later, he would start a journal called *Pardesi Khalsa*. He came back home on 29 August 1914 sailing on SS *Korea*. With Nidhan Singh and others, he had halted at Nagasaki from where he reached Calcutta escaping arrest in the aftermath of the Budge Budge shootout.

Once he reached his village, along with Sanghwal, he formed a Doaba front that was dreaded by the Punjab police. He kept the police forces of Langeri, Sakruli and Nangal Kalan villages on their toes. Additional forces had, in fact, been summoned in this case especially to guard him.

Information about his whereabouts was leaked to the police by Chanda Singh, zaildar of Nangal Kalan, when Langeri had stopped at the hut of a village sadhu, Tulsa Singh.[6] The hut was located on the outskirts of Binjo. The temptation to acquire riches and land lured informers into the trap of passing on information about revolutionaries.

While Piara Singh was inside the sadhu's hut, the police, around twelve to fourteen men, loaded with ammunition, waited for him to emerge rather than launching an attack on him. When he got out of the hut, they followed him to the village and spread the rumour of him being a robber. In the melee, he was caught by a shepherd, who hit him on the ankle, rupturing a blood vessel. He was caught and taken to the police station.

Sanghwal and his Doaba group killed the zaildar, Chanda Singh, that night, disguising themselves as traders as they rode on camels to Nangal Kalan.

The 23rd Cavalry and Its Bombs

Prem Singh, belonging to Sur Singh village of Amritsar, was the head of the Majha detachment. He was instrumental in contacting Dafeddar Lachman Singh and his group of people. Apart from Prem Singh, none of the other Ghadarites were in contact with men of the regiment. Prem Singh, who had taken four donkeys loaded with party literature, had walked up to Delhi in those days to spread the message of Ghadar. A man of indomitable will, he refused to give up when plans at Mian Mir went haywire. Despite the failure of the uprising on the planned day, he was back in the cantonment with the jawans who were not yet dispirited and became willing listeners.

He would come to the premises and teach them how to make bombs and dynamite. Designed by bomb expert Mathura Singh, the bombs containing chlorate and potash were successfully made by them. The murder of Kirpal Singh, the mole who had jeopardized their plans, was also discussed. On the hit list was Bela Singh, zaildar, who had told the sarkar about the Ghadarites' movements.

The bombs were packed safely by the soldiers on the day before their move to Nowganj cantonment located in Harpalpur, United Province.

On 13 May 1915, when the trunks were being thrown on the ground, the soldiers were standing around taking stock of their luggage.[7] The trunk containing the bombs landed on the ground with a big explosion and this would sound the death knell for the men of the 23rd Cavalry, who had not been identified so far.

This blast led to the questioning of the men, who owned up to the bombs and disclosed the names of all accomplices in what would be called the Lahore Conspiracy. The disaffected men were shorn of their uniform and taken to Dagshai where they would be court-martialled, away from prying public eyes.

The Jagatpura Murder

Prem Singh was instrumental in motivating Kala Singh of Jagatpura and Channan Singh of Burchand towards the Ghadarite fold. These men were not returned immigrants but part of the local populace. The Ghadarites raised a consciousness in them, making them rise against the local zaildars and men of power who sided with the British.

Sardar Bahadur Arur Singh, the manager of the Golden Temple, constantly invoked the ire of these men by siding with the British government. He had already escaped an attempt on his life.[8]

The next man targeted by the trio was Sardar Bahadur Achar Singh of Jagatpura, who was sympathetic to the British government. After the demolition of the wall of Gurdwara Rakabganj, he had uttered statements in favour of the British that had greatly peeved the Ghadarites. They killed him in his fields on

4 June in broad daylight and in front of the villagers, who did not come to his rescue.[9]

The Walla Bridge Shoot-Out

If Sanghwal became the centre of Ghadarites in the Doaba region, Dhudhike village in Malwa and Sur Singh in Majha were the other hotspots of dissidence. One attempt to wage war against the regime and loot the Kapurthala arsenal was envisaged by Doaba and Malwa Ghadarites. On this account, a meeting was held on 25 May in which the detachments from the Doaba and Majha regions participated. They felt that the lack of ammunition was a deterrent to accomplishing their plans. They decided to attack the guard posted on the Walla Bridge near Amritsar for ammunition and then attack the Kapurthala regiment. 5 June was decided as the day to execute this operation.

One of the detachments was headed by Banta Singh Sanghwal, who led the men from Doaba.[10] He was accompanied by Ranga Singh Khurdpur, Kala Singh Jagatpuriya and Charan Singh Burchand.[11] The Dhudhike group was headed by Prem Singh, who led the men from Majha. It included Bachan Singh Dhudhike, Rur Singh Talwandi and Bhai Jawand Singh Nangal. They started from Kapurthala, taking different detours. While Sanghwal led his men through Kartarpur and reached Amritsar, Prem Singh and his men crossed Gondwal, Tarn Taran and then reached Amritsar.

But the attempted attack did not take place on 5 June. The 42nd Deoli Regiment deployed on Walla Bridge was sturdy and the men on guard did not slacken in their duty. The Ghadarites went back and decided to come back again on the 11th. However, this time, they did not reach the designated spot at the same time. While Prem Singh and his men reached first, Sanghwal was a little late. Prem Singh left his men and decided to go in search of the other detachment which reached in his absence. And there they waited for the guards, to carry out their plan.

This time, the Ghadarites were determined not to go back empty-handed. The guns and ammunition would be theirs and they devised a plan to act accordingly. They decided that they would wait for the train to pass. The noise emanating from the chugging of the train would be the perfect mask to execute their operations. The night of the 11th would prove to be a night of reckoning for neither did the two guards sit for a breather, nor did they appear lax.

Once at the bridge, the Ghadarites sat undiscovered under the cover of the tall grass waiting for the opportune moment to take on the guards. The right time would be the crossing of the train. At 4 a.m. they could hear the whistle of the goods train and gestured to each other.

Sanghwal and Jawand Singh led their men from the front. Prem Singh had still not returned while the rest prepared for the attack.

The train was approaching and so was their moment of reckoning. Precisely when it crossed the bridge, Sanghwal and Jawand Singh shot the guard at the post. The Ghadarites ran out of hiding. Kala Singh picked up the rifle of the dead man.

The train had passed and now there was no masking the heavy footsteps of the Ghadarites. A havildar emerged from the temporary shelter where he had been resting, waiting for his shift to begin. Kala Singh gave him no time to react and shot him down. Two more men came out, and they were shot too.

Kala Singh and Sanghwal put on the uniforms of the guard and havildar. The rest of the uniforms were packed in a bundle to be taken to Kapurthala.

Meanwhile Prem Singh, who missed the action, got in touch with Bhagwan Singh, the policeman, who was going to help them raid the Kapurthala arsenal. Rur Singh and Bachan Singh reached Kapurthala after crossing the Beas on a ferry where they met Prem Singh and Bhagwan Singh.

One guard who had witnessed the shoot-out but escaped the notice of the Ghadarites spilled the beans of this encounter to his superiors, who sent more men to chase the Ghadarites. The men who had left for Kapurthala escaped but the rest of them—Kala Singh, Harnam Singh, Channan Singh, Sanghwal and Jawand Singh—were their target.

For the next twenty-four hours, they were chased by the police till their arrival in the princely state of Kapurthala. They had covered thirty-eight miles. Their bodies were fatigued. The Kapurthala police had been intimated in advance of their arrival. The men buried their ammunition in the bushes near the river. They left the boat and escaped into a nearby village in search of food and water.

Channan Singh and Kala Singh were arrested near the river while Sanghwal and Jawand Singh managed to escape.

The Murder at Padhri Kalan

Prem Singh once again led his men to murder an informer named Kapur Singh, who had leaked the information about their meeting at Jhar Sahib while they were planning an uprising at Mian Mir cantonment. Along with him were Rur Singh, Inder Singh Padhri, Arun Singh of Sanghwal and Hardit Singh of Dalewal. The man in question was a *shahukar*, a moneylender.

Kapur Singh was killed on 3 August 1915 while he was returning home from the well after taking a bath.[12]

Inder Singh was caught by the police. Later, Prem Singh too could not escape their clutches. He, Inder Singh and Arur Singh were hanged till death. The others were transported for life to the Andamans.

Chapter 28

The Lahore Conspiracy Case Trials

'The blood of the martyrs does not flow in vain! It shall bear fruit!'[1]

Sarabha had written thus on the wall of the Lahore Central Jail with his blood where he, Bhakna and others, the sixty-four accused in the first Lahore Conspiracy trial had been lodged.[2] Seven amongst them were going to be hanged. Two were little more than boys—Sarabha and Pingle. Sarabha was the youngest, a mere eighteen and a half.

Sarabha had been enthusiastic since the start. As a sixteen-year-old, he had joined the Ghadar Party and later, the Ghadar press. His enthusiasm had spiked as he travelled to Punjab to wage Ghadar. His enthusiasm had not ebbed but had grown stronger and his determination, firmer.

Viceroy Lord Hardinge had imposed his will on the lieutenant governor of Punjab, Michael O'Dwyer, who had dealt with the trial in a shoddy manner. The Governor had picked the three judges and formed a commission that had conducted a summary trial in the premises of the Lahore Central Jail on the basis of police complaints.[3] No one had been allowed to watch these hurriedly conducted trials.[4] No press, no relatives of the so-called accused had been allowed in. There were no witnesses, no defence, only the prosecution. Though the judges had given capital punishment to twenty-four, including those who had been arrested the moment their ships touched India, the viceroy had used his special powers and reduced their sentences to life imprisonment.[5] These included Bhakna and Jawala Singh Thatthiyan amongst others.

So far, this regime had not let a word out. It had shown mercy to some but had been cruel and unforgiving towards the others. The mercy pleas made on behalf of Sarbha and Pingle were rejected by the viceroy. The extent of his mercy was partially based on placating the public anger that would boil over once it became public as to how unfairly the trials had been conducted.

The foremost trial, which was known as the First Lahore Conspiracy Case trial, started on 26 April 1915 in which sixty-three people were tried and eighteen were declared absconders.[6] It would last till the middle of September. It would be followed by four supplementary cases and trials of several subsidiary cases. A total of 175 people were sentenced, resulting in 136 convictions. Out of the forty-two death sentences, half were reduced to life imprisonment. The Special Defence of India Act was called into action, which gave the government the power to arrest anyone, put them in jail and then start a trial sans any appeal.[7]

The convictions were quick, sentences crisply laid out and the spirit of justice had been throttled. The charges included waging war against the Crown or conspiring to do so, in and out of India, inciting troops to sedition and mutiny and committing dacoities, murder and abetting murder.

Sarabha was defiant till the very end, unapologetic about his goal of expelling the British from India. He refused to bend before the law and stoically bore the proclamation of the death sentence. He was hanged on 16 November 1915 along with Pingle and five others.[8]

Chapter 29

The Revolt at Singapore

Singapore was a strategically located port under British control. It was important not only because of its geographic location but also because it saw the arrival and departure of ships coming from the west to the far east, which later entered Indian territory. It was a confluence of cultures, accommodating Sikhs, Muslims as well as small numbers of other communities.

Singapore was subject to two different kinds of influences. The first influence was the preachings of the Ghadar. The Sikh population, after it settled in the Far East, had built gurdwaras in Singapore, Hong Kong, Malaya and Penang.[1] When the influx of Ghadarites began from Canada and America, it soon reached Singapore. Men deboarded from the ships bringing their energy, enthusiasm and anger. The army could not remain untouched by this influence, especially the Muslim unit, the Light Infantry and the loyal Fifth, which was posted at Singapore.[2]

Ghadar leaders preached sedition in the army barracks. Mujatafa Hussain was a Ghadarite who was earlier posted as zaildar in the court of wards at Cawnpore and who had spread the message of Ghadar in Manila and later in Singapore.[3] Hira Singh and Gujar Singh Charar were other Ghadarites who had been distributing Ghadar literature in the military settlements of Singapore.

The second influence was the Pan-Islamic, Turkish influence on the men in the barracks. The two regiments posted in Singapore were the Malay State Guides and Fifth Light Infantry.[4] The latter mainly comprised Ranghar Muslims and Pathans.[5] Both the units were disaffected by the anti-British preachings of Turkey when it joined Germany in the First World War.

If *Ghadar* was the voice of anti-British Sikh and Hindu immigrants, *Jehan-i-Islam* was the Muslim paper published from Constantinople that influenced Muslims. *Jehan-i-Islam* was openly seditious in its nature and intent and was circulated alongside copies of the *Ghadar* to different parts of the world.

Enver Pasha, a powerful figure in the Ottoman Empire, wrote in the 20 November 1914 issue of *Jehan-i-Islam*:

> This is the time that the Ghadar should be declared in India, the magazines of the English should be plundered, their weapons looted and they should be killed therewith. The Indians number 32 crores at the best and the English are only 2 lakhs: they should be murdered: they have no army. The Suez Canal will shortly be closed by the Turks, but he who will die and liberate the country and his native land will live forever. Hindus and Muhammmadans, you are both soldiers of the army and you are brothers, and this low graded English is your enemy; you should become ghazis by declaring jihad, and by combining with your brothers murder the English and liberate India.[6]

How could such words not have affected the men!

The first currents of discontent were detected in the regiment of 130th Baluchis, which had been posted out of Bombay as punishment for the killing of a regimental officer. The regiment had been posted at Rangoon and comprised mainly of Muslims. Their plot against the British was detected before it materialized into action. All 200 men were penalized and the uprising was nipped in the bud.[7]

The second wave of disaffection was detected amongst the Malay State Guides. The regiment was thoroughly disaffected and wanted to side with the Ottoman Empire. They wanted the caliphate to send them a warship so that they could leave Singapore. This piece of information was noted down in a letter by Kasim Mansoor, who was a pro-Turkish Gujarati Muslim staying in Singapore.[8] The letter addressed to his son in Rangoon was to be handed over to the Turkish Consulate but it was intercepted by the British[9] at Rangoon and passed on to the government. The regiment was transferred to another place with immediate orders.

Besides the Fifth Light Infantry, the other regiment stationed in Singapore at that time was the 36th Sikh regiment.

When the government thought they had been successful in quelling dissidence in its Muslim regiments, there came a bolt from the blue. The Fifth Light Infantry regiment, which had so far not shown any signs of resistance, had shaken the confidence of the regime in their men. This regiment had recently been transferred to Singapore because the native regiment had been transferred to France on the western front to fight the war.

The regimental men under Turkish and Ghadar influences had decided to launch an attack on the English officers on the night of 19 February 1915. They were unaware of the same kind of attack being planned in Lahore, Ferozepur and other Indian cantonments. But this attack did not take place on the planned date. The regiment was transferred to Hong Kong and they were about to sail on the British sloop, *Cadmus*, on 16 February.

The ringleaders—Jamedar Chisti Khan, Subedar Dundey Khan and Jamedar Abdul Ali—were surprised at this development. But they did not lose hope. The uprising, they decided, would happen on the night of the 15th when they would be called to deposit their arms before the move the next day.[10] The Chinese would be celebrating their lunar new year and it would be the perfect time to execute their plans. The uprising would be masked under the garb of celebrations.

They were lined up to give in their revolvers and unwillingly everyone was placing their weapons on the table. Along with the name, they were noting down the make and type of the weapon.

When Ismail Khan was asked to deposit his revolver, he placed the revolver on the chest of the man collecting the ammunition and fired. One shot was enough to start the chain reaction of multiple shots that were fired in every direction, killing the English officers.

The mutineers then organized themselves into three sections.

Some of them marched towards Tanglin barracks where the German prisoners captured from the *Emden* had been put up.[11] These prisoners had not come out of their barracks and chose not to escape even when the doors of the prison were thrown open. Their support had been taken for granted. This greatly peeved the mutineers, who were banking on the support of the German prisoners to overthrow the British.

The second group approached the bungalow of Colonel E.V. Martin, who was the commanding officer of the Fifth Light Infantry.[12] Some of the English guards of the Volunteer Corps had run towards the port and created an alarm. These eighty-six men of Malay States Volunteers Rifles and the colonel had been held inside the house.[13] The colonel had reached out to the station commander, Major General Readout, and informed him about the mutiny. The major informed the Governor.

The third group had moved towards the city to obstruct the help coming from outside and to kill all the Englishmen they would encounter. They went towards Pasir Panjang (the south-western part of Singapore) killing eight European officers, nine soldiers and sixteen civilians.[14] Women and children were spared, though one stray bullet had led to the death of an officer's wife. They stopped the car of the district judge, killing him on the spot. The car of a businessman was stopped and he was shot point-blank.

The Governor, General Readout and Admiral Martyn Jerram sent desperate wireless messages calling to the ships for help. The Russian, French and Japanese warships had heeded this call and sent their men. The Japanese were the first to arrive. The sultan of Johore sent 150 men to help.[15] Help also came from Rangoon in the form of companies of the 1st/4th Battalion, King's Shropshire Light Infantry (Territorials). They arrived on the night of the 15th itself but nothing was done that night.

On the 16th morning, eighty men from Shropshire, twenty-one from the arsenal division, fifty Singapore volunteers and twenty-five chosen civilians were led by Colonel Burnell.[16] The mutineers, confident of having won the battle on the first day, were roaming around in small groups celebrating their success. There were only a few men guarding the barracks. They were easily overpowered by the approaching contingent, who prepared to wrest back control. The mutineers were overpowered and the barracks taken under control. Colonel Readout too was rescued from his hideout. The mutineers roaming the city were rounded up by 100 special police officers, which included the Japanese force as well.

On the morning of 17 February, more help arrived in the form of men and ammunition. The few groups of mutineers who had evaded arrest the previous day were captured as well. The unorganized resistance of mutineers had been quelled completely by the end of the third day after the arrest of 422 mutineers. However, 300 men were still at large.

While the 18th morning saw the hunt for the rest of the men, the proceedings for initiating cases against the soldiers who had erred were also initiated. Cursory sentences were handed to the men who would be publicly executed. The city people were assembled outside Outram Prison, the venue of the public executions. The men were stood in a single horizontal file and shot in full public view.

The *Straits Times* reported: 'An enormous crowd, reliably estimated at more than 15,000 people, was packed on the slopes of Sepoy Lines looking down on the scene. The square as before was composed of regulars, local volunteers and Shropshire under the command of Colonel Derrick of the Singapore Volunteer Corps (SVC).'[17]

This brought an end to the revolt in Singapore that the British managed to quell, but which was proof that all was not well. The men under their command wanted to get away, were oppressed and wanted to avenge the insults heaped upon them and their communities.

The action then progressed towards Burma where the Ghadarites were working in active connivance with the Germans and the impact of the pro-Turkish, pro-Muslim sentiment was growing.

Chapter 30

The Siam–Burma Angle

As previously stated, the Ottoman Empire, the seat of the caliphate, was regarded with utmost respect by Muslims from all over the world. Pan-Islamism as a movement soon garnered strength and strung the scattered beads of this religion into one thread.

The sentiment of Muslim unity found solidarity amongst Indian Muslims, who looked upon the Ottoman Empire as their saviour and any insult to its integrity was a personal insult to them. Pan-Islamism had been garnering strength in India since the late nineteenth century. It was fuelled by the strength of the written word.

Weekly papers like *Jehan-i-Islam*, since its inception in 1914, had been publishing articles in Arabic, Turkish and Urdu.[1] Its purpose was to discuss politics and promote conversations between Muslim countries. Another magazine called *Zamindar* being published from Lahore too was working on the same lines.

The Indian Muslim mattered and the support of this community was crucial to the British, who had realized the importance of keeping this community in its fold. Pan-Islamism was seen by the British as a means to weaken the traditional Muslim loyalty it had been banking on for years. And this danger looked real after the Russian–Japanese War (1904–05) in which Japan became the first Asian country to defeat the expansionist plans of Russia in East Asia.

The Japanese win had turned people in India ecstatic as wealthy donors collected Rs 65,000 for the widows and orphans of the Japanese soldiers.[2] The British feared that the rise of Japan could have disastrous effects on the growth of Indian nationalism.[3] An Indian Urdu paper, *Watan*, published from Lahore, exhorted Indian Muslims to support Japan.[4] Japan became the destination of some Indian students after their win in this war. Their numbers rose to 100 by 1910–11.[5]

The Turkey–Italian War in 1911 proved to be another litmus test. Muslims around the world supported the Ottoman Empire and their anger erupted towards Italy and its allies after this war broke out. Protest meetings were held in India and funds were raised to help Muslim brethren bearing the brunt of this war. Even Muslims who had meagre possessions to their name came forward to help with the donations. Such was their devotion towards the caliphate. Any insult to their supreme leader was taken personally by them.

The Aid to the Ottoman Red Crescent Society was begun by Indian Muslims to support war-torn Turkish citizens. On 15 December 1912, a medical mission left for Turkey under the aegis of this society.[6] The Tripoli and Balkan wars gave rise to a feeling that Muslims could not be true believers if they were living under English rule and so most of the people of this society were sent to missions abroad. Many volunteers decided to settle down in Turkey itself, also simultaneously making plans to bring Muslims from India to Konya and Adana (cities in Turkey).[7]

Indians wanted the British Indian government to intervene on behalf of Turkey and take sides. When Italy was acting against Muslim interests in Tripoli, stern action was demanded by Muslims on behalf of Turkey. As a result of this, a medical mission was sent by the British government, which included Ali Ahmed Siddiqui and Hakim Faim Ali, to assuage the Indian Muslim sensibilities. A Punjabi Muslim named Abu Saiyid, who had been working in

Rangoon too, had reached Turkey, getting himself involved with the Turkish sensibilities and spreading the word of *Jehan-i-Islam*.

But all did not remain well between the Ottoman Empire and the British government. The international policy of the British led it to make some anti-Turkish remarks that did not go down well with the ordinary Indian Muslim. And from here the seeds of conflict were sown. The British were not only construed as anti-Turkish, they came to be regarded as anti-Muslim.[8] The Germans had been sympathizing with the Muslims and so they were now regarded as their friends. These sensibilities would only sharpen and gain an edge when the Ottoman Empire would side with Germany in the First World War.

Even as Indian Muslims were aligning with Turkey, they were being wooed by the Ghadar Party in Canada and America. Mohammed Barakatullah, an office-bearer and a very important pillar of the Ghadar Party, was a Muslim, who had been managing its Tokyo affairs. Har Dayal too had been writing in favour of Hindu-Muslim unity in *Ghadar*.

Burma occupied a strategic position and after the failed revolutions in Lahore and Ferozepur cantonments, it was seen as a suitable location for the Ghadar Party to start operations afresh. The capital, Rangoon, had been a centre of Pan-Islamic activities before the start of the First World War.[9]

Sometime in 1913, a new Turkish consulate was established in Rangoon.[10] Bengali revolutionaries too were active in Burma long before the arrival of the Ghadarites. Khirodgopal Mukherjee, a Bengali revolutionary, had travelled to Burma in 1908 and opened a centre at Meiktila.[11] Another Bengali revolutionary had travelled to Rangoon in 1913 where he engaged with the Turkish Consul and local Pan-Islamites.[12]

With the presence of a strong anti-British sentiment, a police contingent with weapons and armoury had been positioned permanently to quell any chances of dissent in Rangoon.

The Germans, the Ghadar Party and the Pan-Islamists concentrated their energies on a single goal—to gather the forces of revolt in Burma.

The German Interest in Pan-Islamism

'Now our job is to show up the whole business ruthlessly and tear away the mask of Christian peacemaking and put the pharsical hypocrisy about peace in the pillory! And our consuls in Turkey and India, agents, etc., must get a conflagration going throughout the whole Mohammedan world against this hatred, unscrupulous, dishonest nation of shopkeepers—since if we are going to bleed to death, England must at least lose India,' said Kaiser Wilhelm II, the last German emperor in July 1914.[13]

Germany wanted Turkey's influence in Afghanistan and amongst Muslims in India to grow manifold. When ties between Britain and Germany started falling apart, Germany was comforted with the falling apart of Britain-Turkey ties as well. The rise of Muslim power could lead to the loss of India and an endangered India could destabilize Britain—that seemed to be the thinking. Germany began weaving a strong anti-British policy with the rise of Pan-Islamism and the incidents of terrorism in India.

The Kaiser had firmly believed that when the war would erupt, the Muslims living under the subjugation of Britain and Russia would support Germany.

'If Britain becomes our opponent, attempts will have to be made to instigate a rebellion in India. The same has to be tried in Egypt . . . Persia must be called upon to make use of the favourable opportunity to throw off the Russian yoke and, if possible, to act together with Turkey,' wrote General von Moltke on the day of the treaty signing between Turkey and Germany on 2 August 1914.[14]

Baron Max von Oppenheim, the German diplomat and archaeologist, shared the optimism when he wrote to the German office thus:

> Britain knows that once she is pushed out of India she may never get India back again. If there were deeper unrest in India, Britain would be forced to send a major portion of her fleet to Indian waters to protect the numerous British interests, the British people there, and the British world position. British public opinion would also want it and thus Britain would have to conclude an early peace favourable to us . . .[15]

Enver Pasha, the Ottoman military officer and the main leader of the Young Turk revolution, had given wings to the hopes of Germany when he had proposed his grand plan to them.[16] He wanted German military officers dressed like Muslims to accompany a group of Turkish officers to Afghanistan, who in his opinion were waiting for encouragement to attack India. And the German office had obliged. It had chosen fifteen people to head this expedition. Their plans got a further boost by the formation of Tashkilat-i-Mukhsusa, a central office for the Islamic movement in the Turkish war ministry.

The Siam-Burma Route

When the war erupted, the neutral countries bordering India gained importance for they could be used for anti-British operations.[17] The Ghadarites, those who had been landing at Indian ports, were being arrested on arrival. The government was using the Ingress to India Act against them. Valuable manpower was being wasted. When it came to choosing the land route to India, the names of several countries did the rounds—Afghanistan, Tibet, China, Iran and Siam (now Thailand). Out of these countries, China and Siam were crucial because they had a good number of Indian revolutionaries with an organized network.

China was in turmoil as it was preparing for its own revolution. The leader of the Chinese revolution, Sun Yat-Sen, was on good terms with Indian revolutionaries, Barakatullah and Khankhoje.[18] But though he had promised support to Ghadar men, he was not ready to antagonize the British by letting his country be used for Ghadar activities.

Siam was the only viable option left where a large number of Ghadarites could gather and launch an offensive through Rangoon. The smuggling of arms would be easy and the jungles of Siam offered a perfect camouflage to hide the ammunition that would be brought to China from foreign shores and then moved to Siam. It was also decided that Ghadarites would disembark in China and from there, move to Bangkok on foot.

Siam offered certain advantages. Firstly, there were a large number of Sikhs and Muslims.[19] The land of Siam was fertile and preferred for mining, which made it lucrative as a settlement.

The Sikhs were being affected by the circulation of the *Ghadar* newspaper. Muslims were being brought into the fold by the writings of Enver Pasha in *Jehan-i-Islam*.[20] Some of the Sikhs were wealthy, which meant that they could contribute to the cause of the revolution. Many were shopkeepers and had a strong network of shops in the interior of the city. Also many of them were hawkers. There were two Sikh gurdwaras in Bangkok as well. The wealthiest Sikh in Siam, Buddha Singh, supported the cause of Ghadar and became a strong pillar of the movement.

Secondly, there was a strong anti-British sentiment among the people of Siam that was also being helped by the fact that in the early years of the war, the government took no step to stop the anti-British activities on its soil.

Thirdly, the long inland stretch of the Siam-Burma border was thinly guarded and allowed movement of men and ammunition. The government was busy guarding the ports of India to protect them from invaders. So far, no military activity had been undertaken from the land routes and hence, Siam posed no threat to India.

Fourthly, the railway line being laid on the Siam–Burma border was being supervised by Amar Singh, a Ghadarite. He would get unemployed Indians to work, who could then be incorporated in the attack when an offensive was launched from the Siam side.

Fifthly, Burma had a small military garrison and the military police were mainly Punjabi. Once again, Ghadar literature played its part well in disaffecting these men.

The Germans had captured Santau Island in Japan. Their presence in the region made sure of their ready availability.

All these factors made the Siam-Burma route very favourable to Ghadarites.

German Cooperation in the Siamese Plan

The Germans were going to help Indian revolutionaries with men, ammunition and money. They started offering bribes to Thai newspapers for anti-British propaganda and even started publishing a German newspaper called *Unshan* from Bangkok.[21] The former German consul to Hong Kong was roped in and given money to help with the activities in Thailand. A large number of shotguns were also imported to Thailand.

One of the men who would be leading this movement from the Ghadarite camp was Jodh Singh. Born in Rawalpindi and educated in Amritsar, he had worked with railroad contractors in Lahore, Calcutta and Assam.[22] A few months into the job, he had run away to Chittagong with a Rs 500 cheque he was supposed to encash for his boss. And then he appeared in Portland as a labourer. From Portland, he crossed over to England. He had gone to India House and met Har Dayal there, who was about to leave for the US. He had then moved to Berlin where he was approached by Madam Cama to write for *Bande Mataram*. Before that, he travelled from Genoa to Germany on a passport that depicted him as a German subject and later to America on another false passport secured through the German Consulate. In America, he met three Germans, Wehde, Boehm and Sterneck, who were to take charge of men waiting for them in Bangkok.

Meanwhile, Ghadarites were travelling to China and reaching Bangkok through Amoy and Swatow. They were being asked to wait in Bangkok before making a move towards Burma in small batches to avoid undue suspicion.

The revolutionaries in the making would be given military training in the jungles of Siam. Totalling 10,000, they were to be trained as soldiers and their help enlisted to capture Burma. Along with them, the Burmese police were to be disaffected and taken into confidence. This was the ambitious plan to take in Burma and then wage a war on Indian territories through the north-east. Tunnels had been dug in Pakho, near the Siam border to hide the cache of expected ammunition.[23] Another plan that resonated along with the capture of Burma was the seizure of the Andamans and the release of prisoners who would help the revolutionaries as the prison island would be made a base for future attacks.

Barakatullah formed an effective link between the Berlin Indian Independence Committee, which was mainly interested in purchasing and sending arms to the Bengali revolutionaries, the Ghadarites and the Germans. He had connected the dots and brought all three disjointed factions together.

Heramba Lal Gupta too had coordinated with the Germans on behalf of the Indian Committee and requested for another 8000 rifles, 2000 revolvers and machine guns for Bengalis at home as well as the Indian revolutionaries in Thailand. Money was paid to Wehde and his friend by the German foreign office for the purchase of arms.

Jodh Singh, after receiving instructions from Ram Chandra in Yugantar Ashram, and Heramba Lal Gupta in Berlin reached New York. Boehm and his men reached San Francisco on 9 May 1915 and sailed to Honolulu. Jodh Singh was to follow them later. He was accompanied by Chenchiah and Sukumar Chatterjee on this mission. They had sailed from San Francisco on 23 March 1915 with coded letters for German Consuls at Honolulu and Manila.

The Way to Burma

Sohan Lal Pathak and Harnam Singh Sahri were amongst the first men to reach Burma through Siam. Sahri had been deported from America for delivering arms to the passengers of the *Komagata Maru* and had been waiting in Yokohama to find a suitable assignment. Pathak was one of the members of the shore committee that had dealt with the affairs of the *Komagata Maru*.

Sohan Lal Pathak was born in Amritsar on 7 January 1883 in a family of modest means.[24] He completed most of his education with a scholarship. He wanted to be a teacher but was declared unfit in the training test because of his frail physique. But later, he did end up becoming a teacher in a primary school in Amritsar. After moving to Lahore, he started tutoring students along with his job.[25]

After teaching in various schools and colleges, Pathak moved to Siam in 1909 where he started selling clothes to support himself. After suffering losses, he quit the business. He met Amar Singh who was working as an overseer on the Siam-Burma Railway line. Singh employed him and he started working on the railway line with other Punjabi labourers.

Amar Singh had been living in Siam since 1910.[26] After marrying a Siamese girl, he had become a naturalized Siamese subject. He was a surveyor on the Royal Northern Siamese Railway. His headquarters were in Pakho where the railway line had been extended.[27]

After the failure of his business, Pathak sought monetary help from his family for his passage to America. He started studying pharmacy in a college in Oregon State. He came in contact with Bhakna, Har Dayal and emissaries of the Ghadar Party and gradually got into the folds of the party. When it was time to choose someone to head the Siam–Burma scheme, Pathak was chosen for he had worked in Siam and knew the place well.

Pathak and Sahri were assisted by five others who would leave Siam for Rangoon. These five were Ram Rakha, Chet Ram, Mujtafa Hussain, Ali Ahmed Siddiqui and Abu Sayid.[28] Jodh Singh, Chenchiah and others were on their way from America.

Mujtafa Hussain, or Mul Chand as he was called, was a Muslim under the alias of a Hindu identity. He was a zaildar at the court of wards at Cawnpore.[29] He had travelled to America, from there to Singapore and now to Rangoon. Ram Rakha had left the police force a long time ago. He was in Manila in 1914 where he was joined by Guru Dutt Kumar.[30] From the Philippines he had travelled to Bangkok and now he had come to Rangoon accompanying Pathak. Ali Ahmed Siddiqui was a member of the Red Crescent Society and had been to Turkey.[31] Hakim Faim Ali was the man deputed from the Turkish consulate to preach the message of Pan-Islamism in Burma.

The road from Siam to Rangoon was not easy for these men. Sahri had left for Ban Pin, a town in Siam. Here he had met Pathak and the others. They had planned to go to Rahang, a city near Rangoon but Sahri was hit by a bad bout of diarrhoea. It was only after recuperating for ten long days that he was able to get up on his feet. Amar Singh had come to fetch Sahri and Pathak. Sahri had taken the alias of Ishar Das and had often given the slip to the police by donning a burqa, disguising himself as a woman.[32]

Chet Ram was in Rangoon. He had taken a house on rent on 16, Dufferin Street and a post box as well for the receipt of letters and Ghadar literature.[33] He had also set up a press in Pakho to print Ghadar literature.[34] The gurdwara in Chiengmai was an important place for their meetings as the granthi was in collusion with them.

Abu Sayid and Ali Ahmed Sidiqui had spread the message of *Jehan-i-Islam*. Pathak and Sahri had to ignite the Punjabi police force. The plan was all set and the time to revolt was ripe, but things did not go as planned.

The first fall came when the letters addressed to 16, Dufferin Street came under surveillance.[35] The second fall came when Chet Ram was caught with a bundle of Ghadar literature that was printed at Pakho and being carried towards Siam. It was intercepted at Myawaddy and found to contain 200 copies of *Ghadar* in Urdu, Gurmukhi and Hindi. It contained the message titled 'A Message of Love to Military Brethren', a scathing attack on the British government.[36]

The cover had been blown. The Indian government increased surveillance around the Burma–Siam border and arrested hundreds of revolutionaries. The Siam government too began acting tough. The dreams of revolution were shattered once again.

Despite all the brouhaha in Siam and Rangoon, Pathak was busy cajoling the men of the Mountain Battery in Maymyo with Ghadar literature and issues of *Jehan-i-Islam*.[37] A school teacher, who was Pathak's friend, had become a go-between, initiating meetings between Pathak and the man in charge, a jamadar.

Pathak had met the jamadar several times and he had promised help. On 15 August 1915, Pathak had come to meet the jamadar bearing three automatic pistols and 300 rounds of ammunition when the jamadar got him arrested on the charges of attempting to incite soldiers of the Mountain Battery of Artillery to murder their officers and mutiny, and distributing Ghadar literature.[38] On his person were found revolutionary articles written by Har Dayal, a bomb manual, an old issue of the *Ghadar* newspaper, three automatic pistols and rounds of ammunition.[39]

Pathak was sentenced to death in the trials and hanged in Mandalay Jail.[40] Sahri and two associates were arrested while crossing the Burma–Siam border near Myawaddy on 9 September 1915.[41]

Jodh Singh had arrived in Bangkok with Chenchiah and the Germans. By then the bonhomie between the Germans and Indians had fizzled out. The Ghadarites and the Germans were not aware of each other's actions and there was a lack of cohesion amongst them. According to Boehm, the German, no details of the Siam

expedition were made available to him.[42] The German consul in
Siam too was not taken on board regarding this plan. Jodh Singh
was not able to pinpoint the location where the arms were to be
handed over to them. Any possibility of an action together was not
possible now when suspicion had taken deep roots amidst them.
The promised arms too had not arrived. German officers who were
to impart military training to the revolutionaries in East Bengal
were captured and they gave all the information to their captors.[43]

The arrested men were taken to Mandalay and two sham trials
were initiated on the pattern of the Lahore Conspiracy Case trials.
The sentences were quick, unjust and without any hearings. The
men in question had done nothing concrete. Their plotting and
planning was conceived to be dangerous and some of them were
given death sentences.

In the first Mandalay Conspiracy case, Harnam Singh was
sentenced to death along with forfeiture of property. Chet Ram
was sentenced to transportation for life.[44]

In the second conspiracy case, Mujtafa Hussain, Amar Singh,
Ram Rakha and Ali Ahmed Siddiqui were sentenced to life. Amar
Singh and Jodh Singh turned approvers.[45]

The Isemonger report stated:

> Lack of organization, bad leadership and incapacity to maintain
> secrecy, and the Indian habit of regarding the ideal as the fact
> accomplished no doubt played their part in defeating the
> revolutionaries, but on more than one occasion their designs were
> dangerously near fulfillment and disaster was narrowly averted.[46]

The Siam–Burma scheme turned out to be a dud just like the
other plans of the Ghadarites. With the arrest of all the leaders of
the Siam–Burma scheme, heightened police patrolling along the
borders, confiscation of all revolutionary literature and the press,
things turned stagnant in Siam as well. This opportunity to create
Ghadar too was quelled.

Chapter 31

The Plans of the Berlin Indian Independence Committee

In October 1911, Friedrich von Bernhandi's new book, *Germany and the Next War* addressed the possibility of an alliance between Indian revolutionaries and Germany.[1] This book was translated into English and feted by the freedom fighters. It was the sign they had been waiting for! Yes, Germany was willing to help and come to their rescue.

Dhirendranath Sarkar, a Bengali revolutionary, had gone to Germany from America and conveyed the news to the Yugantar group in Bengal that help was in the offing.[2] The Germans, it appeared, were ready to collaborate and that brought much cheer in the Bengali revolutionary camp.

The German office had sought out Indian revolutionaries residing in Europe for active participation in this cause. Lajpat Rai had refused. Krishnavarma too had said no because he had signed a pact with the British government that he would not indulge in anti-British activities. Madam Cama too had been lying low. Virendranath Chattopadhyaya turned out to be the leader and became the liaison between the Indians and the Germans.[3]

Virendranath Chattopadhyaya had gone to London in 1903 to become a lawyer and had become closely associated with the

India House Movement. He turned out to be the undisputed leader of the Indian Independence Committee in Berlin.[4]

Chatto soon came in contact with an expert in Middle Eastern affairs in the German Foreign Office, Max von Oppenheim. A series of meetings had set the ball rolling for the Indian–German alliance. The pith of these meetings turned into a concrete plan called the Zimmerman Plan.[5] This plan involved an attack on India through Afghanistan, seeking Turkish help to destabilize the Indian government. It also involved a mission towards Turkey that would be headed by Wilhelm Wassmus for providing arms to Indian revolutionaries.

Har Dayal, while in Switzerland, was invited by Barakatullah to come to Berlin and join the Berlin Indian Independence Committee.[6] Out of America and out of his prominent role in active Ghadar affairs, he had agreed and travelled to Berlin.

In Istanbul, Enver Pasha, the influential military commander, had proposed to Germany that revolutionary movements should be organized in North Africa and Afghanistan by sending suitable German officers to those places. Before that, the Turko-German agreement had been signed on 2 August 1914.[7] Germany was confident of its success and a senior official had remarked, 'Attempts must be made to raise the revolt in India in case England becomes our opponent. The same should be done to Egypt. Persia too should be encouraged to take this opportunity to get rid of the Russian yoke and to proceed together with Turks.'[8]

Under these circumstances, a first post was established by Berlin in Istanbul to take advantage of the Pan-Islamic movement.[9] Firstly, it wanted to circulate its propaganda amongst Indian soldiers and pilgrims and secondly it wanted to invade India through the north-west.

Har Dayal had his own grandiose plans that went like this:

We have 10,000 Hindus in the United States and Canada and about 1,00,000 in China and the Malay Peninsula. The nationalist

paper *Ghadar* circulates among them, and they are just now very
much agitated over the Indian question in British Columbia. At
least a few thousand will respond to an appeal for immediate action,
if German support is assured. They should focus all attention on
Kashmir because its mountainous terrain and relative dearth of
military personnel would favour the insurgents.[10]

He was sent to Constantinople to take this mission forward but
when he reached there, he could not be at the helm of affairs.
His friend and host Abu Sayid was bringing out *Jehan-i-Islam* and
Har Dayal wanted to be in charge of the paper. He also wanted to
rename the office of the Berlin Indian Independence Committee
in Istanbul as 'Bureau du Parti National Hindou' but this was also
not done.[11]

Har Dayal had grievances against the Germans for not listening
to him, making him wait and not giving him the importance he
thought he deserved. He returned to Switzerland a disappointed
man, leaving his mission in the lurch. And though Har Dayal
retreated, the Germans did send some missions towards the west
to fulfil its objectives.[12]

The first mission, which comprised fifteen men under the
leadership of Wilhelm Wassmus, marched on 6 September 1914
from Berlin towards Turkey.[13] Iran (Persia) was of considerable
strategic importance in those days because no mission could
be accomplished without passing through its territory since
ammunition could not be air-dropped and militia were not hi-
tech in techniques involving wireless radio. But Iran was wary
of the British and Russians and no bonhomie existed between
them and the Turks. But they did have a sympathetic side for the
Germans. The Democratic Party and some tribal chiefs had a soft
corner for the Germans.

While Wassmus carried on with his men, the Ghadar Party
too wanted to make use of this situation and send their men
towards the west. Acting on the advice of Captain Kadri Bey,

the Ottoman minister of defence, Pandurang Khankhoje and a friend left for Turkey in September 1914. They eventually joined the Wassmus mission, which was held up at Haleb due to some issues. Accompanying Khankhoje were two Indians, Agashe and Promothonath Datta.[14]

Wassmus along with his team and Indians reached the south-west of Iran. Their aim was to destroy British oil installations and weaken local tribes that had been friendly towards the British government. Though the mission was sent with Turkish support, most of the Turkish officials were suspicious of the Germans because for them it meant an increased influence of Germany over Iran, which was not acceptable to them. While Wassmus with his men was in Iran, the First World War came unannounced. It was the Turks and Germans versus the Russians and Britain. The British government wanted to protect its interests in the Persian Gulf. It captured Basra and landed its troops at Fao and Shatt al-Arab. It was then that the caliphate called for jihad and for all Muslims to unite against infidel Christians.[15]

But Pan-Islamism could at best be described as a sentiment for there were differences and distrust among Muslim nations, making it difficult for them to accommodate each other. Petty differences and fear of the other invading their territory kept them on tenterhooks. If Iran detested the Turks and the British and yet loved the Germans, some Arab nations were dependent on Britain for its support while Egypt was anti-British. Some Muslims were sceptical of the infidel Germans and Hindus (the Ghadar Party) who were considered idolaters. Such a dichotomy in beliefs and values never let them get united.[16]

While the Wassmus mission was in progress and had not reached its destination, the second mission was sent by the Germans under Captain Oskar von Niedermeyer towards Kabul. The aim of this mission was to persuade the Emir of Afghanistan to invade India. This mission proceeded on 5 December 1914 from Istanbul, meeting the Wassmus mission at Haleb. From Haleb, both the missions proceeded towards Baghdad and reached there in the middle of January 1915.[17]

Once there, the missions ventured on their individual ways from Baghdad. The Niedermeyer mission left for Tehran and the Wassmus mission with Khankhoje and others went towards Bushire. Khankhoje had taken the boat along with his Indian counterparts to distribute seditious leaflets amongst the Indian soldiers. On the way, they had been caught by a pro-British tribal chief, Haidar Khan, but Wassmus and some people of his team and of course, the Indians, managed to escape. They did manage to reach Shiraz but most of the literature was left behind in British possession.

Wassmus and the escaped men were put up in Shiraz for many months. The Germans had an upper hand in the war at that time and most of the officials in Iran were actively backing the Germans. It was speculated that it was the right time to position an attack on India through the deserts of Kemran and Mekran. At the same time, Barakatullah and Raja Mahendra Pratap were moving towards Kabul for another mission.

The Germans were unstoppable. One after the other, men were being commissioned and missions were being dispatched with vigour. Another mission by the name of Zugmayer-Griesinger arrived in Kerman on 4 July 1914.[18] Here they started training the local military men, taking help from local tribal chiefs and officials.

In January 1916, Khankhoje and some men had gone to Bampur to negotiate with Bahram Khan Bampuri, a local tribal chief who had pledged allegiance to their cause. But they did not know that their plans to cause mischief in the west had been laid bare. Britain had started its own counter-operations and enlisted many of the tribal chiefs in that area, including Bampur. When Khankhoje and his men went to meet Bampuri, they were attacked but they managed to escape.

Khankhoje was captured while making an escape towards the west while the others were captured at Niriz.[19] Only a few could make it back to Shiraz. Soon, German influence began receding in Iran. In August 1915, Bushire was occupied by British troops for a short time. The Russian Army had advanced within 25 miles of Tehran and later occupied Kashan. British forces organized a new unit, South Persian Rifles, and set out for Kerman. Another British expedition had started from Baluchistan towards Southeast Iran. The local chiefs were now with the British. Iran, the strategic location, had been conquered. No offensive could be launched from there. The promise of freedom had given way to tears of disappointment and desolation.

Chapter 32

The Tale of Three Ships

The Berlin Indian Independence Committee in collaboration with the German consulate had made plans to send arms to the Bengali revolutionaries. The plans were outlined by an independent council that consisted of Rash Behari Bose, Bhagwan Singh and Abani Mukherjee, a Bengali revolutionary. Jatin Mukherjee was overseeing operations in Bengal to receive the arms. The Bengal group of revolutionaries were ambitious and the fact that the Berlin Indian Independence Committee was dominated by Bengalis helped them to make plans to receive reinforcements from outside. The plan was to blow up three main railway lines leading up to Bengal with the ammunition received. The Madras line near Balasore was to be cut. The arms were to be stored at Balasore, Calcutta and Hatia. The railway line coming from Nagpur was to be attacked near Chakradharpur and the railway bridge on the Ajay river was to be blown up.

Once America took sides in the war, it was getting difficult for revolutionaries to carry on with their activities since it was no longer a safe haven for operations against the British. America had brought into practice neutrality laws in 1916 that forbade people living in the country from carrying out any covert operations against Britain, which was its war-time partner and an ally. So, the plan to send ammunition could not be initiated from American soil.

A schooner, *Annie Larsen*, and an oil tanker, *Maverick*, were called to carry ammunition in international waters to avoid any suspicion.

Annie Larsen was to take the cargo to Socorro Islands, 400 miles off the coast of Mexico, where it was supposed to wait for *Maverick* and deposit the arms on it. The Bengali Yugantar group had set up a fake import business in Calcutta called Harry & Sons to serve as a front to receive the arms. A German firm, Jebson & Company in San Francisco, had agreed to send the arms that were purchased by the German arms dealer, Krupp.[1] Twenty thousand Spanish-American War vintage US army rifles with cartridges, 200 to 300 automatic pistols, or in other words, 'eleven wagon loads of arms and ammunition' were to be loaded on *Annie Larsen* in San Diego.[2]

Maverick was a repurposed tanker purchased from the Standard Oil Tanker Company.[3] Ghadarites too had a role to play in this scheme. Ghadar men were to board *Maverick* disguised as Persian waiters, with loads of Ghadar literature.[4]

They were to deposit the arms acquired from *Annie Larsen* into the oil tanks of *Maverick*, which was to sail to Batavia (present-day Jakarta) where it would be met by the German consul and a member of the Berlin Indian Independence Committee, M.N. Roy.

This was the plan laid out for both the ships, but it did not materialize the way it was pictured by all. The meeting of *Annie Larsen* and *Maverick* was crucial, but this did not happen. *Annie Larsen* began its journey from San Pedro in California towards the Socorro Islands and reached its destination sometime in March 1915. *Maverick* was not there and so the crew of *Annie Larsen* decided to wait there for some days. The wait turned from days to weeks but there was no sign of the oil tanker. Apparently, *Maverick* did not get clearance from San Francisco until 22 April 1915 but *Annie Larsen* had exhausted its supplies and had left the islands to refuel on 10 April 1915. So, while *Annie Larsen* had been waiting for *Maverick*, it had not yet left port and when it did, it was way too late. There was no chance of a meeting.

Annie Larsen had sailed towards Acapulco, a city in Mexico, made contact with the German consulate and was told to go back to the islands. The schooner sailed all the way back but by the time it reached the islands, *Maverick* had left the designated place after waiting for many days. They were not meant to meet and the designed plan never took any concrete shape.

In late June, *Annie Larsen* finally lowered its sails at Aberdeen, Washington. It was searched and the cargo was confiscated by the American authorities. *Maverick,* according to plan, proceeded towards Batavia without arms, but with Ghadarites and the literature. The five multicultural Persian waiters aboard not only aroused suspicion but also curiosity with the names they had taken up—Jehangir, Khan, Dutt, Deen and Shamsher.[5] The ship was intercepted by Dutch destroyers and was found to be empty. Two of the occupants returned to San Francisco and the others were arrested in Bangkok and sent to Singapore.[6]

Meanwhile M.N. Roy had left for Dili on the island of Timor, which was chosen as the point for delivery, assuming that everything had gone well and arms were on the way but there was no sign of *Maverick*.[7] The ammunition was to be distributed into three segments at Calcutta, Hatita and Balasore.[8] The plan was to blow up bridges, attack Fort William where the disaffected 14th Rajput Rifles were to side with them and take control of the arsenals in the city.

The third vessel, a schooner that tried to sail towards India with the same aim of delivering ammunition was *Henry S.* It had sailed from Manila in the Philippines to Pontianak (Indonesia) on the west coast of Borneo on 14 July 1915. The engine broke down and it could only reach Paleleh in the north of Sulawesi (Indonesia). On the ship were German agents Wehde and Boehm, who had to reach Thailand to train Ghadarites. There was ammunition on board that was seized by customs though the German agents managed to escape. Boehm was arrested in Singapore when he was going from Batavia to Shanghai. Wehde reached Manila, escaping arrest.

Chapter 33

The Hindu–German Conspiracy Trial

When the US pledged support to Britain in World War I in April 1917, the activities of the Ghadarites and their association with Germany came under the scrutiny of American intelligence services. The British had been mounting pressure on the American government for the arrest of Indians indulging in revolutionary activities with German help on its soil. Until February 1917, President Woodrow Wilson maintained that Indian revolutionaries were not violating its neutrality laws.[1] On 6 April 1917, when the US officially became a British ally, a formal warrant for the arrest of Indian revolutionaries was issued.

Ram Chandra, managing the affairs of the Yugantar Ashram in California along with C.K. Chakrabarty, the man who was overseeing the operations of the Berlin Indian Independence Committee, were amongst the first ones to be arrested. By 8 April, most of the Indian revolutionaries, along with German agents and consulate officials Franz Bopp, E.H. von Schack and Wilhelm von Brincken were arrested.[2]

The Hindu–German Conspiracy Trial commenced on 12 November 1917 in San Francisco and lasted till April 1918. It proved to be a lengthy trial involving men, money and a considerable amount of time. The charges levelled included violation of neutrality laws, being hostile towards any country or dominion with which the United States was at peace and carrying on a military expedition against such country.[3]

Over 200 secret agents and witnesses deposed before the district court of California in this trial.[4] The trial cost the British government $2.5 million and the American government $4,50,000.[5]

Fifteen Ghadarites were sentenced to terms ranging from a few months to years. Taraknath Das was sentenced for twenty-two months, Santokh Singh for twenty-one and Bhagwan Singh for eighteen. They were told that after the completion of their sentence if they dabbled in anti-British activities they would be deported and this meant death or life imprisonment. This trial marked the end of the Ghadar Movement in America. But the most vile end was that of Ram Chandra, the editor of *Ghadar*, to whom the reins were handed over by Har Dayal.

Back in 1914 when the Ghadar Movement was in full force, a number of people left the US for Punjab, keeping their possessions with the Yugantar Ashram. With all the main leaders gone, it was only Ram Chandra who remained at the helm. He had taken the voluntary contributions of the people and many land deeds were in his possession. But these did not amount to too much money. The Ghadar Party was in need of money, but voluntary contributions did not raise its stake. It was the association with Germany, with the trumpet of war, that money came pouring in from the German government into the cause of Indian revolution.

German help came through the Berlin Indian Independence Committee that mainly comprised educated Bengalis while the Ghadar Party had a different set-up. Most of the men had a peasant background and they had come to the US looking for work. Things were never amicable between the committee and the party but at some point, they did cooperate for they had a common aim. The India Committee began to have a larger say in matters of importance with the arrival of Heramba Lal Gupta in

New York.[6] This was the time when New York and Washington, D.C. became important centres of Indo-German cooperation. San Francisco was eclipsed. The committee had taken the Ghadar Party into confidence and the purse strings of German help opened up for them.

The monthly expenditure of the Ghadar Party was only $600 while Germans were giving them something between $1000 and $1200. And most of the staff living on the premises of Yugantar Ashram were receiving a meagre two-dollar salary.[7] Money matters were transparent when Kanshi Ram was the treasurer and the party was headed by selfless men like Bhakna, who never wanted anything for themselves but dedicated themselves to the cause. But then, the rules of the game changed.

The party had two separate funds for work. One for the local expenses raised through subscriptions and the other was the national fund. German money flowed into the national fund, which soon became the personal fund of Ram Chandra.[8] He began treating the party like his own fiefdom, was answerable to no one and started splurging money on his flamboyant lifestyle. The simple and pious values of Ghadar men who left everything for the sake of the party did not touch the core of his heart. They suspected him of amassing wealth and building his personal property from party money. They thought he was keeping the German money in different safe deposits to avoid arousing suspicion and complaints against him had started doing the rounds.

The meeting of the Ghadar Party in December 1915 was the final showdown when members openly demanded his resignation, but Ram Chandra refused to step down. The Khalsa Diwan Societies of Victoria and Stockton too condemned the activities of Ram Chandra. At the party meeting on 13 August 1916, the inevitable split happened. The Ghadar Party, which had united people of different identities and religions into one thread, itself broke apart.

Bhagwan Singh became the leader of the majority faction and Ram Chandra, who had the support of some Muslim leaders, led the other. Instead of one *Ghadar*, two newspapers claiming themselves to be the original *Ghadar* started being published. The rival papers indulged in mudslinging and calling each other names.

Ram Chandra still retained possession of the Ghadar buildings at 1017 Valencia Street and 5 Wood Street, San Francisco.

On 23 April 1918, Ram Singh, who belonged to the Bhagwan Singh faction, had smuggled a pistol inside the courtroom. The pistol was tucked in his turban. Ram Chandra had not agreed to many counts of charges framed against him and might have gone free with a sentence less lenient. This was not acceptable to Ram Singh.[9]

As Ram Chandra was about to testify, Ram Singh shot him multiple times in the chest. A US marshal shot Ram Singh the next moment.

It was a sad day in the history of the Ghadar Party.

Chapter 34

The Silk Letters Plot

After the failure of the revolts in Punjab and Bengal, the Germans focused their attention on the pan-Islamic movement and Afghanistan to make inroads into Indian territory.[1]

The German Foreign Office wanted to persuade the Emir of Afghanistan to attack India at an opportune moment and Indian revolutionaries too were interested in reaching Kabul for they thought it would be easy for them to contact their counterparts in India from there and send a cache of arms as well.[2]

Barakatullah wrote to Har Dayal about his willingness to go to Kabul via Turkey as did Raja Mahendra Pratap to the German Foreign Office about his willingness to accompany Barakatullah. Their proposal was welcomed and accepted by the German Foreign Office.[3]

Mahendra Pratap was a landlord hailing from Hathras in Aligarh district in UP. A philanthropist, he had opened some schools in his home district. Associated with the Congress Party, he had left for Switzerland after the outbreak of war. He had met Har Dayal and Chatto and was brought to Berlin in February 1915. The German council was impressed with his lineage and personality and he was made a part of the mission. They were confident that the raja would have an impact on the princely states and once the revolution was aroused, they would side with him.

They were also confident that Indian princes and Muslims would side with Barakatullah for his Muslim antecedents.[4] Mahendra Pratap was designated as the official head of this mission while Werner Otto von Hentig from the German Foreign Office was in charge of the actual affairs.[5] The mission was christened the Hentig–Pratap mission.

The mission left Berlin on 9 April 1915 and arrived in Kabul from Constantinople in the beginning of October 1915 after a long and arduous journey. It was joined in Persia by another German mission group.[6] Har Dayal accompanied them till Istanbul as representative of the Berlin Indian Independence Committee.

Meanwhile, Muslim revolutionaries within India were exploring the possibility of contacting tribesmen across the western frontier who were rebellious by nature and hated the British.[7] The North-Western Frontier Province was home to mujahideen, men who wore their religion on their sleeves. Saiyid Ahmed Shah was the founder of this colony. He belonged to the Wahabi sect in Rae Bareli in Oudh, a Sunni Muslim sect who believed in the principles of Abdul Wahab.

The mujahideens regarded India ruled by the British government as the *dar-ul-harb,* the land of the enemy—a land that was not governed by Muslims and was unfit for Muslims to live in. This community had always preached jihad, the fight against the infidels. Saiyid Ahmed had begun his life as a soldier. He was indoctrinated into Wahabi doctrines and after his visit to Mecca, he went to India and gained a following.

Under the influence of the preachings of the mujahideen, fifteen students from Lahore left for Kabul to be part of the Muslim regime.[8] They were under the impression that a war would be waged on India by the Muslim rulers. They got a rude shock when, instead of a warm welcome, they were arrested and put in detention. The Muslims in the Indian populace were led to believe that a war was in the making and this time it was going to be the Ottoman Empire with help of Afghan rulers coming to free them from the clutches of the British Empire. Not only the ordinary Muslims but the leaders too had been trying to vouch for the munificence of the world Muslim community.

Maulana Obeidullah Sindi, a religious teacher belonging to Saharanpur, had converted from Sikhism and was a believer of Pan-Islamism. He had crossed the North-West Frontier in August 1915 along with his three companions, Abdulla, Fateh Muhammad and Muhammad Ali. Abul Kalam Azad was another Indian who had embraced Pan-Islamism and propagated war against the British. He had taken out Pan-Islamist newspapers and societies between 1912 to 1916. He had close ties with Bengal's Yugantar group and was also instrumental in the establishment of a training school for revolutionary youths in Calcutta.

While Obeidullah was sketching schemes in Kabul, the Hentig-Pratap mission on reaching Kabul got a welcoming reception. King Habibullah was curious but said he could not collaborate with the German plans. As a result, the Germans left in disgrace but the members of the Ghadar group stayed put.

The Germans, before exiting from this mission, helped the formation of the provisional government of India, *Hakumate-e-Muvaqate-e-Hind* in Kabul.[9]

Raja Mahendra Pratap designated himself as the President, Mohammed Barakatullah as prime minister and Maulana Obeidullah as home minister.[10]

This provisional government wanted to garner the support of the world leaders against the British. They sent letters to the Governor of Turkestan and the Czar of Russia. They wanted Russia to break its treaty relations with Britain, and get its help in waging a war against Britain.[11]

Raja Mahendra Pratap came up with innovative ideas to spread his message. He engraved the message on real gold plates and sent several of them to the rulers of princely states. These messages were written in faultless Urdu, presented in an immaculate fashion and signed by Imperial Chancellor Theobald von Bethmann-Hollweg.

The provisional government contacted the Turkish military government as well. The governor of Hejaz was willing to cooperate as he declared jihad and also helped in distribution of the copies of the same in Indian military quarters. This jihadi message was called the Ghalibnama for it was written by Ghalib Pasha, the Turkish military governor.

The provisional government wanted to form an alliance with the Turkish government. Obeidullah addressed a letter to his old friend, Mahmud Hassan, a Sunni Muslim scholar, on this account. This letter was written on a silk cloth and was hidden in the lining of the messenger's coat.

This document on silk spoke about the German-Turkish mission to Kabul, the establishment of the provisional government of India, the presence of runaway students and the circulation of the Ghalibnama. It also spoke of *Al-Janud-Al-Rabbania*s, meaning the Army of God or the Troops of Liberation or the Islamic Salvation Army.[12] This was supposed to be the union among Islamic kings. The President would have the title of General or Al Qaid and the centre was to be Medina. The secondary centres had to be established in Istanbul, Tehran and Kabul and the third-level centres in countries like India, which were under the control of the British, the infidels as they were called.

A cover letter was written to Sheikh Abdur Rahim, the diplomatic representative of the Turkish government, which was sent along with a plan written on silk.

This plot came to light when the messenger was caught along with his four companions by the British. Ghalib Pasha had become a prisoner of war. The war was never waged from Kabul and neither from the North-West Frontier Province. The plans had been leaked, making the British government conscious of the great Muslim attack that never happened.

Chapter 35

An Imprisoned Life

The 321 islands located in the Bay of Bengal around 600 miles away from the mainland comprise the Andaman and Nicobar Islands.[1]

The islands consist of the Andaman group of islands and the Nicobar group of islands. To the southern end of Nicobar stands Indira Point, the southernmost point of the Indian nation.

The Great Andamanese, the Jarawas, the Sentinelese and the Onge tribes are the original occupants of the Andaman group of islands while the Nicobarese and Shompens reside in the Nicobar group of islands.[2]

Nothing much was known about the Andamans before the British occupation of India. French Jesuits who went there in 1711 to incorporate the local people into the mainstream were unsuccessful in their efforts. In 1778, the government of Austria initiated the construction of a fort on these islands that never saw completion.[3]

Soon, British ships began becoming the target of attacks by islanders. The ships were being looted, their men killed or left marooned on the islands. The stranded would eventually be lost to life in the wake of diseases and inclement weather. It became important for the British to occupy these islands to safeguard the lives of its men from these perils.

Along with them, the British brought the concept of a penal settlement, punishment in exile. The first penal settlement was established in 1787 at Fort Marlborough in Benkoelen in Sumatra island, which was later moved to Penang. A penal settlement was set up in the Andamans in 1789, withdrawn in 1796 and again resuscitated in the coming years.[4] Indian convicts were sent to clear these islands and Ross Island was proposed to be the headquarters. The penal settlement occupied the Ross, Chatham and Viper islands.

When initially established, the primary aim of these islands was to ensure that the convicts carried out their sentences in a disciplined way. The prisoners were made to clear jungles for the construction of buildings. They were made to work for nine hours with a pay of one anna and nine paise for food to manage themselves.[5] The climate was humid, the temperatures high and the work exacting. The conditions on the Andamans were inclement for survival. The monsoon months in the islands brought plentiful rain. The months from May to October were especially detrimental for the health of prisoners, for it poured. The wet climate of the region presented conditions for mosquitoes to thrive in abundance. Diseases like diarrhoea, tuberculosis and malaria ruled the roost. Prisoners survived if they were strong enough to overcome the influx of these diseases, which were as common as fever, cough or cold in any other part of the country. If the diseases were not enough to bog the prisoners down, the leeches would surely suck the blood out of their body. The Andamans was not an easy place to be! All this led to a high rate of mortality amongst the convicts.

Along with the men came the women prisoners, who were kept in a female jail, a large enclosure of separate sleeping wards and work sheds. They could be employed for domestic work after spending five years in the settlement and were also eligible for marriage.[6]

The plan to construct the Cellular Jail was laid out in 1890 on the recommendations of the Lyall and Lethbridge Committee.[7] A unique structure with a strong foundation and a firm outlay, the Cellular Jail was completed in 1906.[8] Before its construction, the convicts were housed in barracks in Port Blair, Ross Island and Viper Island. The prison was supposed to be punitive and humiliating, even more dreadful than a hangman's noose. It was not an ordinary prison. It was designed to create fear and horror in the minds of those who would be brought here to serve their sentences.

There were a total of 690 cells and each cell was thirteen and a half feet by seven feet.[9] Every cell was guarded by a door made of iron bars, and there was a small veranda at the front of each cell, about four feet wide. The minuscule space meant that you could only step out and be ushered to fall into a line when instructed. Each cell had a small ventilator, three feet by one and a half feet. There were no windows. The front of every wing faced the back of the other. The design of the jail was designed to minimize interaction between the convicts.

Every wing contained workshops where men were made to do different tasks. It also contained sheds for bathing and toilets. Fresh water was always in scarce supply.

The First Ones to Arrive

The mutiny of 1857 shook the British to the core. Men were arrested in large numbers and could not be accommodated in Indian jails. These were the first prisoners to be sent to the Cellular Jail. Later, ordinary convicts with a jail term ranging from three months to two years were also sent there.[10]

Long before the arrival of the Ghadarites in the Cellular Jail, the concept of sending political prisoners there had evolved. The Bengali revolutionaries arrived in 1909. The instructions to officials of the Cellular Jail were strict and stringent. These men were to be put to hard labour and were not allowed to talk to each other. They were not to be regarded as ordinary convicts.

They were to be called prisoners of the nation and had to be dealt with harshly.

Hoti Lal Verma and Babu Ram Hari, editors of the *Swarajya* weekly of Allahabad, were the first amongst the political prisoners.[11] Barindra Kumar Ghosh, the younger brother of Aurobindo Ghosh, the much-acclaimed Bengali freedom fighter, too joined them.[12] Born in England, Barindra had returned to India to join the Dacca Anushilan Samiti.[13] Ganesh Savarkar, brother of V.D. Savarkar, who stood trial for the Nasik Conspiracy case, was sentenced to a jail term and sent to the Andamans.

Some of the men amongst the first arrivals suffered terribly on account of prison conditions. Indu Bhusan Roy was the first political prisoner to hang himself.

Ullaskar Dutt went into delirium and was given electric shocks that affected his mental health. Later on, he was shifted out where he was able to recover partially but his mental health remained fragile. He even tried to attempt suicide.[14]

It was into such a scenario that the Ghadar revolutionaries were dispatched to serve their sentences.

Chapter 36

The Arrival of the Ghadarites at the Cellular Jail

The activities initiated by Ghadarites in 1915 and their mass arrests in various conspiracy cases shook the government to the core. They were deeply apprehensive of this new breed of revolutionaries who came from foreign lands, were fearless and prepared to die and whose presence in the state was disaffecting people.

The presence of Ghadarites in Punjab jails was a threat to the government. Even when jailbound, they would serve as a constant reminder to people to rise and revolt. Banishing these dauntless spirits to a jail far away was the convenient way to cut the link connecting them to the masses. This meant reducing the risk of a future revolution and putting on hold the making of future valorous men. Their exile to the Andamans removed them from the scene, thus relieving the government of the difficult task of monitoring them. It created a scare in the minds of those who were witness to this transportation.[1]

The men implicated in the Lahore Conspiracy cases, the Supplementary Lahore Conspiracy cases and Mandalay Conspiracy cases were all given severe punishments. The convicts were divided into groups of four or five and lodged in the jails of Multan, Rawalpindi, Dhariwal and Delhi.

A jailbreak was planned by Jawala Singh in Rawalpindi Jail with the help of ordinary convicts. The plan was to blow up the jail superintendent and the staff, thus making way for an escape. The plan was ultimately unsuccessful when one of the convicts spilled the beans. The officials did a search and recovered gunpowder from the jail premises.

An escape attempt by Ghadarites was made at Multan Jail as well. The treatment meted out to them in jail was terrible. They had revolted when they were asked to remove their turbans and wear the mandatory cap that was part of the jail attire.

The British government wanted to send the Ghadarites far away to break their contact with those with whom they were hobnobbing in the jails. They were instigating other convicts to become a part of their plans and the government could not afford another uprising in the jails of Punjab. The first lot of Ghadarites was packed off on a ship setting sail from Calcutta, *Maharaja*, to the Andamans on 7 December 1915.[2]

Once in the Andamans, the Ghadarites did not settle down into a life of compliance and obedience. They were determined to fight for their rights. To begin with, they were determined that they would not work on the *kohlu*, oil mill, for it was meant for animals and they believed that they ought to be given the respect a human being deserved. They had also decided that they would do jail tasks with complete honesty but would not surrender to the unreasonable demands of the jailer and neither would they let anyone else suffer oppression in jail.

There are a number of documented instances of Ghadarites bravely standing up to the jailer and the guards and risking more punishment, but seeking to be treated with dignity.

Parmanand Jhansi, a young Ghadarite, on his arrival, was assigned the task of pounding dried coconut shells despite the rule that the first fifteen days were to be taken as the quarantine period and the amount of work done by a convict was not to be taken into account. When abused by the jailer, Barrie, he slapped him, leading to a punishment of thirty lashes for this indiscretion with a penalty of less food and six months in solitary confinement with fetters on his body.

Bhan Singh had flown all the way from Canada and could speak and understand only English. One day, when he was standing in line to submit and show his day's work, an unprovoked comment laced with racism by the English guard infuriated him, to which he retorted back. When Bhan Singh was presented before the jailer, he was sentenced to solitary confinement of six months along with reduced rations and manacles. When he refused to be manacled, he was given a severe beating.

Master Chattar Singh, influenced by the Ghadarites, decided to kill the principal of Khalsa College, Amritsar, for toeing the British line. He ended up killing the wrong man and was sentenced to the Andamans with the Ghadarites. He was deeply disturbed by the atrocities committed by the jailer and his men. He slapped Superintendent Murray when the latter came for the weekly check-up of the prisoners' weight. Before this incident, Chattar Singh had refused to mow the lawn on Sundays for the particular day was designated for rest, cleaning the cell and washing clothes. Chattar Singh was put into a very small cage in which he could not get up or lie down. His physical condition deteriorated over a period of time.

Sher Singh was once jokingly asked by the jail doctor if he could drink the ten *seers* of milk in a bucket. In reply, the more than six feet tall Ghadarite lifted the bucket and touched his lips along one corner. When he brought it down, there was not a single drop of milk in it. In another incident, he drank the bottle of oil smuggled by Triloki Nath Chakorvorty from the oil-grinding room to save him. He again demonstrated his courage when he devoured finely powdered glass with his food to get himself bloody diarrhoea for he wanted to get admitted to the hospital where Bhai Prithvi Singh was admitted because of his adamant stance of not having food and water.

Before the arrival of the Ghadarites in the Cellular Jail, prisoners had found a peaceful way to protest against the high-handedness of the jailer and his team. The arrival of the Ghadarites only intensified this means of protest—through a strike.

The first strike was undertaken for the cause of Parmanand Jhansi, who had defied the jailer. This strike went on for six months, as long as the sentence of Jhansi lasted.[3] After the death of Baba Bhan Singh, a strike was initially started by Bhakna, later joined by Baba Prithvi Singh, who stopped wearing clothes and using a blanket at night. The cold floors of the cell used to make his body numb but that did not deter him and he carried on. He had lost weight, but he would not relent. About 100 prisoners (Ghadarites and others) joined this strike. This went on to be the longest strike in the history of the Cellular Jail.[4]

A strike was started by the Ghadarites in support of a prisoner named Gujarati Mal, confined to solitary confinement for six months along with fetters. Mal had retorted back when he was subjected to racial abuse. Bhakna once again came to the forefront when he started the strike for Chattar Singh, who was put in a small cage after he slapped the superintendent.

Ram Rakha Bali started an indefinite fast unto death for the refusal of jail authorities to let him put on his *janeu,* the sacred thread. He was bodily lifted and taken to hospital on 1 June 1919. A feeding pipe used to give him milk led to aspiration in his lungs, ending in his death. He was never accorded a proper funeral as his dead body was thrown into the sea.[5] The jailer feared a revolt but he could not suppress the news of another death. The death of Ram Rakha led to a change in the jail rules. The prisoners who came after him were allowed to retain their religious symbols, including the janeu.

Eight Ghadarites attained martyrdom in the Andamans: Pandit Ram Rakha, Bhan Singh Sunet, Rulia Singh Sarabha, Kehar Singh Marhana, Roda Singh Rode, Swar Natha Singh Dhotian, Nand Singh and Surain Singh.[6]

The political prisoners in the Andamans changed the way the jail was run through their incessant struggle against the treatment they had to endure. Their long, unending strikes made an impact and the reverberations could be felt in the entire country. There was deep anger and mistrust towards the government after the fate of political prisoners was discussed in Indian newspapers.

The transformation of the Cellular Jail began when the Indian Jails Committee created by the Indian government investigated jail administration in the country, including on the penal settlement of the Andamans from April 1919.[7] The committee came to Port Blair in 1920 to hear out the grievances of the prisoners. Later in 1920, a general amnesty was declared for political prisoners.[8]

The government transferred the jailer and the superintendent. The domination of warders, *jamadars* and *tandeels* (minor officials) came to an end as they were stripped of their rank.

The prisoners from Punjab, Bengal and Gujarat were the first ones to be released in 1920. Next came the turn of prisoners of the Manicktola, Lahore and Benares Conspiracy cases. Bhakna and his comrades were repatriated to Madras Jail for Punjab was still not ready to accommodate these patriots in 1921.

Thirty prisoners, along with the Savarkar brothers, were not to be released in the first lot but were repatriated sometime later in the year. But this culminated in the abolition of the Andamans as a penal settlement.

The Andaman and Nicobar Islands were occupied by Japan during the Second World War from 1942 to 1945. The Cellular Jail was turned into a national memorial on 11 February 1979.[9]

Chapter 37

Ghadar After 1918

The raging wave of revolts that had threatened to embroil Punjab in its angst had not succeeded. Attempts to threaten the government from Siam (Thailand) too yielded nothing concrete. But it did cost the precious lives of patriotic men who might not have achieved what they wanted to, but left an indelible mark on the consciousness of a nation.

After the closure of the Cellular Jail and the release of the prisoners, those who remained unscathed started building a new life for themselves. The situation in Canada and the USA had completely altered by now.

In Canada, there was no base of the party left after 1918. Many Punjabi immigrants had left the country in the wake of the recession that accompanied the war. Before the recession, there were around 2500 Indians in Canada. After the war, the number stood at around 951.[1] These people were now more concerned with making a living. Grand ideas did not inspire them any more though they took pride in their Ghadar lineage.

In the USA, the Ghadar Party still had a base, but it stood on shaky turf. The Hindu German Conspiracy trial had made the future of Indians in America insecure. If there was animosity against these migrants who were snatching the jobs of the local people and getting prosperous because of their hard work, it magnified with this case, which was splashed in the papers. Indians were not wanted, disrespected and seen as traitors. By the end of 1919, the sentences of many important leaders were coming to an end. Prominent among them were Gopal Singh, Bhagwan Singh, Santokh Singh and Taraknath Das. Das was an American citizen and did not come under the ambit of deportation, but the others were going to be deported.

The war had ended and so had the uncertainty. The American government had sided with the British. But the laws of the land gave Ghadarites an equal opportunity to build their front along with their Irish counterparts and American radicals. Trade unions too supported the cause of Indians against deportation. They joined hands and on 6 March 1919, an association called Friends of Freedom for India was formed. The association began running a weekly paper called *India News Services*.[2]

American papers and magazines that sympathized with Indians worked tooth and nail to highlight the cause. America was, after all, the land of asylum. The press campaign generated considerable publicity in favour of the anti-deportation movement and attracted writers, educationists, editors and the liberal progressive factions of America.

The worker class too was mobilized. Boiler workers, iron ship builders and helpers and the International Ladies Garment Workers' Union passed resolutions on 1 August 1919 opposing deportation. With help from all quarters, the warrants in Hindu cases were finally cancelled. The judgment passed on 19 May 1920 cancelled the deportation proceedings against Santokh Singh, Gopal Singh and Bhagwan Singh.

The three of them had been convicted in a federal court of having violated the neutrality laws of the US by engaging in a conspiracy to activate a military enterprise against the British government in India. They were subsequently arrested on immigration warrants on the grounds that their case came under the clause in immigration law dealing with moral turpitude. The solicitor of the department held that violation of the neutrality laws did not involve moral turpitude and consequently, the warrants were cancelled.

While this turned out to be a big moment of reckoning for the Ghadar Party, the life of Sikhs on the West Coast was difficult after the end of the war. New restrictions were being imposed on them. Their numbers dwindled in America as well after 1918. There were around 7000 Indians in the US towards the end of 1917, but by the end of 1946, these numbers were down to only 1500.[3]

They had no right to vote, neither could they become American citizens (only whites of European descent were eligible for American citizenship), the properties they had bought with their hard work were confiscated and they were subjected to even more racial abuse.

Since the immigrants could not become American citizens, their lands came under the Alien Land Law enacted in 1913, which was amended in 1920. They were considered to be undesirable aliens and were shown to have 2099 acres of land in their possession, which most of them gave on lease.

Another major issue concerning the Sikh population of America was illegal immigration. Harsher measures were being imposed on the entry of Indians from Mexico. Existing Indian immigrants started making money on new entrants by charging them for their entry. These new entrants were now exploited by their own people as they could not get legal employment anywhere. They became a source of revenue for the immigrants. This created animosity within the Sikh community in America, leading to a string of murders.[4]

Within the Sikh community, there was a lack of suitable women of marriageable age in the US. They could not have sought a mate from their own community because the laws forbade them from bringing in any new immigrants. They married poor Mexican women and made their homes, bringing up children of mixed heritage.[5]

The fate of Ghadar under such circumstances, when immigrants were fighting their own battles for survival in Canada and America, was bleak.

Santokh Singh and others revived the party once they were free men on American soil after finishing their terms. The Ghadar Party by then had almost collapsed, the headquarters at Yugantar Ashram was deserted and the rank and file were in disarray. Germany had lost the war and Russia had revolted against the Czar. It was a different world after 1918.

Santokh Singh was attracted by communist ideas and saw in them the promise of being able to change the Ghadar narrative. He later moved to Russia. But before that happened, he once again assembled the broken shards of Ghadar and tried to make something coherent out of it.

The first initiative of the rejuvenated Ghadar Party was to launch a monthly review named *Independent Hindustan* in English in September 1920. Surendra Nath Kar was invited to be the editor. He too was an accused in the Hindu German Conspiracy Case. The journal was published till the end of 1921. The writings were pro-Soviet, written with caution for now they were under the watch of the US government. Kar moved to New York and then to Berlin where he died in 1922.[6] Another eight-page journal was started by the Ghadar Party in August 1923 called the *United States of India.*

In Russia, a military school had been established in Tashkent to train men to march through Afghanistan to free India. Santokh Singh followed his calling and left for Moscow in August 1922 along with another Ghadar leader, Rattan Singh. After his departure, there was no credible leader to manage the affairs of the Ghadar Party.

Santokh Singh and Rattan Singh later left for Punjab through Afghanistan where they met Udham Singh Kasel and Gurmukh Singh, who were in charge of Indian activities in Kabul. A decision was taken about the formation of a party for the spread of the Marxism-Leninism school of thought in Punjab. Santokh Singh proceeded to Punjab while Rattan Singh stayed put in Kabul.

Santokh Singh formed the Kirti Kisan Party in Punjab in 1926.[7] A weekly magazine *Kirti* was started from Amritsar in Punjabi and Urdu. Many Ghadar men aligned with the Kirti party. The legendary Bhagat Singh, the nephew of Ajit Singh, used to contribute articles for this magazine.

Eventually the Ghadar Party in Punjab split. The mild faction backed the Kirti group and the more aggressive faction backed the Babbar Akali movement. The Babbar Akali faction consisted of those Ghadarites who wanted to avenge the death sentences and imprisonments of their peers by killing the informers, the spies and all those who were responsible for failure of Ghadar in 1915.

The Kirti Party was inclined towards communism and had shades of socialism in it. Santokh Singh died in 1927 due to tuberculosis.

In the mid-1930s, many Left groups began working with the Congress Socialist Party. Financial help to the tune of $1400 was provided to the Congress Party in 1931 by the Ghadar Party's dominant faction in the US. Gandhi had managed to strike an emotional chord. The remaining comrades of the Ghadar Party in the US were not interested in Ghadar any more. The gurdwara in Stockton and the Khalsa Diwan Society in the US began holding public lectures dealing with educational, political, cultural and social aspects. The party was non-existent in Canada too.

In Punjab, the men from the Kirti group contested elections on Congress Party tickets in 1937 and managed a clean sweep. Later, they took control of the Shiromani Gurdwara Prabhandhak Committee.

In July 1946, the historic Luce-Cellar Bill was passed in the American assembly, which made Indians eligible for American citizenship.

After India attained its long-sought freedom in 1947, the Ghadar Party was officially disbanded. The very purpose for which it came into existence had been achieved. The premises on 5, Wood Street was handed over to the government of India.

An era of revolution came to an end. Ghadar finally ceased to exist as a name. But the spirit of Ghadar stayed alive. A living, breathing, formless, fiery spirit with a heart and soul.

Chapter 38

The Ghadar Movement: Wins and Losses

The Ghadar Movement was unique in its conception. It was born in foreign lands, in the minds of men who were far removed from their countrymen, who had to face the brunt of being called slaves because their motherland was chained. These men, when they resided in their country, did not quite feel the pressure of being under the British yoke. But once they crossed the seven seas, their outlook changed completely. An awareness that was lacking earlier cropped up in their minds and it was made fertile with the vicissitudes of life. This awareness brought with it stirrings of a revolution that they desired to bring on with all their might.

The kind of passion Ghadar created in its believers was unique. They wanted to sacrifice it all without caring about anything. They did not think about their families and love of home and hearth. This lack of caution and a daredevil attitude was the hallmark of the Ghadarites.

They did not care about a good life and money, for which they initially came to Canada and America. They did not go there to start a revolution that would take away everything. They came to make a better life for themselves and their loved ones. The cost of this life was separation from wives who would wait for an eternity watching the door for shadows unformed. There were children left behind who would wait for their fathers to carry them on their shoulders, who would wake up every morning without knowing life with the protection of a father and slept every night with uncertainties looming large in their minds about the existence of one. Then there were children who were born when their fathers were away. They encountered them through the fragmented memories recounted by their mothers.

The families of Ghadarites bore the brunt of loss multiple times. Firstly, when the men left; secondly, when they came back but did not want to be tied to their homes any more; and thirdly, when they eventually sacrificed their physical form. They were either hanged or transported for life to the Cellular Jail. Some survived but some lost their lives in jail. The families faced the ire of the British government. Their properties were confiscated and these families were left with nothing but scars and loneliness. They walked with the shadow of fear lurking around them for the rest of their lives.

The Ghadar Movement was not only unique in its conception but also in its composition. The men who were being divided on narrow religious lines in their own country had gone beyond the divisiveness and inculcated themselves into one freedom struggle. Though the majority of Ghadarites were Sikhs from Punjab, yet the Ghadar cannot be called a purely Sikh movement. It was a secular movement and its adherents did not believe in caste, creed or religion. Religion for them was a private matter and any show of religious symbols was discouraged.

Har Dayal was a Hindu, so was Kanshi Ram and Rash Behari Bose, Barakatullah was a Muslim and so was Rehmat Ali. Ghadar was a united Hindu, Muslim and Sikh front. It was the amalgamation of all religions. Sohan Singh Bhakna once said, 'We were not Sikhs or Punjabis. Our religion was patriotism.'[1]

While most of the Ghadar men belonged to Punjab, there were Marathi-speakers and Bengalis and people from other states as well. Vishnu Ganesh Pingle, Savarkar, Tilak and many other fighters embodied the quintessential spirit of Ghadar. So were the men from Bengal like Bose, who not only participated in Ghadar but led the men. Sanyal was from Benares while Chenchiah belonged to Andhra Pradesh. Ghadar did not belong to one province or one state. It belonged to the entire country. Their mode of greeting was '*Bande Mataram*' and not the traditional Punjabi '*Sat Sri Akal*'.

The Ghadarites were way ahead of their time. The divine light in them, which let them rise above caste and communal divides, created a consciousness they brought back home. They not only came back with the message of freedom but also the sermons of equality and brotherhood.

Mangu Ram,[2] who was considered to be a low caste in Punjab, joined the Ghadar Party and was astonished that his caste was irrelevant to these men. He slept and ate with the others in Yugantar Ashram and was given the $2 allowance along with the others. He was treated the same. He had suffered abuse back home but in San Francisco, he was one amongst equals. And this man brought the message of Ghadar back home. He became the messiah of the untouchability movement here.[3] On coming back to India, he opened a school in Mugowal village in Hoshiarpur where the first official meeting of the Ad Dharm movement, of which he was officially elected as the president, was held on 11 and 12 June 1926.[4] He later proposed the idea of the Ad Dharm religion and community, which he believed was the original egalitarian society of the country.[5]

The Ghadar Movement might not have brought the longed-for freedom, but it did become a precursor of national independence. Ghadarites, when they came back, created a national consciousness. They brought an awareness that it was shameful to be called slaves and to be citizens of an enslaved nation was a curse.

The Ghadar Movement bridged the gap between the educated and uneducated. There were men who were highly learned and there were the unlettered Punjabi peasants. It emphasized the power of the vernacular. The newspaper *Ghadar* was brought out in Urdu and Punjabi and other languages too. Had the newspaper been published in English, it might not have achieved its purpose.

The booklet *Ghadar Dian Goonjan* was published in Punjabi. It allowed the men to let their raging turmoil take the shape of words. Their expression, though crude, came from their hearts and its essence spread like wildfire, which was understood by those enduring the same hardships.

The Ghadar Movement failed because of many reasons. Ghadarites were high on enthusiasm and failed to see that their opponent was far stronger than them in terms of men and ammunition. They underestimated the power of the empire. They thought that the people of Punjab were awakened and were only in need of a slight momentum to overthrow the empire. But apart from a handful of revolutionaries, the people in Punjab believed themselves to be taken care of by the empire. The consciousness that was brought by the Ghadarites did not prove to be fruitful enough for a mass revolt.

The Ghadarites lacked men and ammunition. German help was too little, too late. The dacoities committed by Ghadar men gave a bad name to their cause. In many cases, the villagers sided with the police, regarding the revolutionaries to be ordinary dacoits. The lack of a leader and a proper organizational set-up did not let them come up with effective strategies to thwart the government's attempts to muzzle them. The informers, stooges and those who accepted clemency spilled the beans about the plans of revolutionaries and acted as deterrents.

The Ghadar Movement, along with its wins and losses, remains an important part of the Indian freedom struggle. When we talk of independence, Ghadar deserves a mention along with other movements before or after, which, like Ghadar, did not get us independence.

Freedom is a collective world that encompasses the struggle, endurance and grit of a nation. People at different times, in different eras, played their part, lost their lives and left an indelible mark on the face of a nation yet to be formed.

Annexure 1: What Became of Those Who Fought

Ajit Singh

He was arrested in 1945 by the Allied forces and, after being kept in an Italian camp for two months, was transported to Germany where he was kept in a prison in very poor conditions. His health deteriorated in the dark and dingy cell. In 1946, his supporters started making parleys with the Indian government for his release, but the government showed no interest. They claimed that Ajit Singh was no longer an Indian but a Brazilian citizen after rescinding his Indian citizenship.

Ajit Singh was extended a cordial welcome by the Indian Workers Association in Britain on 2 January 1947. He stayed in London for about two months to recuperate as by then he was suffering from tuberculosis. When the issues obstructing his homecoming were resolved, he was able to reach Karachi in March 1947. He died in the early morning the day India attained its freedom in August 1947, in Dalhousie. The news of the Partition had left him heartbroken.

Sohan Singh Bhakna

He was released from the Cellular Jail in 1921 and first transferred to Madras Central Jail and later to Coimbatore, where he lent support to the Moplah agitation. Finally, in 1928, he was transferred to

Lahore Central Jail. He met Bhagat Singh in this jail, with whom he used to have long chats. Bhakna joined the hunger strike initiated by Bhagat Singh for the rights of political prisoners.

Bhakna was released from jail in 1930 after he launched his fifth hunger strike for his release and emerged victorious. He got a rousing reception in Amritsar from various organizations and parties.

He later aligned himself with the Kirti Kisan Party, was instrumental in the making of the Desh Bhagat Yadgar Committee and remained politically active. He died on 20 December 1968 in Amritsar.

Taraknath Das

He was sentenced to twenty-two months in prison in the Hindu German Conspiracy case. After his release, he stayed away from any kind of political activity and concentrated on a literary career. He remained associated with many universities and academic institutions. He returned to India for a while and died in New York on 22 December 1952.

Pandurang Khankhoje

Disappointed with the Indian freedom struggle and back from his western quest, he remained in Germany for some time and later moved to Mexico. He started working on the new varieties of corn and also took up work on bettering maize cultivation. He discovered that maize seed had low resistance to frost and drought by establishing an experimental field in the National School of Agriculture. His most important work was the development of hybrid corn. He got a Mexican passport, married and settled down in Mexico. He came to India in April 1949 with his family, his wife and two daughters and left in 1951. He came back in 1956 never to go back this time. He died on 18 January 1967 in Nagpur.

Mohammad Barakatullah

The Afghan government withdrew its support to the provisional government of India and the mission lost its steam. From Afghanistan, he moved to Russia where he remained till 1922. He went to Berlin and began working with Chatto. His association with Ghadar remained strong during these times. He came back to New York City and later moved to California where he passed away because of diabetes on 20 September 1927.

Raja Mahendra Pratap

For some time, he became an Afghan citizen and spent the war years travelling the world. He returned to India and settled in Dehradun. He was elected to the Indian Parliament in 1957. He died in 1979.

Jawala Singh Thatthiyan

He was sentenced in the First Lahore Conspiracy case with Bhakna and other comrades. He was released from the Cellular Jail in 1921 and died in a road accident in 1938.

Har Dayal

He came back from Germany and severed all contacts with the Berlin Committee. There was a complete change in his viewpoint as he distanced himself from the Indian revolutionary movement and moved to Sweden. He did want to come back to England and sought amnesty but it was not granted to him. On 18 March 1924, he again requested for amnesty, without which it was hazardous for him to travel to England. The fear of arrest loomed large over his head. In 1927, he reiterated his request and the British government allowed him into England. But the Indian government was still not ready to let him into the country, especially Punjab province, which considered him highly volatile material.

In 1934, he wrote the famed book, *Hints of Self-Culture*, which was widely acclaimed. Meanwhile Har Dayal came back to England and remained there for eight years, completing his PhD degree. In 1935, he requested the Indian government to allow him a passage. A favourable decision was made and on 25 October 1938, he was given permission to visit India. He died in March 1939. He was only fifty-four years old.

Bhai Parmanand

He was released from the Cellular Jail in 1920. He started a new movement in the fold of the Arya Samaj, the Jat Pat Todak Mandal (Society for the Abolition of Caste System). He died in December 1947.

Virendranath Chattopadhyaya

He led the Indian Independence Committee in Berlin for many years. After the war, he moved to Moscow and authored many books. He died in Russia on 2 December 1942.

Shachindernath Sanyal

After his release from the Cellular Jail in 1920–21, he became active in revolutionary activities and formed the Hindustan Republican Association with Ram Prasad Bismil and Jogesh Chatterjee. He was involved in the Kakori robbery in 1925 for which he was arrested and released in 1937. He died in 1942 before India achieved her independence.

Annexure 2: The Role of Women in the Ghadar Movement

When the men of the family play the role of valiant revolutionaries, women who might have been their wives, mothers, sisters, aunts, friends are conveniently forgotten. Mothers who gave birth to them, wives who stood like a rock and never dithered, sisters who comforted them in moments of their weakness, aunts who prayed for their goodwill, friends who could have been their neighbours, supporters, cheerleaders for their cause. These faceless, nameless women, who took on the reins of the household when the men gave up everything for the nation, remained their pillars of strength in the darkest of times and yet history chooses to conveniently forget them and their role is never acknowledged.

One such dogged woman was Gulab Kaur, who with her indomitable will and steely determination, created a space for herself amongst the bravest by defying the odds and breaking the manacles of the invisible chains of patriarchy.

Born in 1890 in Bakhshiwala village in Sangrur district of Punjab,[1] she was the only child of a hard-working peasant family. She learnt Gurmukhi from the village *mahant*, a religious preacher.

She was married to Bachitar Singh of Jakhepal village, who had migrated to Manila to earn money because of his meagre landholding back home.[2] A citizen of the Philippines in those days was regarded as a non-citizen US national.[3] The Indians, when faced with restrictions in the US, moved to Manila where, after a stay of six months, they would get their citizenship papers made and further move to the US in a circuitous fashion.[4]

The Ghadar Party had a branch in Manila whose head was Maulvi Hafiz Abdullah. After the tragic incident of the *Komagata Maru* when a call was given to Ghadarites to move back to India, the *jathas* (groups) coming from Canada and America halted at Manila and Singapore. The men would give rousing speeches and encourage others to join them. Bachitar Singh too was roused by the speeches and had his name enrolled to board the ship. When the time came to act, he backed out. Gulab Kaur was furious at this treachery of her husband.[5]

Bibi Gulab Kaur was a daring woman who did the unthinkable and unspeakable in those times. She left her husband and went with the other men without bothering that she might be castigated for her action. Whenever the ships came to a halt, Gulab Kaur would get down and humiliate men who would not have the confidence to follow in the footsteps of the Ghadarites. She played a pivotal role in the Ghadar Movement and the activities of the Ghadarites.

She used to be instrumental in getting them rooms by posing as their wife when it was difficult for single men to get them. Her house in Lahore was the first meeting point of revolutionaries where on their arrival, they were given instructions for further plans. After the failure of the Ghadar Movement, Gulab Kaur played a crucial role in the Babbar Akali Lehar.

Later, she moved to Hoshiarpur and made Kotla Naudh Singh village her abode. She remained active and preached in the nearby villages about the lost cause of Ghadar. She was arrested by the police and kept under surveillance after her release. She died in 1941, a few years before India achieved its independence.[6]

Another revolutionary who played an important role in the Ghadar revolution was Agnes Smedley. She was born on 23 February 1892 in Missouri, USA, in a family of modest means.[7]

The big break in her life arrived when she was accepted as a student for a three-month course in the University of California.[8] She crossed paths with Har Dayal in 1912 when he came for a lecture at the university and was greatly impressed with his ideals. Later, she was asked to leave the premises of the university for her socialist ideas, which conflicted with the ideas of the university.[9] She kept in contact with Ram Chandra and Bhagwan Singh, who were instrumental in inducting her into the Ghadar Movement.[10]

She participated in a secret meeting at Yugantar Ashram in November 1917 along with Bhagwan Singh and Taraknath Das, where they passed the resolution for the creation of a provisional government of India. She came in contact with other Indian revolutionaries, such as Virendranath Chattopadhyaya, with whom she ended up staying in a partnership for a brief time.

Agnes Smedley not only created sympathy for the Indian cause amongst the American public, she also formed an association called Friends of Freedom of India in 1920 in collaboration with the Indian revolutionaries. This association fought against the deportation of the Indians who were named and sentenced to different terms in the Hindu German Conspiracy cases.[11]

Later, Agnes moved to China and associated herself with the Chinese revolutionaries and played an important role in the Chinese freedom struggle. She was also associated with a Soviet espionage ring based in Shanghai.[12]

She contributed articles to *Kirti* magazine from Germany, Moscow and China, even though she disassociated herself from the active Indian freedom struggle. She died in China on 6 May 1950 and was buried there.

Annexure 3: The Legacy of Ghadar:
Desh Bhagat Martyrs' Memorial

Desh Bhagat Yadgar Hall (Desh Bhagat Martyrs' Memorial) in Jalandhar was built by the Ghadarites to keep the memory of Ghadar alive. Before the construction of the memorial, the initiative of helping the families of Ghadarites financially was taken up by Baba Wasakha Singh, who conceived the idea of the Desh Bhagat Family Welfare Society in 1920.

After the success of this society, they came up with the idea of constructing a building that would house literature related to the Ghadar Party. After the partition of the country, Jalandhar was chosen as the place to build the memorial because of its central location and it being the hub of the Punjabi press.

Desh Bhagat Yadgar Hall came into existence in 1964. Bhakna had sold a part of his family land, Baba Amar Singh Sandhwan contributed generously and land for the memorial was bought from Rai Bahadur Badri at a discounted rate. A board was constituted in 1936 headed by Baba Wasakha Singh and Bhagat Singh Bilga as the secretary for the construction of this memorial. Desh Bhagat Pariwar Sahayak Committee (Desh Bhagat Family Welfare Society) was renamed Desh Bhagat Yadgar Committee as well.

For the construction of the memorial, Baba Bhuja Singh went to Birmingham, London, Coventry and Wolverhampton, and held a collection drive among Punjabis living abroad. Help also poured in from non-resident Indians living in Canada and America.

Along with the construction of the memorial, two publications came into existence: *People's Path* and *Desh Bhagat Yadaan* (Desh Bhagat memories). The publication of both the journals continued till 1964, after which they were stopped because of a lack of financial assistance. For the construction of the memorial, architect R.V. Sharma refused his compensation, engineers worked without any salary and there was no dearth of men who came to help and supervise.

After several rounds of construction, the memorial now comprises an auditorium, an exhibition hall, a library, a public hall for social gatherings, a theatre for meetings and formal gatherings and residential rooms along with the committee office. The ground floor has an exhibition hall measuring 90 feet by 60 feet and has around 212 portraits of Indian patriots and Ghadarites.

After the construction of the memorial, the party started working on the spread of the message of Ghadar and its relevance. The silver jubilee of the Ghadar Party was the first such event, held in 1964. Surviving revolutionaries from Bengal, Bihar, Uttar Pradesh, Delhi, Kerala, Andhra Pradesh and Madras congregated on 31 March 1964 to commemorate this event.

The second event to be conducted was 'Mela Ghadari Babiyan Da' (A Fair of Ghadarites) in 1992. Baba Bhagat Singh Bilga hoisted the Ghadar flag at this event, which was dedicated to the memory of Vishnu Ganesh Pingle. People from all over Punjab thronged the fair with vigour. The huge numbers of students were an indication that the cause of Ghadar still resonated in many hearts. These were the times when terrorism in Punjab was at its peak. Despite the volatile atmosphere, the mela turned out to be a huge success, drawing cheers from all quarters.

The fair became an annual affair attracting artists, poets, literary people and thinkers from all over Punjab. In the coming years, it incorporated literary symposiums, elocution competitions, quizzes based on the Ghadar Movement and freedom struggle, and plays. The fair stretched to five days and the audiences were enthralled by this shower of arts and culture soaked in the spirit of Ghadar. This annual fair is held every first week of November.

The Bhai Santokh Singh Kirti Library is a very important part of this memorial. The library not only has books and journals about Ghadar, it has in its possession rare handwritten manuscripts of Ghadarites and recorded interviews. It holds a wide range of material on the Indian revolutionary movement. It has accumulated a complete set of old journals like *Kirti* and *Akali te Pardesi*, along with issues of *Ghadar* and *Yugantar*.

Acknowledgements

I am grateful to Col Vikas Bali for sharing valuable material on Pandit Ram Rakha Bali. My senior, Dr Ranjiv Bali, was more than helpful in providing insights about this lesser-known Ghadarite.

To Amarjit Chandan for giving me a home, Chandanwari (my family and I spent a significant part of my life living as tenants in his ancestral house in Nakodar) and for guiding me in the right direction. Prof. Harish Puri, whose book on Ghadar became a milestone for me and to which I referred time and again. Prof. Chaman Lal was gracious enough to answer my every text and kept sending his valuable articles. Navtej Sarna gave his kind permission to reproduce the text translation from *Zafarnama*. Heartfelt gratitude to Amandeep Sandhu for his kind words.

Chiranji Lal Kangniwal for his enthusiasm and encouragement when he came to know that I was writing about Ghadar. Desh Bhagar Yadgar Hall Library for lending me books. Gurdeep Singh for his help in getting me photocopies of some rare books.

My editor, Karthik Venkatesh, for showing me the way when I was completely lost. For making me go all over the text again to do the citation part, for turning the rustic manuscript into a legible book, for trusting and reposing faith in me. Thanks a lot, Karthik!

Ralph Rebello, my copy editor, who went through the manuscript with a fine-tooth comb and made it so much better. Thank you!

Swastika Biswas for the amazing cover.

A big thank you to Naina Tripathi and the marketing team at Penguin for their whole-hearted support.

My literary agent and mentor, Preeti Gill, for acceptance and warmth. For opening the doors of her heart and home to me. The sessions curated by her cultural initiative Majha House, with authors of diverse backgrounds, have not only enriched my soul but ushered me towards hope and optimism.

For my parents, who live in Canada and were there for me via phone calls throughout the writing of this book. They recorded my daily progress, and the beginning and end of each chapter. I lost my dad before the publication of this book. He was a constant source of motivation, encouraging me, pushing me a little further, to work hard and stay on my quest on those days when I was about to give up. He was my biggest cheerleader, wanting me to excel in whatever I did. The love and support of my mom is invaluable to me. My elder brother Roopi has always been so proud of me.

For my beloved daughter, Sehar, and my husband, Varun.

Notes

Chapter 1: Bombay, Bengal and Punjab Under British Rule

1 Khushwant Singh, *A History of the Sikhs, Volume II: 1839–2004* (Oxford University Press, 1999), p. 3.

2 Ibid., p. 81.

3 S.A.T. Rowlatt, 'Sedition Committee Report 1918' (Superintendent Government Printing, Calcutta), p. 2, sourced from Desh Bhagat Yadgar Hall Library, Jalandhar.

4 Ibid.

5 Ibid., p. 18.

6 Ibid.

7 Bipan Chandra, Mridula Mukherjee, Aditya Mukherjee, Sucheta Mahajan, K.N. Panikkar, *India's Struggle for Independence* (Gurgaon, Penguin Books, 1989), p. 127.

8 Ibid.

9 Khushwant Singh, *A History of the Sikhs, Volume II: 1839–2004*, p. 128.

10 Nirode Kumar Barooah, *India and the Official Germany 1886–1914*, European University papers (Frankfurt: Peter Lang/Bern: M. Herbert Lang, 1977), p. 113.

11 Dr Sasha Tandon, *Social History of Plague in Colonial Punjab* (New Delhi, Writers Choice, 2015), p. 19.

12 Ibid., p. 25.

13 Ibid., p. 29.

14 Khushwant Singh, *A History of the Sikhs, Volume II: 1839–2004*, p. 155.

15 Ibid.

16 Ibid.

17 Dr Savinder Pal, *Sardar Ajit Singh: The Exiled Revolutionary* (Chandigarh: Unistar Books Pvt. Ltd, 2019), p. 24.

18 Maia Ramnath, *Haj to Utopia* (University of California Press, 2011), p. 18.

19 Dr Savinder Pal, *Sardar Ajit Singh: The Exiled Revolutionary*, p. 28.

20 Ibid., p. 29.

21 Ibid., p. 31.

22 Sufi Amba Prasad was born in Moradabad in 1858, with a handicap—one of his hands was rendered lifeless since his birth. This handicap did not act as a hindrance to his feisty spirit. He was well versed in Urdu, Persian and English and wrote scathing articles against the Empire. In 1890, he came up with a weekly magazine, *Jame-ul-Uloom*, from Moradabad. A votary of Hindu-Muslim unity, he was imprisoned for six years because of his seditious activities. After this jail term, he came to Punjab and started writing for the newspaper, *Indian*, being published by Lala Pindi Das. This is where he met Ajit Singh and they became comrades in arms. In 1917, he was killed fighting against the British in Shiraz, Iran, where he had exiled himself to escape arrest.

Chapter 2: The Exodus Abroad: Emigration of Punjab Peasantry

1 Harish K. Puri, *Ghadar Movement: Ideology, Organisation, Strategy* (Amritsar: Guru Nanak Dev University, 2013), p. 27.

2 Ibid., p. 17.

3 Sohan Singh Josh, *Hindustan Ghadar Party: A Short History* (Jalandhar: Desh Bhagat Yadgar Committee, 2007), p. 58.

4 Harish K. Puri, *Ghadar Movement: Ideology, Organisation, Strategy*, p. 17.

5 Ibid.

6 Ibid., p. 24.

7 Ibid., p. 27.

8 *Jeewan Sangram: Sohan Singh Bhakna,* ed. Malwinderjit Singh (Barnala: Tarakbharti Parkashan, 2003), p. 13.

9   Ibid., pp. 13–16.
10 Ibid., pp. 16–20.
11 *Sohan Singh Bhakna: Meri Aap-Beeti*, edited and translated from the Urdu by Amarjit Singh Chandan (Copper Coin Publishing, 2014), p. 4.
12 H.S. Dilgir, *Shahid Kanshi Ram*, Shahid Kanshi Ram, Janam Shatabdi Samaroh Committee, Jalandhar, 1982, p. 47.
13 Ibid., pp. 47, 48.
14 Ibid., p. 49.
15 Harish K. Puri, *Ghadar Movement: Ideology, Organisation, Strategy*, p. 17.

Chapter 3: Joining the Army and the Police

1   Harish K. Puri, *Ghadar Movement: Ideology, Organisation, Strategy*, p. 22.
2   Ibid., p. 17.
3   'Saga of a Freedom Fighter's Supreme Sacrifice', *Daily Telegrams*, an interview with Squadron Leader D.K. Bali by Suresh Philip.
4   Ibid.
5   Dr Jaswant Rai, *Kaum Da Sitara: Shahid Babu Harnam Singh* (Chandigarh: Saptrishi Publications, 2019), p. 12.
6   Ibid., p. 53.
7   Ibid., p. 54.
8   Ibid., p. 56.
9   Maia Ramnath, *Haj to Utopia* (University of California Press, 2011), p. 27.
10 Ibid.
11 Ibid.
12 Ibid.
13 Ibid., p. 28.
14 Giani Hira Singh Dard, *Jiwan Desh Bhagat Baba Harnam Singh ji Tundilat* (Jalandhar: Awami Printing Press), p. 3.
15 Ibid., p. 5.
16 Ibid., p. 12.
17 Ibid.

Chapter 4: Revolutionaries in Exile

1   T.R. Sareen, *The Unsung Heroes: Select Documents on Neglected Part of India's Freedom Struggle* (New Delhi: Life Span Publishers and Distributors, 2009), p. 11.

2   Arun Coomer Bose, *Indian Revolutionaries Abroad, 1905-1922: In the Background of International Developments* (Patna: Bharti Bhawan, 1971), p. 15.

3   T.R. Sareen, *The Unsung Heroes: Select Documents on neglected part of India's Freedom Struggle*, pp. 61–63.

4   Ibid., pp. 55–57.

5   Arun Coomer Bose, *Indian Revolutionaries Abroad, 1905-1922: In the Background of International Developments*, p. 16.

6   Ibid., p. 13.

7   Emily C. Brown, *Har Dayal: Hindu Revolutionary and Rationalist* (The Arizona Board of Regents, 1957), p. 23.

8   S.A.T. Rowlatt, 'Sedition Committee Report, 1918', Superintendent Government Printing, Calcutta, p. 5.

9   Arun Coomer Bose, *Indian Revolutionaries Abroad, 1905-1922: In the Background of International Developments*, p. 17.

10 S.A.T. Rowlatt, 'Sedition Committee Report 1918', p. 5.

11 Ibid.

12 Arun Coomer Bose, *Indian Revolutionaries Abroad, 1905-1922: In the Background of International Developments*, p. 262.

13 Ibid.

14 Emily C. Brown, *Har Dayal: Hindu Revolutionary and Rationalist*, p. 29.

15 S.A.T. Rowlatt, 'Sedition Committee Report, 1918', p. 5.

16 Arun Coomer Bose, *Indian Revolutionaries Abroad, 1905-1922: In the Background of International Developments*, p. 21.

17 Ibid.

18 S.A.T. Rowlatt, 'Sedition Committee Report 1918', p. 8.

19 'Madan Lal Dhingra', https://en.wikiquote.org/wiki/Madan_Lal_Dhingra.

20 Arun Coomer Bose, *Indian Revolutionaries Abroad, 1905-1922: In the Background of International Developments*, p. 254.

21 In a letter dated 18 June 1907, Ajit Singh and Lala Lajpat Rai were declared to be causing sedition in Punjab. Lala Lajpat Rai was the proprietor of a paper, *Punjabee*, which was termed seditious. Lala Lajpat Rai's speech at a mass meeting at Lyallpur was declared provocative. It was established that Lala ji was giving Ajit Singh Rs 100 every month from a political fund. Their political allegiance was proved and they were both deported from India.

22 Dr Savinder Pal, *Sardar Ajit Singh: The Exiled Revolutionary* (Chandigarh: Unistar Books Pvt. Ltd, 2019), pp. 30, 31.

23 Emily C. Brown, *Har Dayal: Hindu Revolutionary and Rationalist*, p. 33

24 T.R. Sareen, *The Unsung Heroes: Select Documents on Neglected Part of India's Freedom Struggle*, p. 119.

25 Arun Coomer Bose, *Indian Revolutionaries Abroad, 1905-1922: In the Background of International Developments*, p. 20.

26 Maia Ramnath, *Haj to Utopia* (University of California Press, 2011), p. 25.

27 Ibid., p. 26.

28 Harish K. Puri, *Ghadar Movement: Ideology, Organisation, Strategy* (Amritsar: Guru Nanak Dev University, 2013), p. 22.

29 Arun Coomer Bose, *Indian Revolutionaries Abroad, 1905-1922: In the Background of International Developments*, p. 255.

30 Maia Ramnath, *Haj to Utopia*, p. 28.

31 Arun Coomer Bose, *Indian Revolutionaries Abroad, 1905-1922: In the Background of International Developments*, p. 50.

32 Maia Ramnath, *Haj to Utopia*, p. 28.

33 The Canadian government made its first attempt to restrict immigration from India by placing veiled restrictions and passing an order in council on 8 January 1908:

> The Governor in council may, by proclamation or order, whenever he considers it necessary or expedient, prohibit the landing in Canada of any specified class of immigrants or of any immigrants who have come to Canada otherwise than by continuous journey from the country of which they are natives or citizens and upon through tickets purchased in that country.

This order was meant for Indians because they could not travel directly to Canada. The arrival of SS *Monteagle* in British Columbia in late 1908 led to an uproar as 105 passengers out of the total 200 had not made a continuous journey. Many amongst these were asked to leave the country. This discriminatory order was quashed on 24 March 1908.

34 Arun Coomer Bose, *Indian Revolutionaries Abroad, 1905-1922: In the Background of International Developments*, p. 51.

35 Ibid.

36 Ibid.

37 Ibid.

38 Maia Ramnath, *Haj to Utopia*, p. 29.

39 Ibid.

40 Ibid., p. 27.

41 Ibid.

42 Ibid.

43 Ibid.

44 Ibid.

45 Ibid., p. 28.

46 Ibid., p. 222.

47 Ibid.

48 Ibid.

49 Ibid., p. 223.

50 Ibid.

51 Ibid.

52 Arun Coomer Bose, *Indian Revolutionaries Abroad, 1905-1922: In the Background of International Developments*, p. 68.

53 Ibid., p. 70.

54 Ibid.

55 Savitri Sawhney, *I Shall Never Ask For Pardon: A Memoir of Pandurang Khankhoje* (Penguin Books India, 2008), p. 3.

56 Ibid., p. 6.

57 Ibid., p. 40.

58 Ibid., p. 67–86.

Chapter 5: The Lure of Studying Abroad

1 Suresh Chandra Ghosh, *The History of Education in Modern India, 1757–2012* (New Delhi: Orient Blackswan Private Limited, 1995), p. 6.

2 Ibid., p. 7.
3 Ibid.
4 Ibid.
5 Ibid., p. 8.
6 Ibid., p. 9.
7 Ibid., p. 15.
8 Ibid., p. 24.
9 Ibid., p. 63.
10 Ibid., p. 36.
11 Ibid., p. 45.
12 Ibid.
13 Ibid., pp. 110, 111.
14 Ibid., p. 103.
15 To go abroad was to cross the black waters and public perceptions were against it for fear of losing caste.
16 Suresh Chandra Ghosh, *The History of Education in Modern India, 1757–2012*, p. 104.
17 Myron Phelps, an American lawyer and farmer, offered scholarships to deserving Hindu boys, offering them a place in American universities through his Society for Advancement of India. He founded the Indo-American National Association whose president was Dadabhai Naoroji. It was a joint English, American, Irish and Indian front to fight British high-handedness; Maia Ramnath, *Haj to Utopia* (University of California Press, 2011), p. 104.
18 He immigrated to the United States because of his family facing immense poverty and ended up as a successful potato farmer in Stockton, California. *Gatha Gadariyan di*, ed. Mandeep (Barnala: Randeep Tarakbharti Parkashan, 2013), p. 23.
19 Maia Ramnath, *Haj to Utopia*, p. 20. The Sikh community in Stockton were prosperous and had built for themselves a gurdwara. Jawala Singh had emerged as a leader of the community in Stockton.
20 Emily C. Brown, *Har Dayal: Hindu Revolutionary and Rationalist* (The Arizona Board of Regents, 1957), p. 127.
21 Maia Ramnath, *Haj to Utopia*, p. 20.
22 Ibid., p. 21.
23 Born in Rawalpindi on 2 June 1894, he received his master's degree from Gordon College, Rawalpindi, in English literature and

history. He later joined Khalsa College, Amritsar, as a professor. He joined the Akali Movement and became part of the Gurdwara Sikh reform movement. He resigned from his job later to protest the government taking control of the educational institute; 'Prof Teja Singh, Teacher, Scholar and Translator of Sikh texts', Surender Pal Singh, https://sikhri.org/articles/professor-teja-singh.

24 Ibid.
25 Ibid.
26 Emily C. Brown, *Har Dayal: Hindu Revolutionary and Rationalist*, p. 128.
27 Maia Ramnath, *Haj to Utopia*, p. 21
28 Emily C. Brown, *Har Dayal: Hindu Revolutionary and Rationalist*, p. 128.
29 Chaman Lal, *Ghadar Party Hero, Kartar Singh Sarabha* (National Book Trust of India, 2009), p. 1.
30 Ibid.
31 Ibid., p. 2.
32 D. Chenchiah, *Ghadar Party Reminiscences*, ed. Parminder Singh (Jalandhar: Desh Bhagat Yadgar Committee), p. 9.
33 Ibid.
34 Ibid., p. 17.
35 Ibid., pp. 17–18.
36 Ibid.
37 Ibid., p. 18–19.
38 Ibid., p. 19.
39 *Shahid Kartar Singh Sarabha ate 1915 de Shahid*, ed. Prithvi Raj Kalia (Progressive People's Foundation of Edmonton, Alberta, Canada, 2015), p. 116.
40 Ibid.
41 Ibid.

Chapter 6: The Face of Ghadar: Lala Har Dayal

1 Emily C. Brown, *Har Dayal: Hindu Revolutionary and Rationalist* (The Arizona Board of Regents, 1957), p. 11.
2 Ibid.

3 Ibid.
4 Ibid., p. 13.
5 Ibid.
6 Ibid., p. 14.
7 Ibid.
8 Ibid.
9 Bhai Parmanand, *The Story of My Life*, The Central Hindu Yuvak Sabha, Lahore, 1934, p. 29.
10 Emily C. Brown, *Har Dayal: Hindu Revolutionary and Rationalist*, p. 17.
11 Ibid., p. 18.
12 Ibid.
13 Ibid., p. 19.
14 Ibid.
15 Ibid.
16 Ibid.
17 Ibid., p. 20.
18 Ibid., p. 30.
19 Ibid., pp. 30, 31.
20 Ibid., p. 31.
21 Ibid., p. 20.
22 Lala Lajpat Rai was arrested on 9 May 1907, on the fiftieth anniversary of the 1857 Mutiny and was deported to Mandalay as a pre-emptive measure to avoid disturbance without being charged or tried under the provision of an archaic law.
23 Ibid., p. 33.
24 Ibid., p. 34.
25 Ibid.
26 Ibid., p. 38.
27 Ibid.
28 Ibid., p. 40.
29 Ibid., p. 41.
30 Ibid.
31 Ibid.
32 Ibid.
33 Ibid., p. 45.

34 Ibid., p. 48.
35 Ibid., p. 53.
36 Ibid.
37 Ibid.
38 Ibid., p. 54.
39 Ibid., p. 56.
40 Ibid.
41 Ibid.
42 Bhai Parmanand, *The Story of My Life*, p. 50.
43 Ibid.
44 Emily C. Brown, *Har Dayal: Hindu Revolutionary and Rationalist*, p. 85.
45 Bhai Parmanand, *The Story of My Life*, p. 51.
46 Emily C. Brown, *Har Dayal: Hindu Revolutionary and Rationalist*, p. 91.
47 Ibid., p. 104.
48 Industrial Workers of the World was a labour organization that came into existence in June 1905 in Chicago. It intended to organize workers along the lines of industrial unions rather than on the basis of specialized trade or crafts.
49 Ibid., p. 110.
50 Ibid.
51 Ibid., pp. 112–114.
52 The William Morris Cycle was an organization started by Har Dayal in which one of the members acted as a host and the rest of the members were guests. There was always a particular theme of study or discussion around which the conversation revolved, followed by refreshments. The International Radical Club was the other organization that involved conversations around monthly dinners at San Francisco; T.R. Sareen, *The Unsung Heroes: Select Documents on Neglected Part of India's Freedom Struggle* (New Delhi: Life Span Publishers and Distributors, 2009), p. 42.
53 Ibid., p. 127.
54 Ibid.
55 D. Chenchiah, *Ghadar Party Reminiscences*, ed. Parminder Singh (Jalandhar: Desh Bhagat Yadgar Committee), p. 33.
56 Ibid.

Chapter 7: Racism in Canada and the USA

1   Harish K. Puri, *Ghadar Movement: Ideology, Organisation, Strategy* (Amritsar: Guru Nanak Dev University, 2013), p. 26.
2   Ibid.
3   Ibid., p. 23.
4   Ibid., p. 26.
5   Hugh Johnston, *The Voyage of Komagata Maru* (Vancouver: University of British Columbia Press, 1989), p. 3.
6   Harish K. Puri, *Ghadar Movement: Ideology, Organisation, Strategy*, p. 24.
7   Hugh Johnston, *The Voyage of Komagata Maru*, p. 3.
8   Sohan Singh Josh, *Hindustan Ghadar Party: A Short History* (Jalandhar: Desh Bhagat Yadgar Committee, 2007), p. 90.
9   Gurcharan Singh Sansera, *Ghadar Party Da Itihas* (Jalandhar: Desh Bhagat Yadgar Committee, 1961), p. 43.
10 Earlier, a head tax of $100 was imposed but later, the Chinese Immigration Act was passed in 1903 and the head tax was raised.
11 Harish K. Puri, *Ghadar Movement: Ideology, Organisation, Strategy*, p. 33.
12 The violent riot involved 200 local residents attacking the East Indian population. The cause of conflict was the increased number of turbaned sardars at the Saint John lumber mill who were forcibly put on trains and sent south of Portland.
13 Lord Curzon was the viceroy of India from 1899 to 1905.
14 Lord Minto was the viceroy and governor general of India from 1905 to 1910.
15 Gurcharan Singh Sansera, *Ghadar Party Da Itihas*, p. 44.
16 Khushwant Singh and Satindra Singh, *Ghadar 1915: India's First Armed Rebellion* (R&K Publishing House, 1966), p. 3.
17 Ibid.
18 He was Prime Minister of Canada from 1896 to 1911.
19 Hugh Johnston, *The Voyage of Komagata Maru*, p. 4.
20 Khushwant Singh and Satindra Singh, *Ghadar 1915: India's First Armed Rebellion*, p. 3.
21 Maia Ramnath, *Haj to Utopia* (University of California Press, 2011), p. 22.

22 Khushwant Singh and Satindra Singh, *Ghadar 1915: India's First Armed Rebellion*, p. 2.
23 Sohan Singh Josh, *Hindustan Ghadar Party: A Short History*, p. 103.

Chapter 8: British Honduras as a Potential Destination?

1 Khushwant Singh and Satindra Singh, *Ghadar 1915: India's First Armed Rebellion* (R&K Publishing House, 1966), p. 1.
2 Ibid., p. 3.
3 Hugh Johnston, *The Voyage of Komagata Maru* (Vancouver: University of British Columbia Press, 1989), p. 4.
4 Gurcharan Singh Sansera, *Ghadar Party Da Itihas* (Jalandhar: Desh Bhagat Yadgar Committee, 1961), p. 46.
5 Sohan Singh Josh, *Hindustan Ghadar Party: A Short History* (Jalandhar: Desh Bhagat Yadgar Committee, 2007), p. 91.
6 Hugh Johnston, *The Voyage of Komagata Maru*, p. 6.
7 Ibid., p. 1.
8 Ibid.
9 Ibid.
10 Ibid.
11 Ibid.
12 Ibid.
13 Sohan Singh Josh, *Hindustan Ghadar Party: A Short History*, pp. 92, 93.

Chapter 9: Restrictions on Immigration

1 Khushwant Singh and Satindra Singh, *Ghadar 1915: India's First Armed Rebellion* (R&K Publishing House, 1966), p. 5.
2 Harish K. Puri, *Ghadar Movement: Ideology, Organisation, Strategy* (Amritsar: Guru Nanak Dev University, 2013), p. 37.
3 Ibid., p. 38.
4 This act, originally passed to safeguard the interests of indentured labour, was now used to prevent the Sikhs leaving for Canada. Canada was not listed in the schedule and the Canadian government

did not want immigrants, so it did not pass legislation for their protection; Khushwant Singh and Satindra Singh, *Ghadar 1915: India's First Armed Rebellion,* p. 7.

5 Sohan Singh Josh, *Hindustan Ghadar Party: A Short History* (Jalandhar: Desh Bhagat Yadgar Committee, 2007), p. 61.

6 Ibid., p. 63.

7 Hugh Johnston, *The Voyage of Komagata Maru* (Vancouver: University of British Columbia Press, 1989), p. 4.

8 Ibid.

9 Ibid., p. 17.

10 Khushwant Singh and Satindra Singh, *Ghadar 1915: India's First Armed Rebellion,* p. 12.

11 Harish K. Puri, *Ghadar Movement: Ideology, Organisation, Strategy,* p. 24.

12 Under this act, people from a particular geographical area, which covered most of China, part of Russia, most of Polynesia, all of India, Burma, Siam, the Malay states, Arabia, Afghanistan and the Indian Ocean islands, were barred from emigrating to the US.

Chapter 10: The Struggle to Bring Families to Canada

1 Gurcharan Singh Sansera, *Ghadar Party Da Itihas* (Jalandhar: Desh Bhagat Yadgar Committee, 1961), p. 55.

2 Ibid., p. 54.

3 Ibid.

4 Ibid., p. 55.

5 Ibid.

6 Sohan Singh Josh, *Hindustan Ghadar Party: A Short History* (Jalandhar: Desh Bhagat Yadgar Committee, 2007), pp. 107–18.

7 Gurcharan Singh Sansera, *Ghadar Party Da Itihas,* p. 55.

8 Hugh Johnston, *The Voyage of Komagata Maru* (Vancouver: University of British Columbia Press, 1989), p. 12.

9 Ibid.

10 Ibid.

Chapter 11: The Hindi Association of the Pacific Coast

1   Khushwant Singh and Satindra Singh, *Ghadar 1915: India's First Armed Rebellion* (R&K Publishing House, 1966), p. 12.

2   Ibid.

3   Ibid.

4   Ibid.

5   Hugh Johnston, *The Voyage of Komagata Maru* (Vancouver: University of British Columbia Press, 1989), p. 5.

6   Khushwant Singh and Satindra Singh, *Ghadar 1915: India's First Armed Rebellion*, p. 12.

7   Formed in May 1905 as the Japanese and Korean Exclusion League, it was renamed as the Asian Exclusion League in December 1907 to include Indians and Chinese as well. The aim was to stop the immigration of Asians to the United States.

8   Khushwant Singh and Satindra Singh, *Ghadar 1915: India's First Armed Rebellion*, p. 13.

9   Ibid.

10 Ibid.

11 Harish K. Puri, *Ghadar Movement: Ideology, Organisation, Strategy* (Amritsar: Guru Nanak Dev University, 2013), p. 45.

12 Ibid., p. 43.

13 Lieh Siegel, 'British Columbia: An Untold History', https://bcanuntoldhistory.knowledge.ca/1900/canadas-first-sikh-temple.

14 It was a two-storey building on Second Avenue, Vancouver.

15 Ibid.

16 The Singh Sabha Movement was founded on 1 October 1873 in Amritsar (Singh Sabha of Amritsar) by Thakur Singh Sandhawalia and Giani Gian Singh. The objective of the movement was to revive the teachings of the Sikh gurus, to counter the proselytizing activities of other religions, to produce Sikh literature and to propagate Sikhism.

17 A wave amidst the immigrants to get clean shaven. Harish K. Puri, *Ghadar Movement: Ideology, Organisation, Strategy*, p. 44.

18 Ibid.

19 Khushwant Singh and Satindra Singh, *Ghadar 1915: India's First Armed Rebellion*, p. 14.

20 Hugh Johnston, *The Voyage of Komagata Maru*, p. 6.

21 Ibid.

22 Ibid.

23 Giani Hira Singh Dard, *Jiwan Desh Bhagat Baba Harnam Singh ji Tundilat* (Jalandhar: Awami Printing Press), p. 15.

24 Harish K. Puri, *Ghadar Movement: Ideology, Organisation, Strategy*, p. 45.

25 It was formed with a motive for the social and political regeneration of Hindustanis in Canada.

26 This organization was founded by Ramnath Puri in San Francisco with branches in Astoria and Vancouver. It intended to politically educate Indians on nationalist lines, training in firing guns and the use of other weapons.

27 F.C. Isemonger and J. Slattery, *An Account of the Ghadar Conspiracy* (Meerut: Archana Publications, 2003), p. 9.

28 Gurcharan Singh Sansera, *Ghadar Party Da Itihas* (Jalandhar: Desh Bhagat Yadgar Committee, 1961), p. 91.

29 Ibid.

30 Ibid.

31 Ajit Singh, the uncle of the legendary Bhagat Singh, was deported to Mandalay on 3 June 1907 and was released after six months. He intensified his revolutionary activities after being released in January 1908, but he was under the close watch of the government. His activities made his stay for a long time at one place difficult. Postal authorities were asked to proscribe his letters. He escaped to Persia with Sufi Amba Prasad in August 1909 and started a paper in Persia with the help of Iranian revolutionaries, but he was hounded by the Indian government. He evaded arrest and escaped to Turkey. Later, he moved to Switzerland and got in touch with Har Dayal. Then he moved to France and started living there; Dr Savinder Pal, *Sardar Ajit Singh: The Exiled Revolutionary* (Chandigarh: Unistar Books Pvt. Ltd, 2019), pp. 30–35.

32 Gurcharan Singh Sansera, *Ghadar Party Da Itihas*, p. 91.

33 F.C. Isemonger and J. Slattery, *An Account of the Ghadar Conspiracy*, p. 13.

34 Ibid., p. 14.

35 Maia Ramnath, *Haj to Utopia* (University of California Press, 2011), p. 34.
36 Gurcharan Singh Sansera, *Ghadar Party Da Itihas*, p. 99.
37 Harish K. Puri, *Ghadar Movement: Ideology, Organisation, Strategy*, p. 76.
38 Ibid., pp. 94–95.

Chapter 12: The Launch of the *Ghadar* Newspaper

1 Harish K. Puri, *Ghadar Movement: Ideology, Organisation, Strategy* (Amritsar: Guru Nanak Dev University, 2013), p. 77.
2 F.C. Isemonger and J. Slattery, *An Account of the Ghadar Conspiracy* (Meerut: Archana Publications, 2003), p. 17.
3 Ibid.
4 Ibid.
5 Ibid.
6 Gurcharan Singh Sansera, *Ghadar Party Da Itihas* (Jalandhar: Desh Bhagat Yadgar Committee, 1961), p. 99.
7 Harish K. Puri, *Ghadar Movement: Ideology, Organisation, Strategy*, p. 77.
8 Ibid., p. 85.
9 Sohan Singh Josh, *Hindustan Ghadar Party: A Short History* (Jalandhar: Desh Bhagat Yadgar Committee, 2007), p. 172.
10 Ibid., p. 79.
11 Ibid., p. 80.
12 Ibid.
13 Ibid.
14 Maia Ramnath, *Haj to Utopia* (University of California Press, 2011), p. 39.
15 Ibid., p. 40.
16 Harish K. Puri, *Ghadar Movement: Ideology, Organisation, Strategy*, p. 80.
17 Ibid., p. 82.
18 Khushwant Singh and Satindra Singh, *Ghadar 1915: India's First Armed Rebellion* (R&K Publishing House, 1966), p. 20.
19 F.C. Isemonger and J. Slattery, *An Account of the Ghadar Conspiracy*, p. 20.
20 Ibid.

21 Ibid.
22 Harish K. Puri, *Ghadar Movement: Ideology, Organisation, Strategy*, p. 86.
23 Maia Ramnath, *Haj to Utopia*, p. 41.
24 Ibid., p. 42.
25 Harish K. Puri, *Ghadar Movement: Ideology, Organisation, Strategy*, p. 84.

Chapter 13: The Arrest of Har Dayal

1 Harish K. Puri, *Ghadar Movement: Ideology, Organisation, Strategy* (Amritsar: Guru Nanak Dev University, 2013), p. 153.
2 F.C. Isemonger and J. Slattery, *An Account of the Ghadar Conspiracy* (Meerut: Archana Publications, 2003), p. 35.
3 Emily C. Brown, *Har Dayal: Hindu Revolutionary and Rationalist* (The Arizona Board of Regents, 1957), p. 150.
4 Ibid., p. 155.
5 Ibid.
6 The law stated that any person who had not stayed for a period of three years in the United States was liable to be deported on any account. In the case of Har Dayal, his being a revolutionary and an anarchist were also cited as reasons for his deportation.
7 An organization based in the USA consisting of Britishers and Americans who supported the Russian revolutionaries against the regime of the Czar.
8 Emily C. Brown, *Har Dayal: Hindu Revolutionary and Rationalist*, p. 165.
9 Ibid.
10 Harish K. Puri, *Ghadar Movement: Ideology, Organisation, Strategy*, p. 86.
11 Sohan Singh Josh, *Hindustan Ghadar Party: A Short History* (Jalandhar: Desh Bhagat Yadgar Committee, 2007), p. 169.
12 Master Amir Chand, the prime suspect and a disciple of Har Dayal, had thrown a bomb at the cavalcade of Lord Hardinge on 23 December 1912, which the latter survived. Har Dayal was also incriminated in this case. He knew if he was deported back to India, he would be arrested.

13 Harish K. Puri, *Ghadar Movement: Ideology, Organisation, Strategy*, p. 87.

14 Ibid.

15 Maia Ramnath, *Haj to Utopia* (University of California Press, 2011), p. 47.

Chapter 14: A Ship Called *Komagata Maru*

1   Hugh Johnston, *The Voyage of Komagata Maru* (Vancouver: University of British Columbia Press, 1989), p. 28.

2   Ibid., p. 27.

3   Ibid.

4   Ibid., p. 29.

5   Ibid., p. 25.

6   Ibid., p. 24.

7   Ibid., p. 27.

8   Ibid.

9   Ibid.

10 Ibid., p. 30.

11 Ibid.

12 Ibid., p. 31.

13 Ibid.

14 Ibid.

15 Ibid., p. 32.

16 Ibid., p. 34.

17 Ibid., p. 33.

18 Ibid.

19 Ibid., p. 34.

20 Khushwant Singh and Satindra Singh, *Ghadar 1915: India's First Armed Rebellion* (R&K Publishing House, 1966), p. 24.

21 Ibid.

22 Ibid., p. 25.

23 Ibid., p. 23.

24 Ibid.

25 Hugh Johnston, *The Voyage of Komagata Maru*, p. 19.

26 Sohan Singh Josh, *Hindustan Ghadar Party: A Short History* (Jalandhar: Desh Bhagat Yadgar Committee, 2007), p. 143.
27 Hugh Johnston, *The Voyage of Komagata Maru*, p. 39.
28 He had travelled to San Francisco after meeting the passengers of the *Komagata Maru* after his deportation from Canada in November 1913.
29 Hugh Johnston, *The Voyage of Komagata Maru*, p. 9.
30 Khushwant Singh and Satindra Singh, *Ghadar 1915: India's First Armed Rebellion*, p. 23.
31 Sohan Singh Josh, *Hindustan Ghadar Party: A Short History*, p. 144.
32 Ibid.
33 Ibid.
34 Ibid., p. 151.
35 Hugh Johnston, *The Voyage of Komagata Maru*, p. 45.
36 Sohan Singh Josh, *Hindustan Ghadar Party: A Short History*, p. 157.

Chapter 15: The Long Journey Back Home

1 Hugh Johnston, *The Voyage of Komagata Maru* (Vancouver: University of British Columbia Press, 1989), p. 92.
2 Ibid., p. 94.
3 Ibid., p. 95.
4 Ibid., pp. 92–103.
5 Khushwant Singh and Satindra Singh, *Ghadar 1915: India's First Armed Rebellion* (R&K Publishing House, 1966), pp. 33–34.

Chapter 16: In the Aftermath of the *Komagata Maru*

1 Khushwant Singh and Satindra Singh, *Ghadar 1915: India's First Armed Rebellion* (R&K Publishing House, 1966), p. 29.
2 Hugh Johnston, *The Voyage of Komagata Maru* (Vancouver: University of British Columbia Press, 1989), p. 126.
3 Khushwant Singh and Satindra Singh, *Ghadar 1915: India's First Armed Rebellion* (R&K Publishing House, 1966), p. 29.
4 Hugh Johnston, *The Voyage of Komagata Maru*, p. 126.

5   *Shahid Kartar Singh Sarabha ate 1915 de shahid*, ed. Prithvi Raj
    Kalia, 2015, p. 173.
6   Khushwant Singh and Satindra Singh, *Ghadar 1915: India's First
    Armed Rebellion*, p. 29.
7   *Shahid Kartar Singh Sarabha ate 1915 de shahid*, ed. Prithvi Raj
    Kalia, 2015, p. 175.
8   Khushwant Singh and Satindra Singh, *Ghadar 1915: India's First
    Armed Rebellion*, p. 29.

Chapter 17: The Homecoming of the Warriors

1   Emily C. Brown, *Hindu Revolutionary and Rationalist Lala Har
    Dayal* (The Arizona Board of Regents, 1957), p. 150.
2   Maia Ramnath, *Haj to Utopia* (University of California Press,
    2011), p. 50.
3   Ibid.
4   Ibid.
5   Ibid.
6   Khushwant Singh and Satindra Singh, *Ghadar 1915: India's First
    Armed Rebellion* (R&K Publishing House, 1966), p. 35.
7   Ibid., p. 35–36.
8   *Jeewan Sangram: Baba Sohan Singh Bhakna*, ed. Malwinderjit
    Singh, p. 42.
9   Ibid.
10 *Jeewan Sangram: Baba Sohan Singh Bhakna*, ed. Malwinderjit
    Singh, p. 43.
11 Maia Ramnath, *Haj to Utopia*, p. 51.

Chapter 18: The Reorganization of the Ghadar Party in Punjab

1   Harish K. Puri, *Ghadar Movement: Ideology, Organisation, Strategy*
    (Amritsar: Guru Nanak Dev University, 2013), p. 184.
2   Ibid.
3   Giani Hira Singh Dard, *Jeewan Desh Bhagat Harnam Singh ji
    Tundilat* (Jalandhar: Awami Printing Press), p. 29.

4   Ibid.

5   H.S. Dilgir, *Shahid Kanshi Ram*, Shahid Kanshi Ram, Janam Shatabdi Samaroh Committee, Jalandhar, 1982, p. 103.

6   Ibid., p. 104.

7   F.C. Isemonger and J. Slattery, *An Account of the Ghadar Conspiracy* (Meerut: Archana Publications, 2003), p. 77.

8   Ibid.

9   Chaman Lal, *Ghadar Party Hero Kartar Singh Sarabha*, National Book Trust of India, 2009, p. 18.

10 F.C. Isemonger and J. Slattery, *An Account of the Ghadar Conspiracy*, p. 77.

11 Ibid., p. 78.

12 Ibid., pp. 81–85.

Chapter 19: The Rage at Ferozepur Shahr

1   F.C. Isemonger and J. Slattery, *An Account of the Ghadar Conspiracy* (Meerut: Archana Publications, 2003), p. 79.

2   Ibid.

3   Bhagat Singh Bilga, *Ghadar Lehar De Anfole Varke* (Jalandhar: Punjab Parkashan, 2013), p. 84.

4   Ibid.

5   Shachindernath Sanyal, *Bandi Jeevan* (Atmaram and Sons, 2013), p. 49.

6   Ibid.

Chapter 20: Shachindernath Sanyal in Punjab

1   Shachindernath Sanyal, *Bandi Jeevan* (Atmaram and Sons, 2013), p. 39.

2   Ibid., pp. 51–61.

3   Uma Mukherjee, *Two Great Indian Revolutionaries: Rash Behari Bose and Jyotindra Nath Mukherjee* (Kolkata: Dey's Publishing, 1966), p. 175.

4   Shachindernath Sanyal, *Bandi Jeevan*, p. 80.

5   F.C. Isemonger and J. Slattery, *An Account of the Ghadar Conspiracy* (Meerut: Archana Publications, 2003), p. 76.

Chapter 21: Rash Behari Bose

1 Uma Mukherjee, *Two Great Indian Revolutionaries: Rash Behari Bose and Jyotindra Nath Mukherjee* (Kolkata: Dey's Publishing, 1966), p. 111.
2 Ibid.
3 Ibid., p. 112.
4 Ibid.
5 Ibid., p. 114.
6 Ibid.
7 Ibid.
8 Ibid., p. 117.
9 Ibid.
10 Ibid., p. 118.
11 Ibid., p. 123.
12 Ibid., p. 122.
13 Ibid., p. 119.
14 Emily C. Brown, *Har Dayal: Hindu Revolutionary and Rationalist* (The Arizona Board of Regents, 1957), p. 129.
15 Uma Mukherjee, *Two Great Indian Revolutionaries: Rash Behari Bose and Jyotindra Nath Mukherjee*, p. 123.
16 Ibid., p. 133.
17 Ibid., p. 134.
18 Ibid., p. 137.

Chapter 22: The Dacoities

1 Chaman Lal, *Ghadar Party Hero, Kartar Singh Sarabha*, National Book Trust of India, 2009, p. 25.
2 Ibid., pp. 24, 25.
3 Ibid., p. 25.
4 Ibid.
5 Ibid.
6 Ibid.
7 Ibid.

8   F.C. Isemonger and J. Slattery, *An Account of the Ghadar Conspiracy* (Meerut: Archana Publications, 2003), p. 111.

9   Chaman Lal, *Ghadar Party Hero, Kartar Singh Sarabha*, p. 25.

Chapter 23: The Making of the Berlin Indian Independence Committee

1   Nirode Kumar Barooah, *India and the Official Germany 1886–1914*, European University papers (Frankfurt: Peter Lang/Bern: M. Herbert Lang, 1977), p. 23.

2   The problems in the Indian populace over British rule, the clamour for revolution, the disaffection of the troops made Britain stand on the precipice. India was not only a matter of prestige for them; it was a necessity for them to materialize their expansion plans. They had proliferated their trade not only in India but all over Asia. The British Indian Army that comprised half of Indians (for whom it was a matter of prestige to serve the British) had been sent to Crimea, Persia, China, New Zealand, Abyssinia, Singapore, Hong Kong, Malaya, Malta, Afghanistan, Egypt, Sudan, Burma, Nyasa and Mombasa to guard British interests without the British taxpayer having to pay anything for its maintenance. Russia's geographical location provided an advantage and their expansion plans also made India a bone of contention. Britain saw Japan, its ally in Asia, as a rival wanting a piece of India. And here Britain was, on its own, isolated amidst allies, when it came to India, full of fear of losing it and yet unable to keep the Indian populace under stringent checks.

3   Ibid., p. 60.

4   Ibid., p. 66.

5   Ibid., p. 68.

6   The allies of World War I, which included the United Kingdom, France and Russia, later joined by Italy, Japan and the United States (joined in 1917).

7   The central powers included Germany, Austria-Hungary, Bulgaria and the Ottoman Empire.

8   Ibid., p. 188.

9   Ibid.
10 Ibid., p. 188, 189.
11 Arun Coomer Bose, *Indian Revolutionaries Abroad, 1905-1922* (Patna: Bharti Bhawan, 1971), p. 100.

Chapter 24: The Uprising in Lahore and Ferozepur Cantonments

1   Chaman Lal, *Ghadar Party Hero, Kartar Singh Sarabha,* National Book Trust of India, 2009, p. 26.
2   Maia Ramnath, *Haj to Utopia* (University of California Press, 2011), p. 56.
3   Ibid.
4   Khushwant Singh and Satindra Singh, *Ghadar 1915: India's First Armed Rebellion* (R&K Publishing House, 1966), pp. 42, 43.
5   Ibid., p. 43.
6   Maia Ramnath, *Haj to Utopia*, p. 57.
7   Ibid.
8   Ibid.
9   Ibid.
10 Gurcharan Singh Sansera, *Ghadar Party Da Itihas* (Jalandhar: Desh Bhagat Yadgar Committee, 1961).
11 Ibid., p. 208.
12 Maia Ramnath, *Haj to Utopia*, p. 58.

Chapter 25: The Arrest of Sarabha, Tundilat and Pingle

1   Chaman Lal, *Ghadar Party Hero, Kartar Singh Sarabha,* National Book Trust of India, 2009, p. 30.
2   Uma Mukherjee, *Two Great Indian Revolutionaries: Rash Behari Bose and Jyotindranath Mukherjee* (Kolkata: Dey's Publishing, 1966), p. 149.
3   Ibid.
4   Chaman Lal, *Ghadar Party Hero, Kartar Singh Sarabha*, p. 30.
5   Gurcharan Singh Sansera, *Ghadar Party Da Itihas* (Jalandhar: Desh Bhagat Yadgar Committee, 1961), p. 210.

6 Ibid., p. 211.

7 Uma Mukherjee, *Two Great Indian Revolutionaries: Rash Behari Bose and Jyotindranath Mukherjee*, p. 150.

8 Ibid., p. 154.

Chapter 26: Banta Singh Sanghwal

1 *Ghadar Gatha, 1915*, ed. Buta Singh (Jalandhar: Punjab Prakashan), p. 62.

2 Ibid.

3 Ibid., p. 63.

4 Ibid., p. 64.

5 Ibid., p. 66.

6 Ibid.

7 Ibid.

Chapter 27: Attempts to Reignite the Revolutionary Fervour

1 Gurcharan Singh Sansera, *Ghadar Party Da Itihas* (Jalandhar: Desh Bhagat Yadgar Committee, 1961), p. 209.

2 F.C. Isemonger and J. Slattery, *An Account of the Ghadar Conspiracy* (Meerut: Archana Publications, 2003), p. 125.

3 Gurcharan Singh Sansera, *Ghadar Party Da Itihas*, p. 209.

4 Ibid.

5 F.C. Isemonger and J. Slattery, *An Account of the Ghadar Conspiracy*, p. 129.

6 Ibid., p. 132.

7 Ibid., pp. 132, 133.

8 Ibid., p. 134.

9 Ibid., p. 35.

10 Gurcharan Singh Sansera, *Ghadar Party Da Itihas*, p. 221.

11 Ibid.

12 Khushwant Singh and Satindra Singh, *Ghadar 1915: India's First Armed Rebellion* (R&K Publishing House, 1966), p. 44.

Chapter 28: The Lahore Conspiracy Case Trials

1 *Jeewan Sangram: Sohan Singh Bhakna*, ed. Malwinderjit Singh, p. 47.
2 Ibid.
3 Gurcharan Singh Sansera, *Ghadar Party Da Itihas* (Jalandhar: Desh Bhagat Yadgar Committee, 1961), p. 214.
4 Ibid.
5 Chaman Lal, *Ghadar Party Hero Kartar Singh Sarabha*, National Book Trust of India, 2009, p. 39.
6 F.C. Isemonger and J. Slattery, *An Account of the Ghadar Conspiracy* (Meerut: Archana Publications, 2003), p. 140.
7 Gurcharan Singh Sansera, *Ghadar Party Da Itihas*, pp. 212, 213.
8 Ibid., p. 39.

Chapter 29: The Revolt in Singapore

1 The first gurdwara in Hong Kong was built in 1901 and was called Shri Guru Singh Sabha. In Singapore, the Queen Street gurdwara came into existence in 1912. In Penang, a gurdwara was built in 1903.
2 Khushwant Singh and Satindra Singh, *Ghadar 1915: India's First Armed Rebellion* (R&K Publishing House, 1966), p. 46.
3 Malwinder Singh Waraich and Harish Jain, *Mandalay Conspiracy Case II Proceedings* (Unistar Publishers, 2017), p. 533.
4 Khushwant Singh and Satindra Singh, *Ghadar 1915: India's First Armed Rebellion*, p. 46.
5 *The Ghadr Movement and India's Anti-Imperialist Struggle*, ed. P.R. Kalia, Progressive People's Foundation of Edmonton, 2013, p. 278.
6 Maia Ramnath, *Haj to Utopia* (University of California Press, 2011), p. 181.
7 Ibid., p. 274.
8 Gurcharan Singh Sansera, *Ghadar Party Da Itihas* (Jalandhar: Desh Bhagat Yadgar Committee, 1961), p. 234.
9 Ibid., p. 235.
10 Ibid.
11 Maia Ramnath, *Haj to Utopia*, p. 192

12 *The Ghadr Movement and India's Anti-Imperialist Struggle*, ed. P.R. Kalia, Progressive People's Foundation of Edmonton, 2013, p. 275.

13 Ibid.

14 Ibid.

15 Ibid., p. 276.

16 Ibid.

17 Ibid.

Chapter 30: The Siam–Burma Angle

1 Maia Ramnath, *Haj to Utopia* (University of California Press, 2011), p. 176.

2 Nirode Kumar Barooah, *India and the Official Germany 1886-1914*, European University papers (Frankfurt: Peter Lang/Bern: M. Herbert Lang, 1977), pp. 137, 138.

3 Ibid.

4 Ibid.

5 Arun Coomer Bose, *Indian Revolutionaries Abroad* (Patna: Bharti Bhawan, 1971), p. 66.

6 Arun Coomer Bose, *Indian Revolutionaries Abroad*, p. 80.

7 Ibid.

8 Ibid.

9 Ibid., p. 135.

10 Ibid.

11 Ibid.

12 Ibid.

13 Nirode Kumar Barooah, *India and the Official Germany 1886-1914*, p. 167.

14 Ibid., p. 169.

15 Ibid., p. 171.

16 Young Turks was a conglomeration of various reform groups challenging the autocratic regime of Sultan Abdulhamid II. It paved the way for a revolution (3–28 July 1908) that gave birth to a constitutional government.

17 Arun Coomer Bose, *Indian Revolutionaries Abroad*, p. 131.

18 Ibid., p. 132.

19 Gurcharan Singh Sansera, *Ghadar Party Da Itihas* (Jalandhar: Desh Bhagat Yadgar Committee, 1961), p. 243.

20 Ibid.

21 Arun Coomer Bose, *Indian Revolutionaries Abroad*, p. 133.

22 Maia Ramnath, *Haj to Utopia*, p. 83.

23 Arun Coomer Bose, *Indian Revolutionaries Abroad*, p. 133.

24 Malwinder Jit Singh Waraich, *Jiwaniyan Gadhri Shahid Pandit Sohan Lal Pathak, Babu Harnam Singh Sahri* (Chandigarh: Unistar Books Pvt. Ltd, 2016), p. 27.

25 Ibid.

26 Malwinder Singh Waraich and Harish Jain, *Mandalay Conspiracy Case II Proceedings* (Unistar Publishers, 2017), p. 539.

27 Ibid.

28 Ibid., pp. 529–64.

29 Ibid., p. 533.

30 Ibid., p. 546.

31 Ibid., p. 552.

32 Shahid Babu Harnam Singh Sahri, Dr Jaswant Rai, *Kaum da Sitara* (Saptrishi Publications, 2019), p. 109.

33 Malwinder Singh Waraich and Harish Jain, *Mandalay Conspiracy Case II Proceedings,* p. 536.

34 Malwinder Jit Singh Waraich, *Jiwaniyan Gadhri Shahid Pandit Sohan Lal Pathak, Babu Harnam Singh Sahri*, p. 16.

35 Ibid.

36 Maia Ramnath, *Haj to Utopia*, p. 86.

37 Ibid., p. 88.

38 Ibid.

39 Malwinder Jit Singh Waraich, *Jiwaniyan Gadhri Shahid Pandit Sohan Lal Pathak, Babu Harnam Singh Sahri*, p. 41.

40 Maia Ramnath, *Haj to Utopia*, p. 41.

41 Malwinder Jit Singh Waraich, *Jiwaniyan Gadhri Shahid Pandit Sohan Lal Pathak, Babu Harnam Singh Sahri*, p. 62.

42 Maia Ramnath, *Haj to Utopia*, p. 87.

43 Khushwant Singh and Satindra Singh, *Ghadar 1915: India's First Armed Rebellion* (R&K Publishing House, 1966), p. 53.

44 F.C. Isemonger and J. Slattery, *An Account of the Ghadar Conspiracy*, Appendix N.

45 Ibid. Appendix O.

46 Khushwant Singh and Satindra Singh, *Ghadar 1915: India's First Armed Rebellion*, p. 55. This report was penned by Punjab police officers in 1919 for the perusal of the British Government.

Chapter 31: The Plans of the Berlin Indian Independence Committee

1 Arun Coomer Bose, *Indian Revolutionaries Abroad* (Patna: Bharti Bhawan, 1971), p. 83.

2 Ibid.

3 Ibid., p. 84.

4 Ibid., p. 255.

5 Ibid., p. 85.

6 Ibid., p. 96.

7 Ibid., p. 99.

8 Ibid.

9 Ibid., p. 100.

10 Nirode Kumar Barooah, *India and the Official Germany 1886–1914*, European University papers (Frankfurt: Peter Lang/Bern: M. Herbert Lang, 1977), p. 194

11 Maia Ramnath, *Haj to Utopia* (University of California Press, 2011), p. 177.

12 Ibid.

13 Arun Coomer Bose, *Indian Revolutionaries Abroad*, p. 100.

14 Savitri Sawhney, *I Shall Never Ask For Pardon: A Memoir of Pandurang Khankhoje* (Penguin Books India, 2008), pp. 141, 142.

15 Arun Coomer Bose, *Indian Revolutionaries Abroad*, p. 103–06.

16 Ibid.

17 Ibid.

18 Ibid., p. 104.

19 Ibid., p. 105.

Chapter 32: The Tale of Three Ships

1   Maia Ramnath, *Haj to Utopia* (University of California Press, 2011), p. 78.
2   Ibid.
3   Ibid.
4   Harish K. Puri, *Ghadar Movement: Ideology, Organisation, Strategy* (Amritsar: Guru Nanak Dev University, 2013), p. 105.
5   Maia Ramnath, *Haj to Utopia*, p. 79.
6   Ibid., p. 80.
7   Ibid., p. 78.
8   Ibid.

Chapter 33: The Hindu–German Conspiracy Trial

1   Harish K. Puri, *Ghadar Movement: Ideology, Organisation, Strategy* (Amritsar: Guru Nanak Dev University, 2013), p. 116.
2   Ibid., p. 117.
3   Maia Ramnath, *Haj to Utopia* (University of California Press, 2011), p. 92.
4   Harish K. Puri, *Ghadar Movement: Ideology, Organisation, Strategy*, p. 117.
5   Maia Ramnath, *Haj to Utopia*, p. 92.
6   Ibid., p. 91.
7   Gurcharan Singh Sansera, *Ghadar Party Da Itihas* (Jalandhar: Desh Bhagat Yadgar Committee, 1961), p. 267.
8   Ibid.
9   Ibid., p. 272.

Chapter 34: The Silk Letters Plot

1   Emily C. Brown, *Har Dayal: Hindu Revolutionary and Rationalist* (The Arizona Board of Regents, 1957), p. 204.
2   Arun Coomer Bose, *Indian Revolutionaries Abroad* (Patna: Bharti Bhawan, 1971), p. 107.
3   Ibid.

4   Ibid.
5   Ibid.
6   Emily C. Brown, *Har Dayal: Hindu Revolutionary and Rationalist*, p. 205.
7   Arun Coomer Bose, *Indian Revolutionaries Abroad*, p. 110.
8   Maia Ramnath, *Haj to Utopia* (University of California Press, 2011), pp. 185, 186.
9   Harish K. Puri, *Ghadar Movement: Ideology, Organisation, Strategy* (Amritsar: Guru Nanak Dev University, 2013), p. 112.
10 Ibid.
11 Maia Ramnath, *Haj to Utopia*, p. 185.
12 Ibid., p. 187

Chapter 35: An Imprisoned Life

1   S.N. Aggarwal, *The Heroes of Cellular Jail* (Rupa Publications, 2018), p. 1.
2   Ibid., p. 7.
3   Ibid., p. 8.
4   Ibid., p. 13.
5   Ibid., p. 16.
6   Ibid., p. 17.
7   Ibid., p. 73.
8   Ibid.
9   Ibid., p. 77.
10 S.N. Aggarwal, *The Heroes of Cellular Jail*, p. 34.
11 Ibid., p. 92.
12 Ibid., p. 93.
13 Ibid.
14 Ibid.

Chapter 36: The Arrival of the Ghadarites at the Cellular Jail

1   *Kale Panian di Dastan*, ed. Dalbir Kaur and Prem Singh (Jalandhar: Desh Bhagat Yadgar Committee, 2012), p. 18.

2   Ibid., p. 20.
3   Ibid., p. 219.
4   Ibid., p. 226.
5   A supreme sacrifice by unsung hero, Amar Shaheed Ram Rakha Bali.
6   S.N. Aggarwal, *The Heroes of Cellular Jail* (Rupa Publications, 2018), p. 213.
7   Ibid., p. 240.
8   Ibid., p. 232.
9   Ibid., p. 308.

Chapter 37: Ghadar After 1918

1   Harish K. Puri, *Ghadar Movement: Ideology, Organisation, Strategy* (Amritsar: Guru Nanak Dev University, 2013), p. 231.
2   Maia Ramnath, *Haj to Utopia* (University of California Press, 2011), pp. 131–36.
3   Harish K. Puri, *Ghadar Movement: Ideology, Organisation, Strategy*, p. 230.
4   Ibid., p. 232.
5   Ibid.
6   Sohan Singh Josh, *Hindustan Ghadar Party: A Short History* (Jalandhar: Desh Bhagat Yadgar Committee, 2007), p. 503.
7   Ibid., p. 516.

Chapter 38: The Ghadar Movement: Wins and Losses

1   Harish K. Puri, *Ghadar Movement: Ideology, Organisation, Strategy* (Amritsar: Guru Nanak Dev University, 2013), p. 144.
2   Mangu Ram belonged to an affluent background; his father had a prosperous trade in raw hides, but he was considered untouchable because of his social background. He was not allowed in the elementary school building and was made to squat in the doorway from where he attended his classes. He arrived in California in 1909 and started working in the fruit orchards of Fresno.
3   Maia Ramnath, *Haj To Utopia* (University of California Press, 2011), p. 234.

4   'Ad Dharm', an article by Mark Juergensmeyer, sourced from juergensmeyer.org › uploads › 2013/12 › Ad-Dharm.PP-1.pdf.

5   The followers of Ad Dharm believed in the existence of one God, Adi Purkh. Kabir and Ravi Das, the patron saint of Ad Dharm, were hailed as the revered gurus and the customary salutation was 'Jai Guru Dev'.

Annexure 2: The Role of Women in the Ghadar Movement

1   *Gatha Gadriyan Di*, ed. Mandeep and Randeep (Barnala: Tarakbharti Parkashan, 2013), p. 49.

2   Rakesh Kumar, *Gulab Kaur, Ghadar Lehar Di Daler Yodha* (Ludhiana: Chintan Prakashan), p. 14.

3   Under Article IX of the Treaty of Paris, which ended the Spanish–American War and through which Spain ceded the Philippines to the United States, Filipinos continued as non-US citizens until 4 July 1946 when through president proclamation, the US recognized the Philippines as an independent country.

4   Gurcharan Singh Sansera, *Ghadar Party Da Itihas* (Jalandhar: Desh Bhagat Yadgar Committee, 1961), p. 124.

5   *Gatha Gadriyan Di*, ed. Mandeep and Randeep, pp. 49, 50.

6   Ibid., p. 50.

7   Jagwinder Jodha, *Karantikari Agnes Smedley* (Jalandhar: Punj Aab Parkashan, 2015), p. 7.

8   Ibid., p. 214.

9   Ibid.

10 Maia Ramnath, *Haj to Utopia* (University of California Press, 2011), p. 129.

11 Ibid., p. 131.

12 Ibid., p. 129.

Bibliography

Articles/Periodicals/Theses/Reports

Almquist, Karen Singh, Thesis, 'New Era: The Political Perceptions of the Hindustan Ghadar Party', California State University, Sacramento, 2009.

Bambali, Vijay, 'Ghadri Shahid Ram Rakha Da Pind, Sasoli', *Nawan Zamana*, 25 October 2020.

Chandan, Amarjit, 'Nama Phansiwala'.

Juergensmeyer, Mark, 'Ad Dharm', juergensmeyer.org › uploads › 2013/12 › Ad-Dharm.PP-1.pdf.

Kangniwal, Chiranji Lal, 'Kale Pani Da Shahid, Ram Rakha Bali', *Mela Ghadri Babiyan Da*, a booklet by Desh Yadgar Committee, 2006.

Puri, Harish K., 'The Ghadar Movement and the Contemporary Revolutionary Nationalist Struggle in Bengal and Maharashtra: Exploring the Links and Distinctive Features', Dr Ganda Singh Memorial Lecture, Punjabi University, Patiala, 15 September 2016.

'Saga of a Freedom Fighter's Supreme Sacrifice', *Daily Telegrams*, an interview with Squadron Leader D.K. Bali by Suresh Philip.

Sedition Committee Report, Calcutta Superintendent Government, Printing, India, 1918.

Sidhu, Gurmel S., 'Ghadar Movement: Role of Media and Literature', California State University, Fresno, sikhcentury. wordpress.com 2013.

Books: English

Aggarwal, B.R., *Trials of Independence* (India: National Book Trust, 1991).

Aggarwal, S.N., *The Heroes of Cellular Jail* (India: Rupa Publications, 2018).

Barooah, Nirode Kumar, *India and Official Germany, 1886–1914* (Frankfurt: Peter Lang/Bern: M. Herbert Lang, 1977).

Bose, Arun Coomer, *Indian Revolutionaries Abroad* (Patna: Bharti Bhawan, 1971).

Brown, Emily C., *Har Dayal, Hindu Revolutionary and Rationalist* (The Arizona Board of Regents, 1957).

Chandra, Bipan, Mridula Mukherjee, Aditya Mukherjee, Sucheta Mahajan, K.N. Panikkar, *India's Struggle For Independence* (India: Penguin Books, 1989).

Chenchiah, D., *Ghadar Party Reminiscences*, ed. Parminder Singh (Jalandhar: Desh Bhagat Yadgar Committee).

Darling, Malcolm Lyall, *The Punjab Peasant in Prosperity and Debt* (Oxford University Press, 1928).

Desh Bhagat Yadgar Hall Library, A Guide to Collection of Manuscripts, Personal Testimonials, Letters, Periodicals and Archival Materials on the Ghadar Movement, compiled by Darshan Singh Tatla, Desh Bhagat Yadgar Committee, Jalandhar, 2013.

Dhami, Sadhu Singh, *Maluka: A Novel* (Publication Bureau, Punjabi University, Patiala, 1997).

Ghosh, Suresh Chandra, *The History of Education in Modern India, 1757-2012* (Orient Blackswan Private Limited, 2016).

Isemonger, F.C., and J. Slattery, *An Account of The Ghadar Conspiracy (1913–1915),* (Archana Publications, 2003).

Johnston, Hugh, *The Voyage of The Komagata Maru: The Sikh Challenge to Canada's Colour Bar* (Vancouver: University of British Columbia Press, 1989).

Josh, Sohan Singh, *Hindustan Ghadar Party, A Short History* (Jalandhar: Desh Bhagat Yadgar Committee, 2007).

Lal, Chaman, *Ghadar Party Hero, Kartar Singh Sarabha*, translated by Hina Nandrajog (National Book Trust, India, 2014).

Mukherjee, Uma, *Two Great Indian Revolutionaries, Rash Behari Bose and Jyotindra Nath Mukherjee* (Dey's Publishing, 2004).

Pal, Sarvinder, *Sardar Ajit Singh, The Exiled Revolutionary* (Chandigarh: Unistar Books, 2019).

Parmanand, Bhai, *The Story of My Life* (Lahore: The Central Hindu Yuvak Sabha, 1934).

Puri, Harish K., *Ghadar Movement, A Short History* (India: National Book Trust, 2012).

Puri, Harish K., *Ghadar Movement: Ideology, Organisation, Strategy* (Amritsar: Guru Nanak Dev University, 2013).

Rai, Lala Lajpat, *The Story of My Deportation* (Lahore: Punjabee Press, 1908).

Ramnath, Maia, *Haj to Utopia* (University of California Press, 2011).

Sandhu, Waryam Singh, *Who Were the Ghadrite Babas?*, translated by Iqbal Ramoowalia, Ghadar Centenary Committee, Toronto, 2013.

Sareen, T.R., *The Unsung Heroes, Select Documents on Neglected Part of India's Freedom Struggle, Part I and II* (New Delhi: Life Span Publishers and Distributors, 2009).

Savarkar, Veer, *My Transportation For Life* (Chandigarh: Abhishek Publications, 2007).

Savarkar, Veer, *The Indian War of Independence, 1857* (Chandigarh: Abhishek Publications, 2019).

Sawhney, Savitri, *I Shall Never Ask For Pardon, A Memoir of Pandurang Khankhoje* (India: Penguin Books, 2008).

Singh, Khushwant, *A History of The Sikhs, Second Edition, Volume II 1839-2004* (Oxford University Press, 2020).

Singh, Khushwant, and Satindra Singh, *Ghadar 1915* (New Delhi: R&K Publishing House, 1966).

Sinha, Bejoy Kumar, *In Andamans, The Indian Bastille* (Allahabad Law Journal Press, 1939).

Smedley, Agnes, *Daughter of Earth* (Mineola, New York: Dover Publications, 1929).

Struggle For Free Hindusthan (Ghadar Movement), eds Bhai Nahar Singh and Kirpal Singh (New Delhi: Atlantic Publishers, 1986).

Tandon, Sasha, *Social History of Plague in Colonial India* (New Delhi: Writer's Choice, 2015).

The Ghadar Movement and India's Anti-Imperialist Struggle, ed. P.R. Kalia (Alberta, Canada: Progressive Peoples Foundation of Edmonton, 2013).

Waraich, Malwinder Singh and Harish Jain, *Mandalay Conspiracy Case I Proceedings* (Chandigarh: Unistar Books, 2017).

Books: Punjabi

Bajaj, Principal Prem Singh, *Baba Sohan Singh Diyan Ahem Likhtan* (Samrala: Dildeep Parkashan, 2015).

Bajon, Chuhar Singh, *Desh Bhagat Yadgar Hall Da Itihas* (Jalandhar: Chirag Parkashan, 2008).

Bhakna, Sohan Singh, *Meri Aap Beeti*, edited and translated from the Urdu by Amrajit Chandan (Copper Coin Publishing, 2014).

Bilga, Bhagat Singh, *Ghadar Leher De Unphole Varke* (Jalandhar: 5aab Parkashan, 2013).

Dard, Giani Hira Singh, *Jiwan Desh Bhagat Harnam Singh Tundilat* (Jalandhar: Awami Printing Press, 1962).

Dilgir, H.S., *Shahid Kanshi Ram*, Shahid Kanshi Ram Shatabdi Samaroh Committee, Jalandhar, 1982.

Gatha Gadriyan Di, eds Mandeep and Randeep (Barnala: Tarakbharti Parkashan, 2013).

Gatha Ghadar 1915, ed. Buta Singh (Jalandhar: 5aab Parkashan, 2015).

Ghadar Dian Paidan, compiled by History Sub Committee, Desh Bhagat Yadgar Hall, Jalandhar, 2004.

Ghadar Lehar De Sarokar, ed. Balbir Parwana (Jalandhar: 5aab Parkashan, 2013).

Jeewan Sangram: Baba Sohan Singh Bhakna, ed. Prof Malwinderjit Singh (Barnala: Tarakbharti Parkashan, 2003).

Jodha, Jagwinder, *Karantikari Agnes Smedley* (Jalandhar: 5aab Parkashan, 2015).

Johnston, Hugh J.M., *Komagata Maru Di Itihasak Yatra*, Punjabi Edition, ed. Prof. Jagmohan Singh and Narbhinder, translated by Harcharan Singh Chahal and Ajaib Singh Tiwana (Jalandhar: 5aab Parkashan).

Kale Panian Di Dastan, eds. Prof Dalbir Kaur and Dr Prem Singh (Jalandhar: Desh Bhagat Yadgar Committee, 2012).

Kangniwal, Charanji Lal, *Desh Bhagat Yadgar Ate Baba Amar Singh Sandhwan* (Jalandhar: 5aab Parkashan, 2013).

Komagata Maru Di Kahani Baba Gurdit Singh Di Zubani, ed. Gurdev Singh Sidhu (Chandigarh: Lokgeet Parkashan, 2015).

Kumar, Rakesh, *Gulab Kaur, Ghadar Lehar Di Daler Yodha* (Chintan Parkashan, 2020).

Lahore Supplementary Case, Mandalay and Padhri Kalan Conspiracy Case, ed. Harwinder Bhandal (Jalandhar: Desh Bhagat Yadgar Committee, 2016).

Lala Har Dayal, Selected Writings 1884-1939 (Chandigarh: Lokgeet Parkashan and Jalandhar: Desh Bhagat Yadgar Committee, 2008).

Madhimegha, Prithipal Singh, *Ghadar Party De Suhe Pane* (Jalandhar: 5aab Parkashan, 2016).

Mahilpur, Harjap Singh, *Jail Diary and Other Writings* (Jalandhar: 5aab Parkashan, 2015).

Rai, Jaswant, *Kaum Da Sitara, Shahid Babu Harnam Singh Sahri* (Chandigarh: Saptrishi Publications, 2019).

Sandhu, Wariyam Singh, *Ghadar Leher Di Gatha* (Samana: Sangam Publications and Jalandhar: Desh Bhagat Yadgar Committee, 2013).

Sansera, Gurcharan Singh, *Ghadar Party Da Itihas* (Jalandhar: Desh Bhagat Yadgar Committee, 2015).

Sarokaran Di Awaz, Brampton, Canada and Shahid Bhagat Singh Centenary Foundation, Khatkar Kalan, 2016.

Shahid Kartar Singh Sarabha and Martyrs of 1915, ed. Prithvi Raj Kalia, Progressive People's Foundation of Edmonton, Alberta, Canada, 2015.

Singh, Kesar, *Komagata Maru: A Historic Novel,* ed. Malwinder Singh Waraich (Chandigarh: Lokgeet Parkashan, 2017).

Singh, Nanak, *Ik Mian Do Talwaran, A Novel* (Amritsar: Lok Sahit Parkashan and Jalandhar: New Book Company, 2020).

Singh, Sarabjit, *Ghadar Lehar, Itihas, Rajniti Ate Sahit* (Jalandhar: Deepak Publishers, 2008).

Waraich, Malwinderjit Singh, *Biographies of Pandit Sohan Lal Pathak, Babu Harnam Singh Sahri* (Chandigarh: Unistar Books, 2016).

Books: Hindi

Sanyal, Shachindernath, *Bandi Jeevan* (Delhi: Atmaram and Sons, 2013).

Index

Scan QR code to access the
Penguin Random House India website